REVOLUTIONARY POLITICS
AND THE CUBAN WORKING CLASS

Revolutionary Politics and the Cuban Working Class

BY MAURICE ZEITLIN

HARPER TORCHBOOKS
Harper & Row, Publishers
New York, Evanston, and London

To Marilyn

Contents

Introduction to the Torchbook edition   vii

Preface   liii

Map   1

1. Orientations, Setting, Methods   3

2. Economic Insecurity and Politics   45

3. Race Relations and Politics   66

4. Skill and Politics   89

5. Sex and the Single Worker   120

6. Social Mobility and Politics   132

7. Social Relations in the Plant and in Politics   157

8. Alienation and Revolution   185

9. Political Generations   211

10. Revolutionary Workers and Individual Liberties   242

11. Revolutionary Politics and the Cuban Working Class   277

Index   297

Cuba's Workers, Workers' Cuba, 1969—

A Special Supplement to the Torchbook Edition

❧ The revolution in Cuba is an artifact of the Cuban imagination. In this revolutionary island off our shores, Cuba's leaders aim to create the "twenty-first-century man," and have reasserted the classical egalitarian and liberating vision of socialism. They are engaged in no simple doctrinal quarrel or metaphysical debate with Communist parties in power elsewhere. At issue is the image of socialist man and the conception of socialism. It is an issue which has direct implications for any movement whose ideal is the creation of a society free of exploitation and oppression.

Not only have the Cuban revolutionaries done much in one decade to eliminate some of the worst material consequences of colonial misdevelopment, but they are also trying simultaneously to infuse in the Cuban people an ennobling vision of man, a dream of things to come that compels them to reach beyond themselves and "to make the extraordinary" as Fidel Castro says, "an ordinary part of their lives." Rejecting, in Che Guevara's words, the "scholasticism that has held back the development of Marxist philosophy," the revolutionaries have been pragmatic, innovating, and humanistic. "The ultimate and most important revolutionary aspiration," Che wrote in his essay "Socialism and Man in Cuba," is "to see man freed from alienation." Against the accusation that "the period of building socialism is characterized by the abolition of individuality for the sake of the state," Che replied with "the facts of the Cuban experience" in which "man—individualized, specific, named" is basic. It is this emphasis on the role of the individual—"the actor in this strange and moving drama of the building of socialism, in his twofold existence as a unique human being and a member of the community," as a self-conscious maker of history together with others "who struggle for the same cause"—that distinguishes the Cuban revolution so radically from other socialist revolutions in our time.

The Cuban revolutionaries are the first independent radicals in the world to put through a socialist revolution. (Despite their identification, in the course of the revolution, with the international Communist movement and their fusion with the old Communists, the Fidelistas still hold the initiative within the revolutionary leadership; revolutionary optimism and the rejection of received Communist doctrine are the quintessence of Cuban Communism.) It is the dream of the revolutionaries, in Che's words, to make possible men's "conscious, individual, and collective participation in all the mechanisms of direction and production" and the realization of their fullest human potential. "This will be translated concretely," Che wrote, "into the reappropriation of man's nature through freed work and the expression of his own condition in culture and art."

This vision of socialism was held by all pre-Stalinist revolutionary socialists. It failed to survive in Russia where, with the vast destruction and chaos of the civil war, and the weariness and exhaustion of the masses after the struggle to defend the Soviet revolution, the Bolsheviks took measures which led them unawares to inter their own principles. Temporary expedients and episodic acts of self-defense were transformed into "socialist" principles and the substance of "Communist legality." One-party rule, in no way inherent in the original Bolshevik program, was termed the essence of "socialist" government; and democratic centralism, which Lenin fashioned as an organizational weapon in conspiratorial conditions to wage revolution, became the embodiment of "workers' democracy." Vast social inequality, the encouragement of competition between workers, and the breakdown of class solidarity became "socialist emulation." "Socialism" came to mean a peculiar amalgam of Russian temperament, Soviet experience, and vulgar Marxism; the revolution absorbed Russia's Byzantine heritage and imperial backwardness in the course of overcoming them.

Fortunately, the tasks of the Cubans are not comparable to those faced by the first who dared in Russia, or by the Chinese or Vietnamese Communists. Unlike them, the Cuban revolutionaries came to power in a society relatively free of chaos, and the spirit and energies of its people were not exhausted, but were, in fact, simply waiting to be tapped. The country has a small population compared to its available resources, a fertile and arable land, and the likelihood of continued economic aid from the Soviet Union. Cuba is small, and planning should be less cumbersome and the complexities less difficult to cope with. Her small population and territorial size allow extensive and intensive communication between the government and people, and mass participation in public affairs.

The Cuban revolutionaries—whatever their extraordinary abilities, especially Fidel's—came to power in a society whose prerevolutionary social structure endowed them with vast advantages compared to the leaders of other major social revolutions in this century.[1] Cuba has an opportunity unparalleled in the other Communist countries to develop institutions which allow government ownership and central planning to lead both to economic growth and to the development of diversity, intellectual freedom, and meaningful majority rule—the socialist vision which Che articulated so eloquently.

This is not to minimize in any way the immense problems the revolutionaries have had to face and the extraordinary way in which they have met and solved many of them; and they have done so in the teeth of United States hostility and despite the embargo. The precedent of the Bay of Pigs invasion, the missile crisis and "quarantine" of Cuba, the invasion of the Dominican Republic, and the ferocity of the

[1] Some of the features of the prerevolutionary social structure which were significant in determining the pace and direction of the revolution and reinforcing its humane and libertarian aspects and potential are discussed below, pp. 271-76. See also, my "Cuba: Revolution Without a Blueprint," *Cuban Communism*, ed. I. L. Horowitz (Chicago: Aldine Publishing Company, 1969).

United States war against the Vietnamese make it clear that
the Cuban revolutionaries cannot afford to relax their vigilance.[2]

Overcoming the misdevelopment and underdevelopment of
Cuban capitalism, especially in circumstances which require
the Cubans to continue to expend national energies and
scarce resources on military preparedness, will require sacrifice and austerity, and the same outstanding qualities of au-
dacity and originality that the revolutionaries have shown so
far in making the revolution. Appreciating and understanding the fact that they are involved in "uninterrupted activity"
(Che) and daily struggle to accomplish a thousand small
things are essential to any constructively critical assessment
of the revolution. Fidel, speaking on the revolution's anniversary two years ago, said: "It requires a tremendous effort
to speak on national anniversaries. This does not mean that

---

[2] What does it indicate about the thinking of U.S. officials and
policy planners, the Cubans might wonder, that someone like Hans
Morgenthau, a former top State Department adviser who publicly
opposes United States intervention in Vietnam, could recently write:
"As part of the settlement of the missile crisis of 1962, we pledged
ourselves not to intervene in Cuba, *which is today a military and
political outpost of the Soviet Union and the fountainhead of sub-
version and military intervention in the Western hemisphere, and as
such directly affects the interests of the United States.* On the other
hand, we have intervened massively in Vietnam, even at the risk
of a major war, although *the Communist threat to American interests from Vietnam is at best remote and in any event is infinitely
more remote than the Communist threat emanating from Cuba.* . . .
It appears incongruous that we intervened massively in the Dominican Republic, whose revolution was, according to our government's
assessment of the facts, a mere symptom of the disease, while *the
disease itself—that is, Cuban Communism—is exempt from effective
intervention altogether.* . . . Intervene we must where our national
interest requires it and where our power gives us a chance to succeed.
The choice of these occasions will be determined not by sweeping
ideological commitments nor by blind reliance upon American
power but by a careful calculation of the interests involved and the
power available. If the United States applies this standard, it will
intervene less and succeed more." *Foreign Affairs*, Vol. 45, No. 3
(April, 1967), pp. 423-33, 436. Italics added.

I am tired, but fifteen years of struggle has put a heavy load on the shoulders of a very small group of men, and has created a new situation in which we should divide our functions more and more."

In my conversations with revolutionaries in the summer of 1969, they repeatedly referred to the immediate and concrete jobs that had to get done to maintain the revolution's momentum. When I discussed socialist planning with Carlos Rafael Rodríguez, for instance, a veteran Communist on the Secretariat of the new Party and one of Cuba's top planners (officially, his ministerial title is President of the National Commission of Technical, Scientific, and Economic Collaboration), he said:

"I am not one of those who believe in the 'messianic concept' of the Party—the Party is not the masses. . . . The problem is that while in principle it is certain that we must try to discover democratic means by which to decide, for instance, the variety and types of consumer goods to be produced (such decisions cannot be left to 'messianic mechanisms' or merely be the responsibility of the Ministry or of technicians), it is a luxury to try to establish such modes of planning at this moment in the revolution, when the priorities are so clear and our needs so pressing."

1969 is the "Year of the Decisive Effort" in Cuba. Everywhere posters exhort Cubans to work "with the same discipline, with the same spirit of sacrifice" as the young men who attacked Fort Moncada to begin the rebellion against Batista. The country is mobilized not for defense but for the achievement of economic objectives, the most important and immediate one being the ten-million-ton sugar harvest in 1970, which Fidel has called a "point of honor for this revolution, . . . a yardstick by which to judge the capability of the revolution."

The island is austere. Rationing is tight and consumption restricted. (Children receive one quart of milk a day, adults, unless a medical diet requires it, none; a loaf of bread and a quarter to three-quarters of a pound of rice and beans weekly per adult. Meat, when available, is rationed to three-quarters of a pound a week, though seafood and pizza, both new in the Cuban diet since the revolution, are more easily obtained. Cucumbers and avocados, though not abundant, are available in sufficient quantities, apparently, to satisfy the Cuban diet. Other greens are rare, but Cubans who never ate them before do not notice their absence now. Clothing is also rationed, and department stores display few items.) Unlike the situation during my visit in 1962, however, when the revolution went through its worst period economically (as the effects of errors in planning, inadequate skills, poor transportation and distribution, the drought, and the economic embargo imposed by the United States had a cumulative impact on production and consumption), the present austerity, government leaders claim, is planned. It is the result of the extraordinary and unprecedented rate of investment of 31 percent of the Gross Material Product (GNP exclusive of services), and of the use of scarce foreign exchange to buy capital goods rather than consumer goods.

Plants apparently have no serious shortage of raw materials or spare parts, or of technically trained personnel. This was the view of the administrators and technicians and production workers I interviewed in seven plants (cement, textiles, agricultural equipment, paper, beer and malt, copper mining, and sugar) scattered over five of Cuba's six provinces. (These were drawn from the sample of 21 plants I visited and in which I interviewed workers in 1962.) All of them were working overtime and, their administrators claimed, at close to theoretical capacity. In the textile plant at Ariguanabo, Bauta, outside of Havana (which is one of Latin America's largest), installed capacity is 176,000 meters daily. It had never been reached before the revolution, according to its administrator; last year they produced 175,679 meters, and they have been averaging 172,300 meters in the past several years. The brewery at Manacas was in the process of expansion to 21,600 boxes of beer (24 bottles per box) a day from its present 13,800, and another 95 workers will be added to the present work force of 376 by May, 1970. In the Venezuela sugar central, British technicians were installing a new automated mill, bringing the number to four, and East Germans were putting in new thermoelectric turbines of 3,000-kilowatt capacity each, according to Agustín Hernández, its young administrator. "Once finished," he said, "this will become the largest sugar central in the world." Similar expansion was either going on or already planned in detail at all the plants I visited. Havana has been neglected and looks it, but there is construction in progress across the island. The roads are in good repair, and new highways are cutting up the landscape, tying together previously inaccessible areas, bringing peasants out of their isolation. The public transportation system functions efficiently, and the smell of Soviet gasoline in GM engines no longer hangs in the Havana air. Extensive new ricelands are being cultivated in Pinar del Río; the "cordon" around Havana, begun in April of 1967, reportedly will soon begin to supply all of Havana with its coffee and citrus-fruit needs. Artificial insemination and hybrid breeding are, it is claimed, preparing the way for vastly increased cattle herds. Artificial lakes, or reservoirs (the cordon alone has 19 completed, 20 almost finished, and another 10 under construction), with resort facilities and parks, are now visible in a countryside where drought has been one of the recurrent agricultural scourges. Mechanization is proceeding apace in agriculture, and the Cubans claim to have solved the technical problem of mechanized sugar-cane harvesting recently and to have several experimental models at work which cut, clean, and load the cane. New hospitals and schools, resorts and parks and recreation centers, apartment houses, private peasant dwellings, even whole new towns, as in Pinar del Río or Batabanó, are going up. "The main structure of an expanding economy," as James Reston reported two years ago, "is obviously being built here" (*New York Times*, July 31, 1967, p. 1:5).

Withal, it should be clear that most peasants continue to live in the pre-Columbian *bohios* built from the wood of the palm tree and thatched with its leaves, though the earthen floors of most I saw were now replaced with wood or concrete. The slums have been eliminated, but workers' dwellings are still obviously inadequate, as anyone wandering around the old city of Havana or stopping in any of more than a dozen cities and towns across the island—as I did, without hindrance—will discover. As you cross the city of Matanzas, for instance, on the way to the outskirts, down behind the railroad tracks you can see shacks put together of scraps of wood and any other loose materials their occupants were able to find. There does not seem to have been any improvement here, and the black children running around, for whom the railroad tracks are a playground, remind you rather sharply how much is yet to be done. So does talking to Miguel Mendoza, *carpenter,* 57 years old. With his wife and seven children, he lives in a former storefront room no larger than ten feet square, on Zapata Street No. 24 across from the Colón cemetery in Havana. It has no inside running water, though there is a faucet nearby. One electric light hangs in the room's center. To him, these quarters, to which he moved a few weeks before I met him, were far better than those he had in the past. His wife, looking much older than her 43 years, agreed. The table, the bunk beds, a few chairs, some shelves with a few pots and dishes were, she told me, their first possessions. "We are all revolutionaries, ready to fight and die if necessary," she said. "Before the revolution, we had nothing. Miguel spent his time in the street; now our children are in school. He has secure work; for us there is no scarcity. . . ."

Sra. Mendoza's comment underlines the vast change in the lives of the poor and of the working class as a whole which even the most modest improvements in living conditions has meant; to most workers, who lived lives of great privation before the revolution, to whom unemployment and under-employment were a constant threat, the present does not appear austere at all. This was summed up well (in the typically eloquent and radical departure from conversational language Cubans use when speaking about their revolution) by a chunky, heavy-fisted, but soft-spoken miner at the Matahambre copper mine at the westernmost tip of the island:

"The life under the capitalist system was a life condemned to death below the earth—and your children also; that's what they were good for. They were lucky if they made sixth grade; that was really special. Only the strongest could work. Those without good physiques could not. The revolution came and now your children are completing basic secondary education, and you, if you want to improve yourself, attend classes at the *Facultad Obrera-Campesina* [Worker-Peasant Faculty].

"You went down in the mine in the morning before the dawn and saw no daylight; it was dark when you emerged from the pit. You took a piece of bread and maybe some meat with you into the mine, if you were among the more fortunate ones; and by the time you ate it, it was grimy and decomposed; but you had to eat it.

"So the revolution comes and it is concluded that the miners must not eat below any more, that they must come to the surface to eat. And you get milk, bread, an egg and meat, *gratis*. . . ."

"Look, I don't mean this in any way personally," another miner told me, "but listen, American. There used to be a *barrio* here they are called the *barrio americano,* where only Americans lived, the administrators, technicians, and so forth; and on the door of their social club was a sign, 'Only for members.' Now that's a social club for all of us. We are all members now. Everyone.

"A polyclinic has been constructed—there was no hospital here before, just one room. Now we have one with forty-four beds, built in 1964 or 1965—I'm not sure. There were no chances for you and your kids. Now there is work for everyone; there are eight six-hour shifts—the shifts used to be eight hours—and all the miners are studying, as are their children; and there are workers' sons from the shop who are now studying even to be engineers.

"The only thing the capitalist enterprise left us was the hole in the ground and in our stomachs. There were three hundred for every job."

The austerity program of the Cuban government has not noticeably dampened the workers' morale, because they see it as part of a common effort to develop their country, from which they have already benefited considerably; the rationing, the endless lines, the shortages seem, paradoxically, to have intensified the revolution's élan and heightened social solidarity. Most important, the egalitarian ethos of the revolution has been accentuated by its egalitarian practice.

"Everyone is on the *libreta*" (ration card), a black brewery worker in Manacas told me. "Everyone has his quota, according to his family's needs, no more or less. This, at least, is what I can see for myself. René [the administrator] stands in line like the rest of us. His wife and mine buy at the same store. No one has privileges now. What there is is for everyone."

Wages and salaries reflect the same pattern of social equality. It continues to be the practice in Cuba, contrary to that in the Soviet Union until quite recently, to maintain a narrow gap between the income of production workers and clerical, administrative, and technical personnel. In fact, it may be more correct to say that there simply is no gap, because there is, as yet, no systematic relationship between occupation and income in Cuba. There is a mix between what the workers call the *sueldo histórico*, or the wage they had been receiving in 1961 when wages were frozen, and the new wage and salary scales which have been established in industry, services and in the predominantly publicly-owned agricultural sector. Plants where productivity was high and the workers had strong trade unions before the revolution, earned wages far higher than workers in similar jobs elsewhere that required equivalent skills and training; often unskilled workers in the organized plants earned more than skilled workers where unions were weak or nonexistent. This irrationality in the wage system hit skilled workers the hardest and intensified their sense of exploitation. The establishment of a standardized wage system was, therefore, an imperative necessity, not merely from the standpoint of rational planning but for equity and social justice, and one strongly supported by the workers, so far as I could tell, even in the "privileged" industries.

In my lengthy talks with workers, privately, informally, and in small groups, I probed for resentment, but found none. I expected the workers whose wages were frozen at their "historic" level to resent this; and I especially expected resentment from workers newly transferred into these plants who are earning far less on the newly established scales than veteran workers still on the "historic" ones. Instead, their responses to my questions were quite the opposite, and phrased in terms of justice and equity for the *other* workers. "It would not be proper to take what the privileged workers won from the capitalist enterprises away from them; they fought for themselves, as they had to," a black streetcar conductor now working at the paper mill in Cárdenas told me. Another man, at the cement plant in Mariel, said, "Every worker's goal was to get his son a job here. Fathers, sons, brothers, nephews helped each other get into the plant. We had a very strong union here. You went up the scale strictly by seniority. There was no such thing as self-improvement. You had no opportunity to study. Some guys in the extraction of ore earned seven hundred dollars a month with overtime. Most of them have renounced their overtime pay, though some haven't; it would have meant a great sacrifice. I myself have. New fellows coming into the plant know that they'll earn the same as workers elsewhere with the same skill and danger involved in their work. That's what counts. The fact is that the wage means very little now—"

"Because," I interrupted, "there's nothing to buy."

"Of course, to be truthful, because there is not much to buy. But mainly because so much is free, and my wife is working also. Everyone has work now, so that a family that had only one earner before now probably has a son, maybe even the wife, working. My wife leaves our kids at the *círculo infantil*—she knows they are well cared for, and it costs us nothing."

A worker at the cement plant in Mariel said:

"This is not conceivable by someone outside the revolutionary process [a favorite Cuban phrase now], I suppose. My consciousness has risen. The revolution was not Communist or even socialist, and neither was I. Something moved us all—what, was not clear—but we struggled. Some of us read and talked about things being different someday. Now we have free work clothes, work shoes, education for ourselves and our children, free health and medical attention, free x-rays, and drugs, vacations with pay; and if someone is not able to work because of illness or accident, he gets his full pay, because we are an outstanding plant with the Banner of the Heroes of Moncada. We don't have to worry about the future. Before, that was our biggest preoccupation —what would happen to your kids if you got sick or lost your job? That's over. By 1970, we won't pay any rent, and we hardly pay anything now, anyway—ten percent of our wage. We get free breakfasts in the plant; we'll be getting free lunches soon; and it only costs fifty cents anyway. Transportation is a nickel. If I want to make a phone call, I go to the corner and it costs me nothing. Little by little, we aren't even thinking in terms of individual earnings any more."

Under the newly established scales, the administrator of

the plant earns no more than the most skilled worker, and may earn less. Especially skilled technicians may receive higher salaries than administrators, but these are also within a narrow range of variation. At the textile plant in Ariguanabo, for instance, which is Cuba's most important cotton textile mill, equipped with modern machinery and employing 2,700 workers, the administrator earns $250 monthly. A section technical chief earns $400 monthly. Skilled workers earn $1.75 an hour, which amounts to about $300 a month (figuring an eight-hour day, five days a week), while the lowest-paid *peón* or unskilled worker earns 55¢ an hour, or about $95 a month. At the Venezuela sugar central, which employs 1,700 workers and is the largest central in Cuba, the administrator earns $300 monthly, his assistant $250; the least skilled worker 50¢ hourly, or about $87 monthly; and a skilled worker $1 hourly, or about $173 monthly. These figures are typical of those in the other plants I visited and apparently is the pattern throughout industry.

Outside of industry, the new wage and salary scales have a similar pattern; the salaries of government officials range from $200 or $250 for typical functionaries to a high of $700 a month for Cabinet Ministers. There are certain limited perquisites of office. Many government functionaries have drivers and cars assigned to them for use on government business, mostly four-cylinder compact Volgas or Alfa Romeos, though an occasional Chevy or Ford still serves the Revolutionary Government. Functionaries, especially those dealing directly with foreign visitors, also have expense accounts which allow them to indulge more often than other Cubans in meals at the few remaining plush restaurants frequented still by the wealthy who have not chosen to leave. Public property and accessible to all, such restaurants are a luxury few Cubans can yet afford.

In general, however, from what I could observe, Cubans in the highest positions in government and industry live simply, and the gap between their life styles and those of ordinary workers is no greater, and perhaps less, than that indicated by differential income levels. Expropriated country homes and private yachting clubs, rather than becoming the opulent quarters of a new elite of government bureaucrats and party officials, as has occurred in other Communist countries as diverse as Yugoslavia and the Soviet Union, are now restaurants, resorts, schools, and museums open to everyone. The mansions along Quinta Avenida (Fifth Avenue[!]) in Marianao house scholarship students from worker and peasant families, or are being used as government office buildings.

(The estate and country home of Irénée du Pont, for instance, is a monument to the past, preserved in all its grandeur. The lawns are closely trimmed; its landscaping is impeccable, and the four-square-mile or so estate looks, perhaps, as lovely as ever. The home, with its hand-polished wood, winding staircase, great carved doors, and sunken wine cellar, its fine paintings and elegant furnishings, is much as the du Ponts left it, including family photos over the fireplace and books in the library. The living and drawing rooms are a public restaurant, and the entire home a museum. [In the du Ponts' former library, I found a copy of Everett Dean Martin's *Farewell to Revolution* (1935), and noted a few passages which, in the present Cuban context, are particularly incongruous:

> Revolutionary ideas are justifications for the seizure of power and wealth by violent means. . . . The progress of culture has been achieved not by revolutionary masses, but by lovers of civilization, the inventors, the artists, scientists and philosophers. . . . I doubt if any great problem in history has been solved by revolution."])

The egalitarian social reality of Cuba is most evident precisely where one would expect to find it least evident, inside the factories, mines, and mills, in the social relations between production workers and administrative, technical, and clerical personnel. Informal social relations are direct, and there do not seem to be distinctions of status involving particular and subtle patterns of deference and obeisance to persons in authority. The social barriers (which functionalist sociologists rationalize as inherent in industrialism) between manual and nonmanual workers have disappeared from such modern industrial plants as the cement factory, paper mill, and copper mine I visited. The absence of these barriers is manifested in surface things such as the disappearance of jackets and ties from office personnel and the universal use of *compañero* (we have no word precisely equivalent; a mixture of fellow, mate, companion, and comrade), rather than *señor*.

The comments of a statistician at the paper mill in Cárdenas, in the midst of a spontaneous discussion between several workers and a visiting American sociologist outside the factory diner, point this up:

"Look, I am an office worker. Does that mean anything now? No, I am a worker like other workers. Before, we thought we were something special. We came in our starched shirts and ties, our fine clothes, sat in our air-conditioned offices, and looked down on the millworkers. They could not even pass through our doors without special permission. Now all that has changed.

"I am a worker like other workers. The administrator is a worker among workers. You want to see him, you see him. You do not have to stand and mumble and hope that you will sometime see someone who will take your complaint to the front office. You enter, like a worker who knows he is the owner here, and you ask to see the administrator. Naturally, he has meetings and a great deal of work. He cannot always just stop and speak to you anytime you wish. This is just. But you know that there is a correct reason why he can't see you, and you understand. Usually, this does not happen. You just ask to see him and do, or anyone else whom you might want to see. There are no privileges."

There has been a conscious de-emphasis on the hierarchical authority structure typical of industrial plants elsewhere. There is an attempt to encourage flexible cooperation between co-workers who have different but interdependent tasks, stressing that production is a common effort in the collective interest, and the responsibility of everyone. At the Venezuela sugar central, for instance, a black worker wearing a grease-stained beret, whom I had interviewed seven years earlier, said that "the system of work has changed completely, because we work for ourselves now. The workers, together, resolve the problems of production, in accordance with our knowledge. We have given up overtime pay. The quality of our work is much improved. We guarantee that equipment is maintained in good condition, that repairs are done when necessary, and that production continues. No one has to watch us any more. The administrator has good relations with the workers. He is concerned with the workers' interests and in easing our work. The fact is that we work like hell, throwing ourselves into it [*metiendo la manga y el cola*]."

The quality of relations at this workplace is indicated, I think, by the fact that as I sat in a corner of the mechanics shop talking privately to an old shoemaker now working at the central, other workers kept wandering over to listen or to make their own comments until I stopped asking them to leave simply because it was impolite to do so. After a few moments, the entire shop of 25 workers or more was involved in a spontaneous discussion of my questions, some joining the crowd, others leaving to return to their work. There was not the slightest indication, that I could sense, that the workers felt that it was anything but their right to rest and talk to their visitor.

Of course, the nature of the methods of production at this sugar central make such spontaneity possible. It could not have occurred without destructive consequences at the highly mechanized textile factory, or the cement plant or the paper mill I visited. Yet even there, workers on their breaks would stop to talk easily and openly, without hesitation. At the paper mill, for instance, while I was waiting to see the administrator to arrange for my interviews, I wandered out with my camera and took a few pictures of some teen-agers playing volleyball in the courtyard (who turned out to be apprentices on scholarships from nearby Cárdenas). Within minutes after the kids and I started talking (one wanted to know how to say in English *"Vayase a la casa!"*—"Go Home!"—another what I thought of Cuba's defeat of the U.S. to win the Amateur World Series the day before, and whether my heart was with Cuba or the U.S., etc.), several workers who had come out of the diner joined us; and one of them, the cook himself, recognized me from my visit in 1962. And again, almost seven years to the day after a similar spontaneous gathering there, at the bus stop, a group of workers was formed that soon grew to more than 50, putting in their views about how things had changed in the intervening years. Office workers, several of them women, engineers, and production workers were involved in the discussion, which continued for over an hour.

The workers' sense of ease around administrative and supervisory personnel (typically referred to as *responables*), as well as clerical and technical employees, and the radical narrowing of the social distance between them, is undoubtedly a general consequence, on the one hand, of the recently of the destruction of the old class structure, in which the workers were considered social inferiors and manual work demeaning, and, on the other, of the Revolutionary Government's philosophical and practical emphasis on social equality. However, it is also the direct result of specific practices in the workplace which sustain the egalitarian and nonauthoritarian quality of these relationships.

The authority of those toward the top of the formal structure of the plant is limited and hedged in a number of ways. That "fundamental managerial prerogative" which even the most powerful industrial unions in America have not altered in any essential way—the authority to dismiss workers—does not reside in the hands of the plant officials. Workers cannot even be discharged for cause—negligence, frequent tardiness or absence from work; "back-talk" cannot be penalized by firing or even by fining the offending worker. The typical sanction applied is to transfer the worker—at the same pay—to other, less desirable work in the plant, or ultimately to transfer him out of the plant altogether.[3] "This is a blow," as a young engineer at the cement plant in Mariel put it, "because most workers—at least here—are friends and relatives of each other. They've known each other and worked together a long time. The only thing you can do is talk to him [the worker involved], try to explain to him what he lacks in his work, talk and keep talking. And don't think that those who make mistakes at work aren't often outstanding workers, who do a lot of volunteer overtime and so forth, or that they aren't revolutionaries. They are ready to die for the revolution tomorrow but can't do a day's work today. Like this fellow Jorge, who is really a swell guy. He works watching the cement tank, making sure it stays clean and keeps level, and so on, and he's let the thing overflow three times this year already. Either he's 'studying'—reading on the job—or talking to a *compañero,* who is also not working when he should be. So I've talked to him, and Miguel [the administrator] has talked to him—and, well, he says he'll change, and we can only hope so. . . ."

A brewery worker who had been sanctioned and transferred to another department explained to me:

"The administration understands the workers, and I can say this since I've had my own troubles with them. The administrator is respectful [*cariñoso*] of the workers. So is the Chief of Personnel. Everything is said without insult, if you have to be talked to. I had an argument with some guys here. So I got in a fight. The Personnel Chief broke

---

[3] Labor Law No. 1126 in force since January 1, 1965 permits more severe sanctions, including wage deductions and dismissal. In practice, however, under Labor Minister Captain Jorge Risquet, such sanctions are rarely imposed.

it up and I was pretty mad and said some rough words; I lacked respect and was penalized. I was transferred to another department. I did wrong. They were right."

The decision to request the Ministry to transfer a worker for cause cannot be made by the administrator alone. It requires the combined agreement of the local union leaders, the Communist Party "nucleus" in the plant, and the administrative staff, and the request must then be approved by the Ministry; it is not granted without review. The Party nucleus is made up mostly of production workers, and all of them have been chosen (in a combination of elitist and democratic practice described below) by the workers themselves; the union leaders are elected by the workers and work in the plant also; it is therefore a rare offense which receives even this sanction. Moreover, even in the event that the union leaders agree with the Party leadership and administration, the worker can appeal to the *Consejo de Trabajo,* or Work Council, elected by and composed of the workers in the plant. It is charged with hearing, investigating, reviewing, and deciding on the grievances of individual workers. These Councils grew out of the original *Comisiones de Reclamaciones,* or Grievance Commissions, established when Che was Minister of Industries. Unlike those three-man Commissions, however, which included representatives of the factory administration, the Ministry of Labor, and the workers in the factory, the Work Council is composed entirely of five elected workers representing the workers in the plant. These *Consejos* are apparently regarded by the workers as genuinely representative councils which adjudicate individual grievances fairly and efficiently.

As to the trade unions, however, from what I could observe, and from the vague and infrequent references to them by the workers I interviewed, they seem to have "withered away." The workers do not have an *independent organization* which takes the initiative in the plant, industry, or country as a whole, to assure, let alone demand, improved working conditions or higher wages; no organization exists, as an autonomous force, to protect and advance the immediate interests of the workers, as they see them, independent of the prevailing line of the Communist Party or policies of the Revolutionary Government. The distinction in practice between the role played by the Ministry of Labor and that of the CTC-R, the Workers Federation—if it is clear in formal terms—is not clear to ordinary workers. Nor, indeed, does this distinction seem clear to some of the government officials and national leaders I spoke with.

One reason for the unions' failure to play a sufficiently independent role as workers' advocate is that many union officials (such men, for instance, as Conrado Bequer, former head of the Sugar Workers Union, or Jesús Soto, former Organizational Secretary of the CTC-R), who were independent trade unionists before the revolution, have taken positions in the government which demand entirely different roles of them, as administrators, planners, and political leaders. The newer union officials had limited experience, if any, as trade union leaders before the revolution, and their conceptions have been shaped largely in terms of the developmental objectives of the revolution. This is true on the local as well as the national level. While I discovered several ex–trade union officials in the plants I visited, they were not now involved in the leadership of the union. Many, even on the plant level, had been part of the *Mujalista*-run labor bureaucracy and had been thrown out of their positions early in the revolution. They had never been genuine workers' representatives, in any case. Others had simply taken on new tasks as the revolution developed.

At the Matahambre copper mine, in a conversation I had with several workers, one of them recalled their past union leaders this way:

"My boy, look, what we had in the mine before, put simply, as we miners say in our vulgar way, was a bunch of *marrecones* and sons of whores. The union officials were worse than useless to us; they wore revolvers on their hips and kept *us* in line, not the company. You ask why we tolerated such [poor working] conditions here and this is the answer. Most of them have already gone to the United States. Those that really tried to fight the company got their heads cracked; the good ones couldn't survive."

The unions exist on the local and plant level and have a variety of functions, the central one of which is the protection of the workers' interests in the plant. The unions function essentially, however, less as workers' independent organizations than as committees delegated by the workers to represent them on a day-to-day level concerning working conditions, as well as to provide for the distribution of scarce resources to the workers on a fair basis. One important function of the unions, for instance, is to investigate the living conditions of its members, establish priorities in accordance with the relative comfort or dilapidation of their dwellings, and decide on the allocation of housing as it becomes available. (Other, rather more idiosyncratic services are rendered by the unions also. At the cement plant in Mariel, for instance, I was informed by one worker that "the union bought a cow from our dues, and we keep it in a field nearby and take turns caring for it—which really is little work. We milk it and have plenty of milk for ourselves [despite the rationing].") On the plant level, the unions are active in proposing and initiating changes in the conditions of work which alleviate stress and make work less demanding. At the Ariguanabo textile plant, for instance, the union was responsible for proposing and establishing an arrangement to allow the workers to smoke during working hours. Since smoking is so hazardous there, especially in the cotton mill, this change was an important one to the workers.

"Look," a 64-year-old worker who began work there in 1937 (six years after it opened) remarked, "we work more freely. The workers are trusted. In the old days if they caught you smoking, that was it. You got thrown out. Now we have a place to take a break, to rest, to light a cigarette and talk when we feel the need. Someone else tends your machine when you take a break, and you do the same for him. There is a certain companionship at work now."

Since such changes may also be initiated by the workers through general assemblies of the entire work force, or in given departments, called not only by the union itself but also by the administration, the Party nucleus, or the Workers Council, the specific social function of the union as *the* organization of the workers devoted to protecting and advancing their interests has tended to disappear. In a revolutionary context in which the identity of interests between the workers and the administration is stressed continually (a sign on the desk of Agustín Hernández, the administrator of the Venezuela sugar central, reads: "The prestige and authority of the administrator will be directly related to the real links he has with the mass of workers in his unit"), and the workers themselves believe in it, the distinction between the Party, Workers Council, general assembly, and the union as means of furthering their interests has become vague in their minds. Nor, they say, do they feel the need for an independent organization. They have (what to an observer from the U.S. seems to be) a naïve faith in the harmony of interests between themselves, the administration of the plant, and the Revolutionary Government. The differences that do arise can be resolved, the workers insist, by free discussion and without conflict.

This may be true at the moment, and I think from my own observations that it is, and probably will be as long as sufficiently rapid economic growth seems assured by present policies. However, the problems of development are difficult and intractable, especially in the perilous international conditions in which the revolutionaries must resolve them. Tendencies toward the bureaucratization of decision-making in industry are strong under ordinary conditions. Pressed by Cuba's need for accelerated growth, such tendencies could be increased; administrators, anxious to fulfill and overfulfill

quotas, and to respond to the political demands made on
them by the Revolutionary Government, might be tempted
to concentrate more and more decisions in their own hands
and to utilize increasingly tougher methods to discipline the
workers. This, of course, is contrary to the present premise
and practice of the revolutionary leadership. Like its emphasis on flexible cooperation in the plant between co-
workers, the leadership's egalitarian emphasis, and its refusal to countenance special privileges, is also a conscious
decision. Again, however, the possibility exists that under
the social pressures of what Che called "the weeds that shoot
up so easily in the fertilized soil of state subsidization," of
vested interests that may emerge (risen careerists, bureaucrats, and political opportunists), and of some members of
the old privileged strata incorporated into positions of
authority in the economic administration, government, or
Party, the thrust toward social equality clearly evident at
present could be subtly, even unconsciously, deflected.

To prevent such "bureaucratic deformation" of the revolution, as Lenin termed it, whether in industry or government, Lenin argued (*against* Trotsky) that the workers had
to have the freedom to organize to protect both their immediate interests on the job and their relative share of the
national income, and that their spokesmen had to have the
freedom to represent those interests, while at the same
time defending the revolutionary regime. (In practice, Lenin
and his comrades were to curtail rights that they upheld
in principle.) The Cuban leaders recognize this principle,
and assert, at least privately, that they are not satisfied
with the present situation in the unions. I was told by Carlos
Rafael Rodríguez, for instance, that he feels that the unions
have been inadequately concerned with the defense of the
day-to-day interests of the workers and overconcerned with
spurring the workers to meet production targets. In his book-
lined office in the headquarters of the Communist Party's
Central Committee in Havana, he said that "what was

originally Che's antibureaucratic thesis [to keep the political leadership functions of the Party and the specific union functions separate] became an antidemocratic thesis. The unions are transmission belts of the Party directives to the workers but have insufficiently represented the workers to the Party or the Revolutionary Government. They cannot merely be instruments of the Party without losing their purpose. Administrators, after all, can also be *hijos de putas* [sons of whores], and if they are, the workers have to be able to throw them out—and, for that matter, do the same with any bureaucrats. . . ."

The workers I spoke to throughout the country in long, often very probing conversations felt confident that they could "throw out" any *hijo de puta* they felt was maltreating them. While the concrete changes in working conditions scarcely seem to be profound alterations of the workers' role in the productive process, the cumulative impact of such changes has given the workers a sense of well-being and freedom at work, rather than estrangement from it. The cynicism which is the characteristic informal philosophy of manual workers elsewhere, and expresses their resentment and sense of exploitation, apparently has disappeared among Cuban workers. The conditions under which they work *have* changed radically. Even where, as among formerly "privileged workers," their standard of living outside the plant has not improved materially, or may even have lowered, the health and safety conditions in the plant have improved considerably, and the pace and intensity of the work have lessened, bringing them a better life on the job. Most workers, therefore, seem to identify strongly with the revolutionary leadership and to be really willing to work extra hours without overtime pay, and to do voluntary work in the plant or in agricultural production, planting coffee or citrus-fruit trees or cutting sugar cane. As one worker put it to me, "Everyone wants to be able to tell his grandchildren that he was in the harvest of the 'ten million.' "

However, one consequence of their present economic security (or the abolition of what Max Weber called "the whip of hunger") and of their sense of freedom in the plant is that while productivity measured by what each worker produces per day (because he works longer hours) and per unit wage cost has risen considerably, according to government figures, productivity per man-hour apparently has not. "Absenteeism" also continues to be a problem throughout industry. Captain Jorge Risquet, the Minister of Labor, claims that "a vanguard with Communist conscious- ness [*conciencia*] at work has been developing, but at the same time there is still a rear guard whose conduct reflects the ideology of the capitalist past. . . . As the number of centers winning the Heroes of Moncada Banners rises, and as volunteer work, the 'advanced workers' movement [of outstanding workers honored by their fellows], develops, and more and more workers renounce overtime pay, all of which are expressions of the growth of Communist con- sciousness, there has also been an accentuation and spread of absenteeism, negligence, and inadequate use of the work- day. . . ."

Risquet attributes the residue of "capitalist ideology" among the workers, interestingly enough, not to those who were workers before the revolution, or are the sons of workers, but to those who were previously self-employed petit bourgeois, "lumpen," or vagrants, who must now work in industry. In part, it is probably true that such new workers have not yet adapted to the discipline of industrial work, and that this is a contributing factor to the absenteeism and lowered productivity. It is also certain that the adminis- tration of production is still in the hands of inadequately skilled and trained individuals in many places throughout the country, as workers have risen from the ranks rapidly to assume administrative and technical responsibilities. And while the effect of the embargo imposed by the U.S. and the changeover to Soviet technology is no longer a major problem, this still continues to pose serious obstacles to productive efficiency, requiring often crude and improvised methods to be used.

There is an unavoidable dialectic here between the growth of consciousness and the abolition of alienation—of which the revolutionary leaders are quite aware. The workers have lessened the pace and intensity of their work—where possible—because that in itself is an important gain of the revolution. Consciously or unconsciously, they seem to have decided that the benefits of increased production should not come at the expense of their improved life on the job. Until now, the Revolutionary Government has responded to this dialectic by attempting to deepen consciousness. The emphasis has been on persuasion, exhortation, education, rather than on the imposition of punitive sanctions. "Even though they are *legally in force,*" as Risquet puts it, "fines, suspensions, etc., are typical capitalist sanctions . . . which are equally obsolete and harmful, and we have refrained from imposing them and will continue to do so. . . . If we think that sanctions are the only way or the best way to combat these antisocial manifestations, we are wrong. Sanctions must be the last resort. Education and re-education through collective criticism and the help of other workers are the basic weapons in this struggle. . . ."

The workers meet regularly to discuss production goals. The goals of their factory, mine, or mill in the National Plan are submitted to them at the year's beginning. The goals for the plant as a whole and for particular departments are discussed, section by section, and, in most plants, in a general assembly of the entire work force. Once approved or modified by the workers—usually to increase the targets—the plan returns to the relevant Ministry (there are now five industrial Ministries in place of the former unified Ministry of Industries) for further study, and then is sent back to the plant for the workers' final approval. The workers I spoke with evidently considered themselves deeply involved in this process and claimed that the assemblies, run jointly by the administration, union, and Party leadership, were genuine exchanges of ideas and that the plan was often substantially changed by their suggestions.

The revolutionaries have thus far rejected punitive sanctions; and they have rejected what they consider to be "capitalist" or material and individual incentives—which is the path the Soviet Union took and has accentuated further recently by introducing criteria of profitability at the level of the enterprise to govern production. Fidel has spoken out strongly against what he considers to be capitalist tendencies in the Soviet Union and Eastern European socialist countries, and his heretical call to "build communism simultaneously with building socialism" is the doctrinal principle guiding the revolutionary leadership. It is the quest to build what Che called "the new man," rejecting "Communist economics without Communist morality."

"The capitalist society," to quote Risquet again, "is based on the power of money; it is guided by the principle that a man is worth as much as he owns. A thief lucky enough to amass a fortune becomes an illustrious man and he might even get to be president of the republic. Our society is based on merit. And the most precious things a man can amass are his record and the awareness that he has fulfilled his duty and the tasks of his generation, his homeland, and his revolution."

This conception of socialist morality is at the heart of the Cuban revolution's uniqueness among Communist states, because it is combined with an egalitarian practice and a rejection of individual and material incentives in favor of collective and moral ones. Talking to Cuban workers throughout the country, it becomes quickly apparent that these are not merely revolutionary slogans, but commitments deeply felt by many. In their descriptions of what it means to be a Communist, and what is required to merit membership in the Party, the workers emphasized moral qualities.

As the cook at the paper mill put it, "You cannot join the Party unless the workers who know you best and work with you think that you are deserving. You must be of good morality. You must be an advanced worker, you must have the respect of your fellows in everything and be an example of discipline and sacrifice."

Most important, while it is hard to know in even the lengthy interviews I had how much is cliché and how much consciousness, many of the workers themselves emphasize that they are engaged in the construction of a new society, shorn of the exploitation of man by man and based on the premise of producing for the common good rather than individual profit. It is evident that they have talked about these questions, and thought about them. This came out clearly in my discussion with several miners. The mine's administrator, Captain Jesús Parra, a young mulatto wearing a sleeveless undershirt, grimy and sweaty with Matahambre's red earth, had just stated that "the reason for our being is for the benefit of the workers" when a miner broke in to give an example in the new Law No. 270. It gives the workers in a plant that wins the Banner of the Heroes of Moncada retirement and disability benefits equal to 100 percent of their wages. Otherwise workers retire at 70 percent of their pay, up to $250 a month. I suggested that this sounded like a "material stimulus" rather than a moral one —which brought a startled look to the worker's face. Captain Parra grinned. "Do you *really* consider that a 'material incentive'?" he asked. "I do not think so. We understand that other socialist countries have fallen into capitalist habits and forms. But we have learned from this. We have applied collective, not individual, measures. Only a small minority of the workers do not merit the collective benefits which go through them to their families. Workers cannot have their wages reduced as a sanction. They cannot be fired. They know they have work. It is a moral principle of the revolution that we cannot *punish* the families of those who avoid their responsibilities. But shall we also *reward* those few equally?"

"Didn't Fidel say something about building Communism simultaneously with socialism?" I asked.

The previous miner, rather tough, responded:

"I don't understand. It seems to me to be simple justice. Those who do not sacrifice, who sit on their shit, do not merit such rewards. Only those who sacrifice do. And it is us, not some distant government or Jesús [the administrator], who decides who merits and who does not. We know, after all, who works. We decide, department by department, who has done his share and who hasn't. And it isn't as if they don't have a chance to change their situation. We talk to them. We try to explain to them that the old ways are no good any more. That the bosses are gone. That we work for ourselves now and that they are cheating on *us*. And they *do* change. How many of the twelve hundred miners here do you think did not benefit from Law No. 270? A handful, a few, not more than a dozen. Is there something wrong with this? How can this create privileges? It is the majority who gain."

At this point, professor that I am, I gave a brief lecture about developments in the Soviet Union and its use of Stakhanovism. "The principle of individual and material rewards," I said, "became the basis of their development, rationalized by the slogan 'From each according to his ability, to each according to his work'; texts from Lenin and Stalin were cited to justify and allow the growth of ever-wider gaps in status and material welfare between ordinary and privileged workers, the heroes of socialist labor, and especially between the workers and technicians, scientists, administrators, and even party bureaucrats. Was it not based on the same principle of individual merit and sacrifice that the ideals of socialism were distorted in such a way?"

Everyone was listening very carefully. Jesús Parra broke

the silence. "This will not happen here. We, as I have already said, are conscious of errors elsewhere in the socialist world. Our emphasis, as the *compañero* says, is on collective benefits, not individual ones, benefits which cannot be bought and sold, which cannot enter the marketplace, and which cannot be hoarded and accumulated, but which can only better the lives of all the workers in their work, and in their lives as a whole. The changes in the conditions of work in this mine, and in every workplace in this country, directly benefit all workers. The free education, medical care, nominal rents, the work clothes and shoes and hot meals provided *gratis*—these are earned by all the workers and received by all the workers. Such is the way we choose to go."

Contrary to Captain Parra and the miners, however, the 100 percent retirement benefits are clearly material incentives rather than moral ones, and have—at least so far—benefited only a small fraction of the workers in the country, somewhere around 6 percent, according to government sources. While this is, from what I could tell, a rare departure from the central emphasis on moral suasion and collective benefits, this tension between contrasting paths of development under socialism is critical for the future course of the revolution. The revolutionaries have not chosen to adopt the existing models of Soviet development, or succumbed to the pressures of those who urge them to do so. I can guess from discussions with "highly placed" sources, though, that there continue to be serious differences within the leadership on this question; and that there are those who argue that absenteeism and inadequate productivity are reflections of the lack of individual incentives, on the one hand, and of insufficient "discipline," on the other; if they win, Cuba will be taking the road already trod by the Communists elsewhere.

There are signs that "labor brigades" organized along military lines, as well as the actual utilization of "conscript labor," are already quite important in agricultural work, especially in sugar-cane harvesting. Of course, that the Army is engaged in "productive work" is not in itself reason to believe that "paramilitary forms of labor organization" are increasing. It is difficult to sort out the tendencies and countertendencies in any revolution, especially the Cuban, since its leadership continues to be independent, pragmatic, and experimental, bound in reality by little of the "Marxist-Leninist" dogma espoused by Communists elsewhere. The Fidelistas' independent leadership of the struggle for power, despite the old Communists' derogation of it as "bourgeois romantic" and "adventurist," and their success at putting through a socialist revolution 90 miles from the United States, when the Communists were urging a more moderate course and slower pace, have taught the Fidelistas to question the revolutionary judgment of the Communists, as well as to accentuate their own independent and pragmatic politics. Yet the counterpressures are great. It would be easier in the short run to abandon their dreams of an egalitarian and nonauthoritarian socialism and adopt Soviet political economic models. Neither Soviet nor "Western" economists think the revolutionaries can successfully utilize moral suasion and collective rewards to motivate and maintain the commitment of the Cuban people to development.

At the moment, the revolutionary leadership continues to experiment with competing forms of factory administration and labor organization, ranging from paramilitary labor brigades in agriculture in some parts of the country to politico-bureaucratic and quasi-syndicalist forms elsewhere. Typically, the administrators are essentially political cadre, appointed by the Ministry for their reliability and qualities of leadership rather than their technical capacity—though they may also be technically trained, and are expected to study the productive process in their plants with care. The administrator is the chief authority in the plant in formal terms. In practice, however, his authority is shared (to an extent a short visit cannot reveal) with the Communist Party nucleus, of which he is typically also a member, and the union. In places, the Committee of Advanced Workers, selected as outstanding workers by their peers, may also exercise considerable influence over the practical administration of work. The mixture of political and administrative roles is greatest where workers have emerged from the ranks since the revolution and moved into top administrative positions in the same plants they have worked in for many years. They may have been involved in the resistance against Batista, active in the 26th of July movement, and in the leadership of the union local once the revolutionaries took power. This was the pattern, for instance, for Miguel Pérez la Rosa, about 50, the administrator of the cement plant in Mariel, and René Riera, in his mid-thirties, the administrator of the brewery in Manacas.

The latter, employed in the brewery since 1957, where he worked on the bottle conveyor belt, had been General Secretary of the union local, then was appointed personnel head, and also became the organizational secretary of the Party nucleus before being appointed administrator.

Miguel, who has worked in the plant for 27 years, was a mechanic when it was nationalized (and he still was in 1962 when we interviewed him), moving to head of production, and then to administrator. "We tossed the old bosses out ourselves," he told me. "That is, we politely invited them to leave. The Vice-President of the company was here, and so was the manager, Walter Foster, and we said to them, 'Please, your job has finished. You may go now.' And so they went. I was never a Communist, had nothing to do with them, but I was active in the 26th of July cell here and involved in bringing this place to a standstill on the 9th of April [1958], in the general strike. Somehow, one of the major parts got broken. The fellows who led the strike, about six or seven of them, were taken prisoner, though I escaped."

The administrative practice of sharing authority with the

workers' committees, and the effectiveness of worker-administrators in maintaining revolutionary élan, has led to experiments in some plants which formally recognize or reach
beyond this situation. The administrator is elected by the
workers, rather than appointed by the Ministry, and the
plant is run by an Administrative Council composed of
elected workers, who continue to work in production, and
members of the Party and/or its youth group. While the
workers on the Council are elected at large, the Party
representatives are selected by the members of the Party
nucleus. (The Party membership itself is selected as follows:
The workers in the plant nominate those who they believe
merit Party membership, because of their outstanding qualities as workers and because of their "advanced" consciousness, "Marxist-Leninist" ideology, study and self-education,
and devotion to the revolution. When the Party nucleus has
investigated them thoroughly, an explanation and justification
of the reasons why some are accepted and others rejected
for membership is given to the workers at large, and the
decisions may be "ratified" or questioned by the workers,
requiring the Party to investigate further those who the
workers claim should not have been rejected. The Party
may then admit them to membership or decide against it,
again clarifying their reasons at a meeting of the workers in
the plant—but the final decision remains the Party's.)

None of the plants I visited are administered directly by
the workers' Administrative Council, and I do not know
how widespread this practice is. Reportedly, the Guido
Pérez brewery (formerly Hatuey), in El Cotorro outside
Havana, has been run this way since December, 1968;
and the productivity of the brewery's 380 workers is reported to have risen "significantly," and a heightened élan
to be present, since the workers took control.[4]

---

[4] Arthur McEwan, Assistant Professor of Economics, Harvard
University, who visited the brewery in the summer of 1969, is my
source for this information.

The significant question is less how typical this form of workers' control is at present than what it means concerning the views and plans of the Revolutionary Government. Will they interpret the increased motivation and productivity of the workers at plants like Guido Pérez to mean that workers' control over production decisions in the plant, over the conditions and methods of work, ought to be broadened? Will they generalize this experience and attempt to deepen the democratic content of the revolution by encouraging such forms of workers' control throughout industry? Will they go on to involve the workers themselves, through elected representatives, in at least the same sorts of decisions on the level of specific industrial sectors as they do make in the plants? Will there be an attempt to devise forms for the participation of workers' representatives in the actual formulation of the National Plan? At present, despite the apparently ample participation of the workers in discussions and decisions concerning the *implementation* of the objectives of the national economic plan set for their plant, the workers have no role whatsoever, to my knowledge, in determining the plan itself. They have nothing to say over investment priorities; the decision as to what and how much is to be produced is made by the central planning bodies of the Revolutionary Government responsible to the Council of Ministers.

Theoretically, of course, the Revolutionary Government's policies and the creation of the national economic plan are guided by the Communist Party, which is supposed to be the political organization of the masses and responsible to them. Yet despite the fact that the Party seems to be respected by the workers, and considered by them to represent and respond to their interests (if the interviews I had with countless workers throughout the country are typical), there is little question that in practice the Party is responsible to itself—and, above all, to Fidel—and not to the citizenry at large. In the seven years since I last visited Cuba, little has been done to create a political organization which is responsible to the people. The Central Committee of the Communist Party was not chosen by the rank and file of the Party throughout the country, and there seems to be no inclination to carry out such elections within the Party itself. On the contrary, the first national congress of the newly created Communist Party had been scheduled for 1969, but was canceled, with the "explanation" that there was too much work to do, that it would divert energies from the ten-million-ton harvest. There was no public debate about this decision, and there has been none about fundamental questions concerning the revolution for several years.

In the past, especially when Che was active in the revolutionary leadership, genuine differences between government leaders were still publicly debated, if in muted tones. The pages of *Revolución,* the newspaper of the 26th of July, and of *Hoy,* the old Communist Party newspaper, clashed openly over issues as diverse as the revolutionary responsibility of the artist and the road to revolution in Latin America. *Cuba Socialista,* the theoretical journal of the embryonic Party, and other journals such as *Verde Olivo, Nuestra Industria,* and *Trimestre* frequently had articles debating such critical questions as the role of a bank under socialism, the relative merits of central versus decentralized planning, and material versus moral incentives. Today, public debate is absent. The Communist Party newspaper, *Granma,* and the edition published by its youth group are equally unilluminating and uninformative about how the views of the revolutionary leaders may differ on domestic and foreign questions.

The only views that reach the public on a national level are the official views of government leaders, and only after the debates—which reportedly involve the expression of a wide range of views on policy questions—have been resolved in private among the members of the Council of Ministers. A relevant example of this process occurred while I was in

Cuba. The Revolutionary Government passed Law 1225, on September 1, 1969, which requires that everyone in the labor force carry an identification card listing his occupational and employment record, and making the maintenance of such records on their employees mandatory for all administrators. Without prior authorization from the Regional Office of the Ministry of Labor, no one may change his place of employment, and administrators may not employ new workers without such authorization. This is an essential economic measure which, however, has inherent political implications. The Revolutionary Government, if it is to be able to plan economic development rationally, requires accurate information on the composition and mobility of the labor force; it must be in a position to correlate wages, productivity, prices, and the growth and movement of the labor force, so that employment and investment are kept in proper balance, without the intervention of the market and the consequent disemployment, unemployment, and underemployment of men and resources. However, this unquestionably entails some limitation on the freedom of individuals to choose where they live and work, and will involve a system of formal controls. There was extended debate on this question in the Council of Ministers, between those in favor of greater regimentation, or "labor discipline," and those favoring procedures to facilitate the free change of jobs, within the minimal limits required by planning. The debate was apparently resolved by a compromise which requires the administration of the place of work to state in writing to the worker within sixty days the reasons for not permitting him to leave his present position. (I say the debate was "apparently" resolved because the Statute had not yet been officially promulgated.) The worker may then appeal to the Workers Council, which may overrule the administration, permitting the administration, however, up to two years to find a substitute for the worker if his skills are essential and difficult to replace.

The range of differences expressed in the Council of Ministers concerning the contents of this law was not made public in Cuba. Nor has there been public discussion of it in centers of work throughout the country, as is customary with other laws (such as those on workers' emulation) which specifically require the participation and consent of the mass of workers for their practical implementation. Yet here is a practical revolutionary measure which is the epitome of the inherent tension between socialist planning and individual liberties. The system of controls necessary to implement and enforce the law has an inherent authoritarian potential which, as elsewhere throughout a socialist society, can only be kept in check by the conscious creation of mechanisms to check that potential; it requires the establishment of formal procedures which permit planning and individual liberty to complement rather than contradict each other. The surest way to resolve this tension with the least damage to either social or individual needs is to encourage free and full discussion in workers' assemblies, in public meetings, and in the mass media, so that meaningful alternatives can be debated and chosen by the people themselves. This would increase the likelihood, on the one hand, that questions would be examined thoroughly and the range of options explored, and, on the other, that revolutionary measures would be understood, approved, and implemented with the least difficulty.

The fact is that, despite their experimentalism and originality in many areas, the Cuban revolutionaries have so far done little to establish institutions that will guarantee that competing points of view can be heard within the revolutionary socialist consensus; that meaningful alternatives are debated; that policies are initiated, as well as implemented, by the citizenry at large.

This does not mean, so far as I was able to observe, that dissent is repressed or that ideas cannot be expressed freely —even ones hostile to the revolution. Cuba is a remarkable revolutionary country, where the Voice of America and Spanish-language counterrevolutionary broadcasts by exiles, as well as regular programing on such Miami stations as WGBS, can be heard on the radio anywhere. People listen to these broadcasts without noticeable hesitation and without interference. Old Hollywood movies starring Ronald Reagan or John Wayne show on late television, and films from Japan, England, France, Italy, Mexico, and Brazil, as well as Eastern European countries, may be seen at the neighborhood theater. The libraries at the universities, and the National Library in Havana, have many fully accessible anti-Communist volumes. Among those at the National Library (José Martí) are: M. Djilas, *La Nueva Clase: Análisis del Régimen Comunista;* Fulton Sheen, *Communism and the Conscience of the West;* Hilaire Belloc, *El Estado Servil;* Imre Nagy, *Contradicciones del Comunismo;* Victor Kravchenko, *I Chose Freedom;* J. Edgar Hoover, *Masters of Deceit;* G. N. Shuster, *Con Mi Silencio Hablo: la Historia del Cardenal Mindszenty;* and Eli Stanley Jones, *Cristo y el Comunismo.* Journals and newspapers, in English, German, and Spanish, are available, including the current issues of the *New York Times,* the Los Angeles *Times,* the *New Statesman,* and *Excelsior* (from Mexico). Less current, but obviously still dribbing in are the Latin American editions of *Time* magazine, *New Republic, Nation,* and *New Politics.* There is a relatively good representation of works on the Cuban revolution, including my own writing; Paul Baran, *Reflections on the Cuban Revolution;* the U.S. Department of State, Bureau of Public Affairs, *Cuba* (the "white paper" written by Arthur Schlesinger, Jr.); the German edition of Boris Goldenberg, *The Cuban Revolution and Latin America;* and Theodore Draper's *Castro's Cuba.*

In art, the experimentation with a mix of modern and classical forms is evident in the exquisite ballet of Alicia Alonso and the films directed by Alfredo Guevara. The novels of Edmundo Desnoes and Norbeto Fuentes, the drama of Anton Arufat, and the poetry of Heberto Padilla, none of which by the remotest criterion would fit the test of what passes for "socialist realism" in other Communist countries, are published by the Union of Cuban Writers, the Casa de las Americas, and other agencies. To be sure, some of the more experimental works are criticized, often severely, by other writers, who are self-styled defenders of "revolutionary art." Thus, Fuentes' novel on the anti-Batista struggle in the Sierra Escambray was condemned as "counterrevolutionary" by the pseudonymous writer Leopoldo Avila in the pages of *Verde Olivo,* the official journal of the armed forces, as was Padilla's poem, "In Difficult Times," and others in his collection, "Out of the Game." The Union of Writers and Artists published these works, awarded them literary prizes for which they were chosen by an international jury, and included the critiques which denoted them as "counterrevolutionary."

"Marxism-Leninism" has been elevated to official philosphical status; it is a required course at the University and the Worker-Peasant Faculty, yet "input-output" economic analysis and functionalist sociology are also studied at the University; and the selection of readings is representative of these disciplines in the United States. Those who want to qualify for membership in the Communist Party are supposed to be free of "religious doctrine," but the churches are open, and services offered without hindrance. I attended mass at the San Carmen Church, for instance, and witnessed the baptism of the infant son of a young black couple; they, and the priest, were obviously pleased to have me take their photo and their names and addresses, and promise to send them copies.

Discussions I had with the workers ranged over domestic and international questions. There was little indication that any subject was taboo or point of view sacred, or that people attempt to hide their dissatisfaction with the revolution. In the midst of one such discussion at the Venezuela sugar central, in which the workers had been detailing the benefits to them of the revolution, one leaned over to another, gave him an elbow in the side, and commented, "And you want to go to Miami, huh?"

Wherever I went, Cubans seemed to speak freely about whatever they wished, despite the fact that in literally every block in Havana, and similarly in towns and cities across the country, there is a Committee for the Defense of the Revolution, charged with being informed fully about the actions of their neighbors. In Havana alone, 973,494 members of the CDR are involved in "revolutionary vigilance." Close to three million members of the CDR are active in the entire country. Among their activities, aside from "vigilance," are urging people to get chest x-rays, and women to get vaginal smears, and checking to see that they do, repairing neighborhood housing, collecting old newspapers and used cans and bottles, and "recuperating" other raw materials, coordinating volunteer labor in agriculture, and seeing that the streets are kept clean, flowers planted, and children in school. The CDRs seemed to be an accepted part of the neighborhood, according to my random talks with CDR volunteers and their neighbors, not unlike air-raid wardens and civil-defense volunteers in our own country during the Second World War.

The CDRs do engage in surveillance, however, as does the secret police under the Ministry of the Interior, and Cuba reportedly has several thousand political prisoners (there are no official figures) in camps said by their relatives and friends to be located in every province (though I could not verify this personally during my brief visit). What constitutes a "political crime" is not specified by law. There continue to be no formal safeguards of freedom of speech and association, or of personal, civil, and political rights. In practice, Cubans typically seem to feel secure in their persons and to speak freely, even with strangers, despite the absence of institutions and juridical procedures designed to protect the individual and guarantee his freedom from unreasonable search and seizure or arbitrary arrest and punishment. Of course, even when such institutions are long-established, they are still fragile; "guarantees" may be irrelevant when a government is determined to eliminate serious political dissent, and to utilize vague "conspiracy" charges to harass, intimidate, and imprison its political opponents, as is happening at the moment in our own country. Nonetheless, to the extent to which the liberties that exist in practice in Cuba continue to depend on what Fidel has called "the revolution's generosity," the situation is inherently unstable and dangerous.

In the recent trial and conviction (January, 1968) of the so-called "microfactionists" led by Aníbal Escalante, former organizational secretary of the prerevolutionary Communist Party (PSP), several of the government's charges were sufficiently vague to encompass even *pro*revolutionary dissent from the present policies of the Revolutionary Government. Aside from the specific charge that they presented "false, calumnious data about the plans of the Revolution to Officials of foreign countries [Czechoslovakia, East Germany, Soviet Union] with the intent of undermining the international relations of Cuba with other governments, [and took] secret documents from the Central Committee and the Ministry of Basic Industry," the charges are essentially that Escalante and his comrades differed with the Revolutionary Government's policies and attempted to convince others of their views. They were accused of "furthering ideological differences" in the Party, despite the fact that "on numerous occasions" several of them had been "called in to discuss their *ideas* and *attitudes* which were opposed to the line of the Revolution" (my italics). The Statement of the Central Committee summarizing the charges concluded, finally, that "the arguments utilized by such elements, by coinciding with those of the pseudo revolutionaries of Latin America and the imperialists' themes, actually situate this group within the complex of forces opposing the Revolution." Escalante was sentenced by the Revolutionary Tribunal to fifteen years' imprisonment, the others to shorter sentences.

To say the least, this trial might have had a chilling effect on the expression of opposing views even within the Central Committee itself, and in the country at large among revolutionary cadres; and it sets a precedent for the imprisonment of revolutionaries who deviate from the Party line. The fact that Escalante was unpopular for his previous attempt to control the formation of the Party and restrict access to important positions only to old Communists loyal to him made his imprisonment easy; it does not seem, from my conversations with leading government figures and revolutionary intellectuals, to have been interpreted as a precedent that could be applied to them as well. But this is precisely the danger. Once "attitudes, ideas, and arguments" can lead to imprisonment, the potential for the repression of any and all who express competing views, even the most loyal revolutionaries, has been established. It is good, but not enough, to say, as Fidel did after the trial, that "the revolutionary courts were not as severe as some would have wished, but in the final analysis, unnecessary severity has never been a characteristic of this revolution." The experience of the Soviet Union is sufficient evidence that "unnecessary severity" is not easily controlled, whatever the intentions of the revolutionary leadership, once the precedents and procedures (including secret trials like that of Escalante and his comrades) are set into motion.

Seven years ago, at the time of the first "Escalante affair," which led to Escalante's public denunciation but not imprisonment, Fidel's major lesson to the Cuban people in a nationally televised and broadcast speech was that "the suppression of ideas was a myopic, sectarian, stupid, and warped conception of Marxism that could change the Revolution into a tyranny. And that is not revolution! . . . And what must the Revolution be? The Revolution must be a school of courageous men, the Revolution must be a school in which there is liberty of thought!" What lesson do Fidel and his fellow revolutionary leaders want drawn today?

The threat to the revolution from the United States is real and unavoidable, but the revolution's social base among the workers and peasants is secure. There is no serious internal opposition to the revolution; there is no threat from within. The revolution has been a profoundly liberating experience for the Cuban people; they are conscious of themselves as historical actors, and have learned to believe in themselves, to take the implausible for granted and the unprecedented as certain—as "no one," they will tell you, "who has not lived within the revolutionary process can understand."

"The most transcendental changes are within us," they say, "the ones that you cannot see, that are visible only to ourselves. No one who knows the Cuban past as only we can, of whoredom and corruption, of the infinite capacity to deceive oneself and others, to sell oneself to the highest bidder in all things, to lack faith in anything but the vulgar and to accept the obscene as natural—no one who lived this past as we did can doubt the great changes in our beings.

"What was Cuba?—an insignificant whorehouse for the West, a country known only for its sugar and the delights of the flesh, a country of 'simple blacks and *tropicales*,' and now we are trying to create 'the new man.'"

Such talk of creating the "new man," while it has its element of Spanish overstatement, self-flattery, and romanticism, is real. To create that "new man" will require not merely new economic but also new political forms. It will require the consciousness and the will of the revolutionaries; indeed, it will require an effort even more "decisive" for the revolution's future than the present one to produce ten million tons of sugar. Without it, they will not create that form of socialism which Che dreamt of. "The socialist society that we want," he said, "is absolutely democratic; it is based on the needs and the aspirations of the people, and the people have a major role in all decisive points."

The revolutionary leaders have consciously rejected the Soviet model of "how to construct Communism." Cuba is "the black sheep of the family," as Fidel put it, "because it does not follow the beaten path even if that path leads nowhere!" But that Soviet path included not only material incentives and vast inequalities, but also the use of force to repress dissent and the establishment of a monopoly of political power in the hands of the Communist Party. Social inequality and authoritarian controls reinforce and strengthen one another. If the revolutionaries in Cuba reject the one, they must reject the other. "Our task," Che told me in 1961, "is to enlarge democracy within the revolution as much as possible. As you have well said, we are pragmatic. . . . We feel that the government's chief function is to assure channels for the expression of the popular will. What forms this will take, we cannot say yet. This will depend on the political system to be elaborated."

Elaborating this political system is now on the order of the day. The revolutionaries have avoided this task so far in part because of their fear of prematurely institutionalizing forms which will freeze their relations with the people, and prevent that spontaneity and improvisation and the sense of common effort and participation which has characterized their activity so far. The revolutionaries have acted to a great extent, as I wrote several years ago, as if unconsciously guided by a paraphrase of the German socialist Rosa Luxemburg's famous revolutionary axiom: "Mistakes committed by a genuine revolutionary government are much more fruitful and worthwhile historically than the infallibility of the very best central committee." Most important, they have no models which they simply can adopt wholesale. Political forms in the Communist countries, especially in the Soviet bloc, have led, in Che's words, "into dogmatic extremes, into cold scholasticism, into isolation from the masses"; they do not want to "create salaried workers docile to official thinking nor 'fellows' who live under the wing of the budget, exercising 'freedom' in quotation marks."

"We are," Che wrote, "seeking something new that will allow a perfect identification between the government and the community as a whole, adapted to the conditions of the building of socialism peculiar to our country, and avoiding as much as possible the commonplaces of bourgeois democracy transplanted to the society in formation (such as legislative houses, for example). There have been some experiments intended to gradually create the institutionalization of the revolution, but without too much hurry. The major thing holding us back has been the fear that any formal mechanism might separate us from the masses and the individual, making us lose sight of the ultimate and most important revolutionary aspiration: to see man freed from alienation."

Anyone who thinks the answers to the revolutionaries' dilemma are easy has not thought seriously about the questions. The establishment of socialist democracy will require the same pragmatism, experimentalism, and boldness, and the "same strong feelings of love for the people" (Che) and revolutionary optimism that have brought them this far, and have allowed them to transform the prerevolutionary social structure more profoundly and rapidly than has any other "socialist" revolution anywhere. Some questions that they must deal with, while yet involved in a struggle for development, are: How can they guarantee a free press when there is no private ownership of enterprises? What sort of representative system—and what kind of judiciary—is compatible with public ownership of the means of production and central planning? How are the technical requirements of expertise and authority in a planned economy to be reconciled with popular election of government officials? What forms will prevent bureaucratic control of the new society? And how can they do all this while defending the revolution?

Whatever the answers the revolutionaries give to these

questions in practice, it is unquestionable that they must choose soon between that "beaten path that leads nowhere" and one far more difficult for not having been trodden before, toward the establishment of socialist democratic political forms commensurate with the revolution's egalitarian and liberating content. "Then," in the vision that Che bequeathed the revolutionaries, "they will come to sing the song of the new man with the authentic voice of the people."

Preface

🖏 THIS book is based on data drawn from interviews with industrial workers in revolutionary Cuba in the summer of 1962 at a time when, as we know, the United States government ordinarily prohibited American citizens from traveling to Cuba. The needs of scholarship and of our government's foreign policy scarcely coincided. Indeed, I have written this book on the assumption that the Cold War and the needs of American policy should not dictate the problems, premises, or analytical framework of scholarship, nor inhibit scholars from writing on socially relevant and "controversial" subjects. Since the U.S. government did allow correspondents special permission to travel to Cuba, I made both of my trips to the island as a correspondent, in 1961 for Radio KPFA, Berkeley, of the Pacifica Foundation, and in 1962 for *The Nation*.

Throughout the summer of 1962 my wife, Marilyn, and I traveled the length of the country interviewing workers in 21 plants scattered over its six provinces. (See map.) Marilyn's companionship and her willingness (while pregnant) to endure the rigors of three months of travel over rough roads, in semi-tropical climate, lodging in uncomfortable quarters and living on the rather meager diet that was then available in Cuba in order to share the interviewing with me went far beyond the bounds of duty. Without her aid, this study would not have been possible.

Neither would it have been possible without the cooperation I received from the Revolutionary Government and its various bureaus, especially the Ministry of Industry and its head, *Comandante* Ernesto "Ché" Guevara. *Comandante* Guevara had his ministry provide me with the necessary credentials to enter any factories, mines, or mills I found necessary, and to take from their work—for whatever time required—any workers I wished to interview. I am grateful to the Revolutionary Government for its courtesy, and to the many other individuals, too numerous to mention, in various government offices who gave me substantial aid. The cooperation of the workers we interviewed was, of course, the *sine qua non* of our research, and I am indebted to them for their willingness to speak freely and frankly to a couple of visiting "Yanquis." I hope that after reading this book they feel that it was worth sitting through those rather long and often irritating interviews.

This book began as a doctoral dissertation (to which it scarcely bears resemblance) in the Department of Sociology of the University of California at Berkeley. I want to thank Seymour Martin Lipset, who was chairman of my dissertation committee, for his willingness to guide me through the least exciting parts of the work that led to this book—namely, the dissertation itself. He and Martin Trow, the committee's second departmental member, contributed substantially to whatever merits this book may possess. This is true, as well, of all those professors with whom I have been privileged to study.

My colleague, Sidney Verba, gave me helpful advice in the construction of the interview schedule; Frederick Stephan's aid in designing the sample was inestimable, as was my benefit from the methodological acumen of Michael Aiken. My thanks are also due to Mike Smith, who drew the excellent map showing the location of the plants in which the workers were interviewed, to Vicki Weiner, who transcribed the interviews with the workers onto cards, and to Silvia de Cabezas, who typed most of the final manuscript of this book.

In part, this study was supported financially by the Center of International Studies, Princeton University, and I want to acknowledge that support and the encouragement of the center's director, Klaus Knorr.

I owe much to the following individuals who read various parts of the manuscript and made valuable comments and suggestions: Michael Aiken, Robert Alford, C. Arnold Anderson, Marion Brown, Peter Blau, David Chaplin, Robert

L. Crain, Ivan R. Dee, Julian Franklin, Jerald Hage, David Harrop, Guy B. Johnson, Gerald Marwell, J. P. Morray, James Petras, Peter Roman, and Norman Ryder. Anonymous readers of the manuscript for Princeton University Press, as well as for journals in which parts of this book have appeared earlier also made valuable suggestions that I want to acknowledge here. William McClung guided the manuscript along in its early stages at Princeton University Press, and Roy A. Grisham, Jr. edited the manuscript, for which I am grateful.

I am especially grateful to Richard Hamilton, Barrington Moore, Jr., and James O'Connor, for their careful reading of the entire manuscript, and for their exceptionally helpful comments.

I am also grateful to the following journals for their permission to adapt some of my earlier articles for use in this book: *The Nation, American Sociological Review, American Journal of Sociology,* and *Social Forces.*

Approximate Location of Plants in Survey of Cuban Industrial Workers

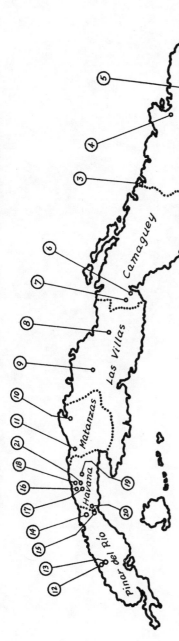

ORIENTE
1. Planta Eléctrica, Santiago de Cuba
2. Enidio Díaz (Santa Regina), sugar central
3. Argelia Libre (Manati), sugar central
4. Nicaro nickel processing plant
5. Hermanos Díaz, petroleum refinery (formerly Texaco), Santiago de Cuba

CAMAGUEY
6. Venezuela (Stewart), sugar central
7. Uruguay (Jatibonico), sugar central

LAS VILLAS
8. Tabaco Torcido, Unit 51 (cigar factory), Placetas
9. Cervezas y Maltas, Unit 4 (beer and malt brewery), Manacas

MATANZAS
10. Guillermo Gerlin, Papelera Técnica Cubana (paper mill), Cardenas
11. Planta Eléctrica José Martí, Matanzas

PINAR DEL RIO
12. Patricio Lumumba Planta de Sulfometales, Puerto de Santa Lucía
13. Matahambre copper mine
14. Fábrica de cemento, Unit 1 (formerly Portland Cement), Mariel
15. Derivados del Cuero, Unit 101 (boot factory), Guanajay

HAVANA
16. Populares (cigarette factory), Vedado
17. Cervezas y Maltas, Unit 1 (beer and malt brewery), Marianao
18. Nico López petroleum refinery (formerly Esso and Shell—now combined), Regla
19. Derivados del Cuero, Unit 205-01 (shoe factory), Managua
20. Hilados y Tejidos Planos, Ariguanabo (textile mill and printing), Bauta
21. Cubana de Acero (agricultural equipment), Víbora

CHAPTER 1

Orientations, Setting, Methods

Introduction

🖢 THIS is a revolutionary era whose distinctive feature "is the entry of the masses as participants in the making of history."[1] The Cuban workers have played a decisive role in their revolution—the first socialist revolution in the Western Hemisphere, and the only socialist revolution that has taken place in a capitalist country in which wage workers constituted the most numerous and perhaps most cohesive class in the population. How the workers see the revolution has been and doubtless will be basic to its continued vitality and to the course taken by the revolution's leaders. A study, therefore, of the shared experiences which led the workers of Cuba to favor or oppose the revolution is of primary historical, social, and theoretical relevance.

Revolutionary politics has a long and venerable tradition in the Cuban working class dating to the very foundation of the Republic itself. The workers were among the most dedicated advocates of the cause of colonial liberation from Spain; anarchosyndicalist ideology was widespread if not dominant among them in the early decades of the twentieth century; the workers formed the major social base of the Communist-led anti-imperialist movement of the late twenties and early thirties that culminated in the abortive popular revolution of 1933-35—a revolution which had as one of its principal declared aims the abolition of United States control of the country's political economy. Until the advent of the Cold War, the Communists were predominant in Cuban labor's leadership and, even with their purge in 1947-48 from official positions in the *Confederación de Trabajadores de Cuba* (CTC), the island's central labor organization, the Com-

[1] Lewis S. Feuer, ed., *Marx and Engels: Basic Writings on Politics and Philosophy* (Garden City, N.Y.: Anchor Books, 1959), p. xviii.

munists retained the allegiance of an estimated 25 percent of the workers. Thus, the Cuban revolution and socialist ideology had a significant base in the working class long before the revolution's leaders began to think and speak of themselves and their revolution as "socialist."

This book, then, is a modest attempt to ascertain some of the major social determinants of pro-Communist and revolutionary political attitudes in the Cuban working class, through multivariate quantitative analysis of survey research data gathered in interviews with Cuban workers during the summer of 1962. Thus, this is the first (and only to date) study to utilize the empirical methods and theory of contemporary sociology for sustained and systematic inquiry into the causes of the differential response of the workers to a social revolution—while that revolution itself was still "young."

In his essay on the sources of Marxism, *The Unfinished Revolution*, Adam B. Ulam writes that

> No sociological surveys enable us to ascertain exactly the ideas of the French and English proletariat during the period of the great economic transformation. The wealth of memoirs, political reports, and even rudimentary economic surveys helps, but the picture of the impact of industrialism is still like the proverbial iceberg: a small part of it visible in the form of theories, statistics, and political and social movements; the greater part of it, the feelings and thoughts of the people affected by industrialization, is submerged. We are forced to speculate about the latter from an analysis of the former.[2]

Our primary concern in this study is to analyze the social determinants of the workers' political attitudes. Yet to some extent the richness of individual motivation—the conscious and expressed reasons the workers have for how they feel about the revolution—is obscured by such an analysis.

[2] (New York: Random House, 1960), p. 72.

Since we personally interviewed Cuban workers and re-corded the verbalized "feelings and thoughts of the people affected" by the Cuban revolution, since we *did do* a socio-logical survey of the Cuban "proletariat," excerpts from these interviews will be presented wherever relevant in the workers' own words, commenting upon the revolution as they see it. Thus we hope, at least, that Professor Ulam's lament about the lack of sociological surveys of the French and English workers during the industrial revolution will not have to be repeated in quite the same anguished terms by students of the Cuban revolution whose wish it is "to ascertain exactly the ideas" of the Cuban workers.

What the workers actually said in our interviews is not only of historical but also of analytical relevance because the very language the workers use to define their situation de-fines for us, at least indirectly, their perceptions of social reality—perceptions which themselves become determinants of their political behavior. Their language gives us some in-sight, at least, into "the phenomenology of the revolutionary consciousness, the world as it is experienced in crisis by the revolutionary workingmen."[3]

In any study of political attitudes based on survey re-search, one is perforce compelled to focus on the recurrent, the generalizable, and the quantifiable, and much is left un-examined and unsaid that undoubtedly was and may still be of decisive political importance. Among the "determinants" of Communist and revolutionary support in the Cuban work-ing class, for example, it should hardly require saying that the *content* of revolutionary socialist ideology itself is of central relevance; for it promises to the workers a new and transformed world of equality and plenty and social justice, of the abolition of the exploitation of man by man, of a socialist society run by the workers themselves—a society that is *theirs for the making* through social revolution. More-

[3] Feuer, p. xix.

over, not only the content of socialist ideology but also the talent of the movement's leaders, their tactical skills, their knowledge, their daring and courage, both physical and intellectual, their oratorical gifts and organizational abilities, their personal persuasiveness and integrity—all these qualities of a movement's leadership enter into and may have a determining effect on the political course the workers will take. The whole gamut of qualities that competing political organizations and movements present to the workers—and what types of workers they try to organize and appeal to—will condition their success. A variety of factors, in other words, proper to the Communists and revolutionaries themselves and to their opponents, rather than to the social structure as a whole or to the working-class structure in particular, are obviously significant in "real life." They enter into the very creation and persistence of a distinct working-class political culture, and into determining workers' political attitudes and behavior. No really adequate understanding of the workers' attitudes is possible without the systematic exploration of these facets of the working-class movement. In this study, I have not dealt with them, and I claim only to offer *some* understanding of the sources of revolutionary politics in the Cuban working class.

Nor is an adequate understanding of the workers' political attitudes possible without knowing the history of the workers. "History itself" (a metaphysical term I dislike but whose meaning is clear) was a major source of working-class attitudes toward the revolution and toward the Communists before the revolution. The major struggles the workers were involved in, the tales propagated in the working-class subculture and the meanings given and the memories retained of these events, the men who figured as important leaders and later as heroes or martyrs of working-class battles, and as symbols of working-class struggle, the compromises and conciliations of their leaders, the workers' victories and their defeats, all in one way or another entered the workers' consciousness and influenced—even now—the workers' political behavior in ways which cannot easily (if at all) be detected through survey research methods. I have tried, though, in my chapter on political generations to do something along these lines.

To put the matter somewhat differently, while I have used survey research and multivariate analysis to try to discover some of the determinants of the political attitudes of Cuban workers and of workers' political radicalism in general, I am not convinced that out of such types of analysis there will emerge some day a general theory of workers' political radicalism. Our substantive hypotheses and their verification must be related to a given historical reality in which the variables examined take their effect. Not only are the independent variables themselves rarely alike in comparative analysis, but they affect human beings who have had different historical experiences and who, therefore, may well respond differently to apparently identical stimuli. I have tried, therefore, in this study to closely link my theoretical generalizations to the specific historical experiences of the Cuban workers.

History is significant even on the simplest levels; for had a study using survey methods been done of working-class politics in Cuba some forty years ago, an "index of attitude" toward the anarchosyndicalists who were then dominant in the labor movement would have been necessary, rather than toward the Communists who were still in their infancy. And we cannot argue, a priori, that anarchosyndicalism would have appealed to the same types of workers as Communist ideology. This raises the question: Is it valid to consider attitudes toward the Communists before the revolution as an index of *political radicalism* among Cuban workers? We know, after all, that the Communists gained stature among the workers not merely as revolutionaries but as good unionists, as honest leaders who were able to successfully pursue militant and forceful union policies that (to use their own phraseology) were in essence straight "economism." And especially in the anti-Batista struggle, the Communists were scarcely a radical political force but were displaced by the 26th of July movement. I do not discount this, but believe that such straight union appeals as the Communists undoubtedly had were complemented by the general Communist image as a revolutionary alternative to Cuban capitalism. Unlike most other Latin American Communist parties, the Cuban party *did* lead not only militant and violent confrontations with the armed forces of Cuba, but had nearly led the workers to power in the abortive revolution of the thirties. The content of Communist education, indoctrination, and agitation among the workers was anti-imperialist, anticapitalist, and revolutionary socialist. Thus, in "concrete reality," their roles as honest unionists and revolutionary socialist agitators were inseparable. It is highly likely that procommunism among the workers in prerevolutionary Cuba was permeated with revolutionary socialist values. My reading of the history of the Cuban working class convinces me that this is a legitimate assumption, and it is this assumption that I make throughout this book. There was no other socialist party of national significance in the working class during the lives of most of the workers we interviewed for this book; therefore, it is not likely that the few anarchist or social democratic workers whom our question about prerevolutionary attitude toward the Communists would miss would seriously alter our findings and interpretations.

Orientations

The major working hypothesis of this study is a simple one: just as a society's class structure is a major basis of its political diversity and cleavage, so too is *intra*class social differentiation politically significant, and by exploring the structure of the working class it will be possible to locate fundamental sources of its political behavior. This does not mean that *inter*class differences, or conflicting class interests, are in any way secondary to the internal structure of the working class as the source of its politics. Quite the contrary. Any conflict between classes tends to erase or minimize the significance of *intra*class differences and to maximize *inter*class differences. Nonetheless, as Roberto Michels once put it: "Working-class history abounds in examples showing how certain fractions or categories of the proletariat have, under the influence of interests peculiar to their sub-class, detached themselves from the great army of labour and made common cause with the bourgeoisie."[4] The principal task of our study, then, has been to identify such "fractions" or "categories" of the working class in Cuba and to observe whether or not and in what manner they have led to their members' differential political behavior.

This study is based on the generic sociological assumption that the individual's position in the social structure determines, to a great extent, the nature, intensity, and variety of social pressures to which he will be subject, that different types of social roles both recruit (or select) and train (or form) different types of social individuals and, therefore, the view of the world they carry around in their heads. The variety of social interaction, patterns of communications, deprivations, and conceptions of themselves that individuals experience varies significantly in accordance with these different social roles and, in turn, result in observable differences in their behavior—from the most intimate and personal values and attitudes to the most public of political stances. To the worker, his *work* is at the very center of his life and *the social pressures to which he is exposed at work play a major role in determining his political views*. Much of his evaluation of the "class struggle" or labor-management conflict, of the general quality of his society and his place within it, whether he believes himself exploited or emancipated,

[4] *Political Parties* (Glencoe, Ill.: The Free Press, 1949), p. 290.

whether he believes his interests are opposed to those of the owners and managers of industry, or that capitalism might better be replaced—by revolution if necessary—by another economic and social system he calls socialism or communism—much of his political behavior can be explained by observing the position he has in the structure of the working class, and the consequent variations in the pressures and deprivations to which he is subject.

Deprivations, as I shall show, in themselves explain little or nothing, for it is the structure of social relationships in which the worker is implicated that determines, in the first place, how he perceives these deprivations (if he perceives them at all) and their objective impact on him. What he perceives and what he experiences of the world, and therefore what he thinks about the world, will vary to a great extent with the role he plays in the process of production, with its concomitant social relations and patterns of interaction and communication.

Take the question of income, for example. Is there some reason why income in itself should relate to a worker's politics? Does the range of social pressures that he experiences significantly vary from those of workers in different income brackets? Does higher income mean conservative politics? And unemployment or underemployment? Are these experiences that qualitatively differ from the experience of the economically secure worker? Unemployment, we shall see, is not merely a deprivation in itself but has a direct effect on the situation from which the worker views the world. It changes his social location. What does this imply? Does the unemployed worker quit participating in union activities and withdraw from politics, or does he become activated by his situation? Is he more or less amenable to revolutionary appeals than the employed worker? What did the experiences of recurrent unemployment and widespread underemployment in prerevolutionary Cuba mean for the workers' responses to Communist agitation and to the revolution itself?

Did unemployed Negro workers respond the same way as their fellow white workers? If not, why not? To what extent did the collective situation of Negro workers in general affect the particular situation of the Negro unemployed and their perceptions of their unemployment? Long ago, Marx said something about the exploited Irish workers who, while in the process of organizing, were bringing their "revolutionary fire" into the English working class and thereby transforming the character of the class struggle. Is there a parallel to the Negro workers of Cuba? Were Negro workers more likely to support the Communists in the labor movement in the decades preceding the revolution, and are they now more or less likely than their fellow white workers to support the revolution? What is the basis of their political differences?

Take, for instance, the question of the skilled worker. The cleavage between skilled workers and the semi- and unskilled workers is quite nearly as old as industrial capitalism itself, and the types of trade unions, political movements and parties supported by them have varied considerably within each country. In many countries the skilled workers have been the moderate and "conservative" ones in their class, while the unskilled have formed the basis of the "extremist" or revolutionary parties and unions. In other countries the pattern is reversed. Why? Under what conditions, or in what sort of situations, are the least deprived and most "successful" workers likely to be even more radical than their less fortunately situated semi- and unskilled working-class peers?

Will the worker's social origins affect his political views? Will his experiences growing up in a peasant or agricultural laborer's household, or in a petite bourgeois, white collar or industrial working-class family affect his political views—despite the fact that he is now a worker like other workers? If his father was a small trader, say, will he not bring different views with him into the working class—views assimilated in association with his parents and early peers—that will differ from those of his fellow workers who are the sons of workers, and require him to make adaptations not required of them? Will not the very same experiences have a different impact on him than on them? The question is, what kind of an impact, and why?

Or take the question of sex. Here are men and women at work, both doing the same sorts of jobs, working in the same kinds of plants. Will their politics be the same? If not, why not?

Whether the worker happens to work in a big plant or small plant and where that plant is located, the region and size of city and the type of neighborhood in which he lives in the community, and therefore the heterogeneity or homogeneity of his political environment, will subject him to still different pressures which, in turn, may interact with the personal satisfaction he draws from his work, and how he conceives his role in social production.

Do their attitudes toward their work affect the workers' political views? How? What political differences, if any, are there between workers whose dissatisfaction with their work derives from different sources?

Finally, there is the question of history and the workers' role in it. What effects, if any, do the workers' early experiences in the labor movement, and the historical experiences through which that movement is then passing, have on their lifelong political behavior? In particular, what effects did their insurrectionary and revolutionary experiences during the abortive revolution of the 1930s have on the Cuban workers? And how did the anti-Batista struggle affect their responses to the Fidelista revolution?

These are some questions raised by the political experience of the working classes of different countries; and we try to answer them in the context of prerevolutionary and postrevolutionary Cuba—questions which are significant not only because of their obvious historical interest, but also because they are questions that are relevant to the development of valid social theory. They are questions which require our attention because of their social relevance, and because in the process of trying to answer them we may contribute to the understanding of the variables at work in determining political behavior.

The Setting

This study is based on interviews my wife and I had with a national, random sample of workers in Cuba in the summer of 1962. This was a critical period for the revolution (as almost any period of any revolution is), since the revolutionary leadership was in the process of rediscovering its own direction and dissociating itself from the modes of rule associated with the so-called old Communists. Throughout the country a series of actions took place which resulted in the elimination of old Communists from positions of power and influence—without yet severing the ties between the "old" and "new" Communists. This may have resulted in a crisis of conscience for many veteran Communist supporters in the working class—a working class which was long led by the Communists and which, as we said, even in the period of illegality, still maintained the "secret support" of an estimated fourth of the workers. The period following the "purges" of 1962 was also one of increased administrative flexibility, of a return to local initiative which gradually had been usurped by the center, namely, the Communist apparatus in the Integrated Revolutionary Organizations. It was a period of heightened invasion fears, less than a year from the Bay of Pigs events, and preceding the Missile Crisis of October by a month. All of this was felt in direct and indirect ways by the workers—from nationalist and revolutionary exhortation to mobilization of the militia. During this very period, the Cuban economy had been experiencing grave difficulties—perhaps the gravest in the three and a half years since the establishment of the revolutionary regime. The 1962 *zafra* was far below expectations and earlier revolutionary harvests; there were severe scarcities in foods and consumer goods, the transportation and internal distribution systems were inefficient, and raw material and spare part shortages were noticeably affecting production in some industries. Some plants were working part time, while others were forced (as in hemp production) to close down completely. The general scarcity of goods, the production problems, the intense social pressure to be "revolutionary" and the local abuses and poor administrative methods of many officials only recently fired from their posts must obviously have had its effects on the workers' morale and view of the revolution.

On the other hand, there were major accomplishments to the credit of the Revolutionary Government in health care, education and welfare improvements for the workers, in the dignity given work, in the changed in-plant relations between administrative and technical personnel and production workers, and in the elimination of corruption and gangsterism in the unions, that apparently made the scarcities and difficulties less onerous than they might have been.

Thus, on one hand, this was a period in the revolution which in some ways was a particularly difficult one for the workers, one likely to evoke discontent especially among the least politically interested and involved; on the other hand, it was a period of revolutionary euphoria, nationalist enthusiasm, and combativeness; a spirit of social solidarity appeared to be present among the workers akin to and more intense than what can be observed among workers at the height of a major strike anywhere. A year before we did the interviewing for this study, for instance, immediately after the abortive invasion of 1961, it was reported by the London *Observer* correspondent (April 30, 1961) in Cuba that:

At the moment, the working classes and the militia would follow Dr. Castro anywhere and in anything. Talk of "defending the country to the last drop of blood" is not for them an idle thought. There is a wide degree of national unity.

Another observer, Ruth Knowles, a petroleum specialist who lived in Cuba for eight years before the revolution and who spent more than a month in Cuba touring the island *during the same period we were interviewing the workers* for this book, reported in the *Wall Street Journal* (November 9, 1962) that "In Cuba the labor unions and the young people back him [Castro] fanatically and there are many groups who are living better than they ever did before."

The important point here, from the standpoint of our study, is that the Revolutionary Government had by the time of our interviews (1962) clearly consolidated its power; the original relatively undifferentiated popular euphoria had by now long been replaced by relatively clear lines of social cleavage generated in response to actions taken by the Revolutionary Government; it was now more than three years since the establishment of the Revolutionary Government, two years since the nationalization of private, American-owned industrial enterprises, and more than a year since Fidel Castro had declared the revolution to be "socialist." It was, in other words, a period in the "youth" of the revolution, when decisive differences in social class support for and disaffection from the revolution already had emerged, yet when a new social structure, with clearly established institutions and norms, had not yet fully crystallized. Whatever might be the possible future form and content of the new social structure in Cuba, as of the time of our interviews with the workers it was clear that the old class structure was in disarray and dissolution and a new one had not yet emerged. Therefore, a study of the differential appeals of the ideology and social content of the revolution to industrial workers could now be meaningful and valuable.

This study is based on interviews with a randomly selected national sample of industrial workers. Before describing the technical details of the sampling and interviewing method, therefore, it is necessary to discuss a fundamental method-ological criticism which might be made of this study, a criti-cism which, were it true, would raise serious problems in the evaluation and utilization of our interview data.

The methodological criticism might be phrased as follows: Is it possible to utilize the methods and data of survey re-search to arrive at reasonable indicators of opinions and atti-tudes in the context of a police state? Since the interviewers were United States citizens, it might be argued that the inter-viewed workers could have reason to believe they or any American residing or doing research in Cuba as late as the summer of 1962 must have been, at the very least, "accept-able" to the regime. In an issue of *Cuba Socialista*, for ex-ample, something of a theoretical organ of the regime, the Committees for the Defense of the Revolution, organized in factories, and neighborhoods, are described as a "system of collective revolutionary vigilance, in which everyone knows who everyone is, what each person who lives in the bloc does, what relations he had with the tyranny, to what he is dedicated, whom he meets and what activities he follows." Thus, it might be argued that in such an atmosphere inter-views are hardly effective indicators of opinions or attitudes.

This is a thoughtful and relevant, but incorrect assessment of the possibility of doing the study we did, when and where we did it. I have no doubts that in many respects the atmos-phere in Cuba was hardly the most conducive to inter-viewing workers (especially for American interviewers, since the United States and Cuba were already in conflict with each other), and that many individuals may have had legitimate fears of stating their views openly. In fact, because there were obviously some workers who were suspicious, even frightened, of the purposes of the interview, we made every effort to establish rapport quickly and put the respondent at his ease, by stressing emphatically that the interview was voluntary and completely anonymous. Occasionally, a respondent would ask that his words not be recorded until the interview had terminated, and we agreed readily. It should be noted also that the interviews ranged from 45 minutes to three and a half hours in length, averaging about an hour and a quarter, in a private atmosphere (see below) and that a great effort of the will would be required in that situation to give answers consistently which were thought to be suitable to the government and the interviewer. It would require a certain level of dramatic skill to feign enthusiasm or to manifest feelings where these did not really exist. Moreover, it must be said that the refusal rate was very low (eight of 210 respondents selected), and that in only a few instances did opponents of the regime evince either hesitancy or fear in speaking their minds freely. Cubans are highly voluble, volatile, and loquacious, regardless of their political views.

Moreover, the objection that Cuba was a "police state" or totalitarian country when we did our interviewing must be put down, insofar as I am concerned, as at best a very serious exaggeration. It is true that things had tightened up considerably in Cuba in the year since the invasion. This was certainly to be expected of a country whose leaders had some evidence that their country was the possible target of another major foreign attempt to overthrow them. During our stay in Cuba there were several false invasion scares, a number of bombings in public buildings, a mortar attack on the hotel housing foreign diplomats, technicians, and visiting dignitaries, which narrowly missed the apartment we were staying in at the time, and so on; and within a month of our return to Cuba, there occurred the "missile crisis" of October 22-28, 1962. Thus, the country in a significant sense was on a war footing, whether based on real or imaginary fears of invasion. *Organized* dissent was not possible in Cuba at this time and yet it was our observation throughout the country that Cubans could and did speak freely about whatever they wished, without fear of government reprisal.

By the time of the cut of the Cuban sugar quota by the U. S. government on July 6, 1960, for example, it was widely believed in the United States that Cuba already had become a police state. Thus, it is relevant that Lloyd A. Free, Director of the Institute for International Social Research in Princeton, New Jersey, who was responsible for a public opinion survey carried out in Cuba during April and early May 1960, wrote:

> Much to our delight, we found that very few respondents refused to answer our questions, probably in part because the wording was indirect and innocuous on the surface. And, as the report will show, a great many at least among the overwhelming majority who did answer all of our questions talked very frankly, indeed. We cannot be sure, of course, that the great bulk of respondents who expressed support for the Castro regime were telling the whole truth (in view of the intolerance of the political climate toward dissenting opinions); but we can be absolutely certain that the substantial proportions which expressed opposition or criticism were not only being courageous but honest.[5]

We found essentially the same situation in Cuba during the summer of 1962 when we did our own interviewing. Just prior to our arrival in Cuba, Fidel Castro had made a major speech denouncing what he termed the sectarianism of the old Cuban Communists, their antilibertarian actions and disregard for the rights of others, and declared that "The Revolution must be a school of courageous men. The Revo-

[5] Lloyd A. Free, *Attitudes of the Cuban People Toward the Castro Regime, in the late Spring of 1960* (Princeton: Institute for International Social Research, 1960), p. ii. This study was designed by Free and Hadley Cantril.

lution must be a school in which there is liberty of thought!"[6]

Consistent with this attitude, bookstores throughout Cuba still sold whatever remained of books by Western scholars, as well as polemically anti-Socialist and anti-Communist books: books, for instance, in Spanish, such as *Religion en alcance de todos, La iglesia catolica frente al comunismo,* and Lerner and Cassel's *Teoría general de Keynes.*

The *Biblioteca Nacional,* Cuba's central public library, was still receiving more or less regularly such U.S. publications as *Time, Life, U.S. News, Look,* and the *New Leader,* as well as such journals as *The New Republic* and *The Nation.* British newspapers such as the London *Observer* and the *Manchester Guardian* were also available. The full spectrum of political opinion, then, could be read in the foreign press by anyone with the knowledge and inclination to do so.

The libraries of the University of Havana, the Central University of Las Villas, and the *Biblioteca Nacional* at this time had general scholarly collections comparable to those in our own college libraries. Among the many polemically anti-Communist books (in Spanish) in the *Biblioteca Nacional,* for example, here were some catalogued under "Communism" (with their call numbers):

335.43: Ponce de Leon, *Los Monstruos que Acechen.*

337.47: S. J. Walsh, *Imperio Total.*

At the University of Havana library:

335.E: Max Eastman, *Reflexiones sobre el fracaso del socialismo.*

335.4K: Arthur Koestler, *El mito sovietico ante la realidad.*

943.7S: Dana Adams Schmidt, *Anatomía de un estado satélite.*

[6] See my two articles, "Labor in Cuba," *The Nation,* Vol. 195 (October 20, 1962), 238-41; and "Castro and Cuba's Communists," *The Nation,* Vol. 195 (November 3, 1962), 284-87, for a more detailed presentation of my observations in Cuba during the course of my research.

There were also such varied works as Trotsky's *Terorismo y comunismo*, Hans Kelsen's *Teoria comunista del derecho y el estado*, M. Ketchum's *What Is Communism?*, Arthur Schlesinger, Jr.'s *The Vital Center*, Blas Roca and Earl Browder's *La conferencia del cancilleres de la Habana*, and Raúl Roa's *En pie*. (The last two, because of their revisionism and anti-Soviet polemics, respectively, could be particularly embarrassing to two prominent Cuban politicians.)

It was still possible to hear broadcasts from the United States clearly on ordinary radio in many parts of Cuba, and the government had not attempted, so far as we could observe, to prevent this in any way. American movies glorifying the American way of life, Hollywood-style, still played at almost every Cuban movie theater and on afternoon television.

It was quite easy to find vocal opponents of the regime—especially in Havana. Taxi drivers and bus boys, department store clerks and grocers would, with the slightest encouragement, engage in a vituperative denunciation of the government. One could travel, as my wife and I did, from one end of the country to the other, knocking on doors at random, talking to people in their homes, in public squares and parks, in factories and schools, on the university campus or in buses and theatre lobbies, without being interfered with—talking and questioning, and even giving the United States government's viewpoint on international affairs.

In one factory after we finished our interviews, a group of workers cornered us to ask some questions of their own. Since it was closing time, the crowd soon grew to over 50 workers who raised questions about everything from the inevitable American "Negro problem" to Soviet nuclear testing. And they received a brief lecture on our federal system of government in explanation of the President's difficulties in enforcing the Supreme Court's desegregation decision, and an opinion that the Soviet resumption of nuclear testing had led to increased tensions and given credence to the view that the

Soviet Union is an aggressive power. An exciting interchange continued for more than a half hour until the bus arrived to take the workers home.

We believe that Cubans could and did inquire and speak freely about whatever they wished—at this time. On the other hand, the newly reorganized curriculum of the University of Havana already required that every student must take one year of a course entitled "Dialectical Materialism," regardless of what he was studying. The textbooks in most courses were direct translations of Soviet texts. The great majority of books sold on news stands and in bookstores were then from the Soviet bloc countries, China and Yugoslavia. More important, the Cuban newspapers, radio, and tv were, essentially, instruments of the government, and there were no noticeable differences among the opinions expressed by the various editorial writers and news commentators (many of whom lifted their "opinions" bodily from Tass). A view of international issues was constantly given in the mass media which glorified the Soviet Union and denigrated the United States. Cuban newsreels seemed to us masterful propaganda documents which emphasized the seamier side of American life.

There were no formal safeguards of freedom of speech and association or of personal, civil, and political rights, of the kind traditional to Western political democracies. Such freedoms as did exist depended only on what Fidel has called "the revolution's generosity to its opponents." There were certainly no established institutional mechanisms or judicial procedures designed to protect the individual and guarantee his freedom from unreasonable search and seizure or arbitrary arrest and imprisonment. The members of the government, the Cabinet ministers, were responsible not to the general citizenry—who did not elect them and who had no direct voice in their selection—but only to themselves and the handful of revolutionary leaders—Fidel, Raúl, "Ché,"—who appointed them.

These leaders were, in fact, the government. They were the decision-makers; and there were no *formal* channels by which the people could directly influence them or recall them. (One must not forget, on the other hand, that the people were armed; wherever one went, one could see ordinary citizens, including long-fingernailed women in high heels, with rifles or submachine guns slung over their shoulders. If this is not an institutional mode of ensuring the responsibility of government figures, it is nevertheless, a certain source of countervailing power. Moreover, the great informality of government leaders, the emphasis on social equality, and the frequent contact between the leaders and ordinary citizens in a variety of contexts serve as important reciprocal channels of communication and influence.)

It is quite obvious from the above that the potentialities for totalitarian rule were strong in Cuba during the period of our interviews. Yet that *potential* had yet to become a reality. Thus, we were able to carry out our interviewing without disturbance or interference and obtain, we believe, data quite as valid as those obtained in any survey research.

In any case, this is an "explanatory" study rather than a descriptive one, and our focus is on internal variation between subgroups in an effort to specify the variables which may differentiate the political behavior of the workers from each other. Thus, whatever the general situation, insofar as it applied more or less equally for all the workers, this in no way vitiates our attempts at discovering the internal variations and explaining them.

Finally, I think it is relevant to cite the comments of Professor Dudley Seers, the well-known British economist, who was in Cuba engaged in research while we were doing our survey. He referred to some of the preliminary findings of the present study in his book *Cuba: The Economic and Social Revolution*, and wrote:

His [Zeitlin's] findings are not inconsistent with the general impression we all [Seers and his co-authors] formed during our stay in Cuba, where we traveled the length of the island and conversed with hundreds of people. (In general, *there was clearly little hesitation on their part about speaking their minds.*)[7]

Interview and Sampling Method

Our interviews were carried out with a randomly selected sample of 210 industrial workers employed in 21 plants widely scattered throughout the island's six provinces. I chose the plants from a list of all mines, mills, and factories functioning in Cuba under the direction of the Ministry of Industries.[8]

The plants were selected by means of a self-weighting random sample in which the probability that a plant would be chosen was directly proportional to the number of workers employed in it. This sampling method tended to exclude the smaller industrial work-places (known in Cuba as "*chinchales*") which abounded there.[9]

[7] Dudley Seers, Andres Bianchi, Richard Jolly, and Max Nolff, *Cuba: The Economic and Social Revolution* (Chapel Hill, N.C.: University of North Carolina Press, 1964), pp. 394n70 and 31. (My italics)

[8] Thus, excluded from the possibility of appearing in the sample were the approximately 120,000 industrial workers employed in some 250 industrial plants under the direction of the Department of Industrialization of the National Institute of Agrarian Reform (INRA). There were 202,799 industrial workers employed in the industrial plants under the direction of the Ministry of Industries. Thus, 62 percent, or close to two-thirds of Cuba's employed industrial workers, constituted the population from which the sample of workers interviewed for this study was drawn.

[9] In detail, the technique utilized was the following: (*a*) Using a list of all industrial plants and the number of workers employed in each, as compiled by the Ministry of Industries, the number of industrial workers was added cumulatively and the subtotals noted. (*b*) Twenty-one six-digit random numbers were drawn from a table of random numbers, and 21 plants were then selected whose cumulative

In each plant, we selected ten workers by one of three methods: (*a*) by visiting each department personally and selecting from a list of the jobs in that department; (*b*) by selecting from a list of all workers employed in the plant

---

subtotals were at least as large as or larger than each of the random numbers.

In each of the plants a predetermined fixed number of workers (because of time and resources available: 10 workers per plant) were selected at random to be interviewed. In each plant, the probability that a worker would be selected was, of course, inversely proportional to the number of workers employed in it.

The sample consisted, then, of 210 industrial workers selected at random from a population in which each worker had a known equal probability of being selected for the sample. Eight workers refused to be interviewed, and were not replaced by others, thus giving a total of 202 actual interviews as the basis of this study. As a check, the refusals were tabulated for the appropriate classification in which refusals themselves could be construed as significant answers (viz., "hostile" to the revolution), and in all instances the relationships persisted or were strengthened. We obtained the age, sex, race, average months worked per year before and since the revolution, and, of course, place of work, of each "refusal."

The above method of sampling may be expressed in the following formula:

$$P = m \, (s/N) \cdot (k/s) - km/N$$

where

m equals the number of industrial plants selected to be in the sample.

s equals the number of workers employed in a given plant selected for the sample.

k equals the fixed number of workers randomly selected to be interviewed in each plant.

N equals the total number of workers employed in all plants from which the sample was drawn.

P equals the probability that a worker in the population would be selected to be interviewed.

The method of sampling was employed to assure the inclusion in the sample of workers actually involved in industrial production using machine power and machine methods of production, rather than handicrafts methods of manufacture. In general, the larger the plant, the more likely that it was actually an industrial center. This was done for the theoretical and practical reasons that (*a*) one focus of this study is on the relationship between the impact of the revolution on the workers' estrangement from their work and their attitudes toward the

on the shift or shifts during which the interviewing was done; (c) by selecting among the homes in the industrial community in which the workers employed in the plant live. We

---

revolution. Therefore, it was particularly necessary to interview "industrial" rather than handicraft workers; (b) from a simple practical standpoint, had we taken a simple random sample of all plants, without weighting for size, we would not have been able to complete our interviewing, but would have spent most of our time scurrying from one tiny plant to another. As it was, we spent a considerable amount of time in traveling around the country, simply to interview workers in the 21 plants we selected; (c) the likelihood that workers interviewed in a factory of 50 or less workers, say, would talk to many others in the factory about the interviews, some of whom were yet to be interviewed, and thereby contaminate the results from these interviews, would be much greater than in the larger ones. It need hardly be pointed out that this method of sampling the working class does not affect the explanatory purposes of our study. "Representativeness," as Hans Zetterberg points out, "should not be confused with randomization. Randomization can be used to obtain representativeness. However, it is also used as a method of controlling irrelevant factors when testing a working hypothesis." (On Theory and Verification in Sociology [New York: Tressler Press, 1954], p. 57.)

The size of the sample on which this study is based (N = 202) has made it difficult, and occasionally impossible, to control for certain theoretically relevant variables and attributes in some contexts where these might be appropriate and desirable. I have, in many instances, made such controls even though this resulted in cells having as few as a dozen workers in them. In most cases, I think, the weight of alternative types of evidence presented, and our theoretical expectations reinforce inferences from these small percentage bases.

It should also be emphasized, of course, that any index of attitude (especially of such complexity as an attitude toward a revolution) has deficiencies, and interviews are inherently limited in their accuracy. Generalization from such data to broader conceptual or empirical domains further dilutes the accuracy of the information provided by the interviews. For these reasons, conclusions about relationships between the variables examined here should be considered tentative and the study a preliminary and exploratory basis for future studies of political behavior during a revolution using survey research methods. Hopefully, these will be in greater depth and have fuller resources available than were available to the writer. Given the unique nature of our data and the unique opportunity they offered to enhance our understanding of political behavior, the methodological risks involved are, I believe, justified.

used method (*a*) in 15 work-places, (*b*) in five, and (*c*) in one work-place.[10]

The advantage of employing method (*a*) for selecting the workers to be interviewed is that we were able to see the workers' reactions throughout the plants visited—the reactions of the workers chosen to be interviewed as well as of the other workers present at that moment in the various departments. Observation of the general reactions of the workers—of reserve or suspicion, curiosity or friendliness—was obviously an important aspect of this study. Moreover, so as to be certain that the worker selected was, indeed, the worker interviewed, this method of selection was preferable. Perhaps if Cuba had not been the center of controversy and the focus of United States hostility during the period in which this study was done, this method would not have been necessary. Fortunately, this was not only a precautionary measure but also was beneficial to our research since it provided, as has been said, the opportunity for direct observation of the interaction between the workers and administrative personnel. Moreover, because my wife and I carried out all interviewing ourselves, this allowed us to have a much clearer understanding of the significance of the interview data, as a result of personal interaction with the respondents, ob-

[10] The latter method was employed only in the mining town of Matahambre in Pinar del Río. The selection was not demonstrably random. It was impossible to pull men out of the mines during their work. We made an attempt to select names from the list of workers not working during that shift, and to go to their homes and interview them there. However, there were then no addresses and fewer street names in Matahambre and this proved impossible. We found it necessary, therefore, to go to neighborhoods in the community in which a high concentration of miners lived, choose a house, and inquire whether or not a miner lived there. If a miner did live there, and was home, then with the miner's consent, we interviewed him. Obviously, this is not the most reliable method of assuring a random sample. The inadequacy here consists in our inability to know what degree of confidence to place in the randomness of the Matahambre sample.

servation of their work contexts and, often, their living surroundings and their homes.

My wife and I interviewed the workers (in Spanish of course), each of us separately interviewing five workers per plant. All interviewing was carried out in complete privacy, in a location provided within the plant, such as a classroom or storage room or office. Before the interviewing, we told each worker interviewed, as well as anyone else concerned, in a variant of the following words, that the writer was

> a correspondent for a liberal, objective American newsweekly called *The Nation* that is published in New York City. We have permission from the Ministry of Industries, your administrator, and the union delegate to interview ten workers here. We have chosen you to be interviewed by selecting at random from a list of the jobs in this department (or all workers in this work-place). That means we do not care to know your name or to be able to identify you personally in any way. These questions are simple and do not require special knowledge. We just want your opinions about some things in your work and in Cuba in general. All your answers are between ourselves and are completely anonymous. We would very much appreciate your permission to interview you.

Every precaution was taken in the interviewing to discover and to prevent dissimulation. Dissimulation, as well as unconscious distortion, must be taken into account in the evaluation of all interview data, in whatever type of study. Internal checks for consistency, as well as external checks on reliability, must be built into any interview schedule, wherever possible, and this was done in this study. The interviews were carried out according to a formal set of questions on a mimeographed interview schedule that I prepared. It was quite clear to the worker that he was being formally interviewed in accordance with predetermined questions, and that notes on his answers were being taken throughout the interview.

But we also used stylized *probes* in these interviews to make it especially difficult for the workers interviewed to give answers that they did not actually feel to be true. For example, if a worker were asked: "Do you think that your children have the same opportunities, better opportunities, or worse opportunities than others to live comfortably and happily?" and he answered: "All children are equal now," he would then be asked some variant of "How is it possible for all children to be equal? Please explain what you mean." And such probes were used freely throughout the interview as a source of additional data and as a check on the workers' answers.

The interview schedule was organized in such a way as to begin the interview with questions which were, on the surface, far removed from political questions of any kind. These were questions pertaining to length of residence in a particular place, or length of time working in the workplace, and so on. With the exception of the extra emphasis on anonymity, on the establishment of rapport, and on special probing to ascertain the truthfulness of a response, the interviews were carried out in accordance with established canons of sociological interviewing.[11]

11 The assistance of the Ministry of Industries was enlisted in the realization of this study. I explained the theoretical and historical purposes of this study to the then Minister of Industries, Major Ernesto "Ché" Guevara. It was his approval which made this study possible. He attached no conditions to our work, and no restrictions whatsoever were placed on our travel, or the kinds of questions we might ask. We explained the purposes of our research, submitted a copy of the mimeographed interview schedule, clarified the purposes (but did not change the wording) of a number of questions which appeared to the Minister to be "loaded," and received permission to enter any plant we wished, and to have workers taken from their work for as long as was necessary for the interviews. We were given credentials by the Ministry to identify us to administrative and labor union officials at the plants visited, and were, after that, left to carry

Aside from doing our interviewing in the midst of a revolution, we also were faced with having to interview in a language and cultural setting other than our own. Whether we successfully overcame the obstacles this situation posed to accurate communication is an unanswerable question. One illustration of the difficulty of cross-cultural interviewing that I think is particularly instructive comes from our pre-test of the interview schedule in a plant just outside Havana. That is, before actually beginning the interviews that would "count" for our sample, it was necessary for us to see how well the questions we intended to ask the workers were understood by them, and if they elicited the kinds of responses we were looking for. The workers' responses to one question particularly startled us. Several of the first ten workers we interviewed in the plant failed to identify either Fidel Castro or any other revolutionary leader when we asked them: "Aside from personal friends or relatives—of all the people you hear or read about—could you name three individuals whom you admire very much?" Yet these same workers indicated quite clearly during the interview that they considered themselves revolutionaries. Why should this question have failed to evoke the anticipated response from revolutionary workers? To find out, we went back to those workers (*i.e.*, who had indicated they were favorable to the revolution by their responses to other questions, but still had not mentioned a revolutionary leader in response to this question). "Why" we asked, "if you deem yourself a revolutionary, didn't you name Fidel or Ché, or another

---

out the research at our own convenience. There was no predetermined schedule of when we were to arrive at any plant, nor, it was evident, had any administrators been informed to expect our visit. On several occasions administrators or personnel chiefs telephoned to the Ministry of Industries in Havana to check our credentials and our insistence that we had permission—which was apparently unbelievable to administrators trying to raise production levels—to take 10 workers from their work for as long as necessary.

leader of the revolution, as a person whom you admire very much?" The explanation was simple. As one worker put it: "Ah, but you said this individual could not be a *personal friend*, and who could be a closer friend to a man, than someone like Fidel or Ché who has done so much for me and my family? He is a friend, close to the heart." Thus, it became necessary for us to add the following explanatory statement to our original question: "When we say 'personal friends' we mean people whom you see pretty regularly, whom you might visit at their homes, say, at any time if you wanted to. We don't want *their* names. We want you to think of people you hear or read about and name three individuals whom you admire very much."

Now, in order to get at the workers' attitudes toward the revolution, we asked a variety of questions, almost any one of which usually started the worker off on a verbal stream of consciousness which might pull in many aspects of the revolution about which we intended to ask specific questions later. Sometimes, we needed to do no more than introduce ourselves in order to get a worker talking about his experiences since the revolution. One worker, for example, tore off his shirt to show me the scars on his back that he claimed were the result of wounds inflicted on him by henchmen of the Batista regime during the anti-Batista struggle. Another worker, a 67-year-old maintenance man at the Nicaro nickel plant who had been an agricultural worker until recently, took a weathered, sweaty card from a few he had wrapped in paper in his pocket, and handed it to me. "This," he said, "is my membership card in the CTC. I have kept it these many years, to remind me of the clean unions we had until Mujal destroyed them. Now, the unions belong to us again. This man who is the union leader is a man who has come to share with the workers. He has no privileges like they did before. . . . Now, he is equal and acts equal." One worker remarked to my wife, who was visibly pregnant, that she was quite fortunate. "Your child," he said, "will be born in the United States of America, a free and glorious country, not like ours, which is run by the Russians." An oil refinery worker, whom I selected to interview, said he did not have to go to a private place for the interview. "Everyone here knows where I stand," he said. "I have passports for my entire family, and I will leave Cuba, my sad country, just as soon as there is room on a plane for us." Another worker motioned to me to be quiet, before our interview began, and stood on a stool to examine the light bulb above our heads, claiming, he said, to discover whether a microphone was hidden there. He then proceeded to speak loudly and clearly about his disdain for the revolution, "a revolution I fought for, but Fidel betrayed to the Communists. . ." A worker at the brewery in Manacas who quite bluntly told my wife of his hostility to the revolution, gave her his name and home address so that we might send him a copy of any articles we would write about our visit to Cuba, and took our address, to look us up in the United States, if he decided to leave his home. A worker at the Uruguay sugar central asked whether he might ask us a question before the interview itself began: "Why," he asked, "does your government make an old Cuban worker suffer with his ulcers?" "How can *our* government be blamed for *your* ulcers?" we asked, rather startled. "Well, then, why doesn't the U.S. trade with Cuba? Where am I to get my medicine, which is a product of the United States?" We sent Rupierto Jaramillo a large bottle of Cremalin liquid on our return to the United States.

An oil worker at the nationalized Esso-Shell refinery in Regla introduced himself as a poet, when my wife asked him what sort of work he did as they were walking to a spot outside the plant for the interview. He wondered, he said, if we might be able to publish a revolutionary poem he happened to have with him, when we returned home. Not only because of our promise, but because it indicates his feelings well,

we offer the reader a poorly translated verse from the poem
of this worker whose name, alas, we forgot to get:

> Sow, sow, *campesino*
> For you indeed are reaching the dawn
> Dismay no more, now
> Already your destiny is yours
> You have triumphed in the war
> But this, too, is your battle
> To hold in check
> Those who do not love their land.

The fact is that only a very few individuals did not make
their opinions of the revolution clear in the course of the
interview, by stating them directly and spontaneously—since
we never asked any direct question requiring them to do so.
On the basis of the overall impression of the worker's position, for example, as we gained it from the entire interview,
we noted whether the worker was, in our estimation, favorable, indecisive, or hostile to the revolution. We could not
use such an index, of course, in our actual analysis since it
would then be impossible to separate out other attitudes as
variables to relate to the variable of attitude toward the revolution—variables, for example, such as the worker's attitude toward his work or toward civil liberties for the revolution's outspoken critics. Out of curiosity, though, about how
our overall estimate coincided with the actual index constructed in order to gauge their attitudes toward the revolution, a variety of relevant attitudinal variables were factor-
analyzed and we found, to our satisfaction, that the only
variable which loaded higher than the individual components
of the index of attitude toward the revolution, was this overall estimate itself.

I selected five questions that, I think, taken in concert,
adequately indicate how the workers view the revolution,
and combined them into an index of attitude toward the
revolution. Of these five questions, two were "open-ended"

questions to which the variety of responses possible were limited only by the worker's imagination, and three were forced-choice questions. The open-ended questions were:

(a) Speaking generally, what are the things about this country that you are most proud of as a Cuban?

(b) What sort [clase] of people govern this country now?

Question (a) is borrowed from another study which was in progress when I was designing the interview schedule for this study. In their study of political attitudes and democracy in five nations, Almond and Verba used question (a) to tap what they call "the general dimension of 'system affect,'" by which they mean "generalized attitudes toward the system as a whole: toward the 'nation,' its virtues, accomplishments, and the like."[12] This, therefore, is a question particularly appropriate for use in our own study to tap the generalized attitudes of the workers toward the revolution.

One hundred and fifteen of the workers in our sample gave answers to this question that were clearly favorable to the revolution. We counted responses as "favorable" to the revolution only if they could be regarded as clearly indicating support, or if they explicitly stated support, of the revolution; for example, mention of the revolution itself, of the "socialist government," of specific economic and social reforms of the Revolutionary Government, of increased work security since the revolution. All others, whether more or less "neutral" responses or "clearly hostile" ones, were simply classified as "not clearly favorable."

For example, the workers could be especially blunt, as was a young worker at a paper milling plant in Cárdenas, whose answer was simply, "Of nothing, chico . . . I don't like Communism," or as a West Indian worker (with two teen-

---

[12] Gabriel Almond and Sidney Verba, The Civic Culture: Political Attitudes and Democracy in Five Nations (Princeton: Princeton University Press, 1963), pp. 101-103.

age daughters in the militia) at the nationalized Portland
Cement plant in Mariel, explained (in English): "I stay
only because I have two daughters who will not leave—
otherwise I'd go away. No one bothers me, I just do not like
it. Why? I can't say why. I guess I just prefer the old
Cuba. . . ."

Occasionally, the pain that his own answer gave the worker
was evident, as with the words of this sugar worker: "Listen
to me. I fought in the hills alongside of Camilo [*Cienfuegos*]
and Ché. I fought Batista. I fought for liberty. The criterion of my acts is that I am a worker. I do my work, now.
But I resist it. This government is quelling freedom of expression. I have seen more here already than I wanted to
see. I am afraid and discontent and pained with many things.
I have a third position. I am neither for nor against the
revolution as it now stands." "Politically," said another
worker, "I am proud of nothing here. I was studying before
the revolution. I never liked politics, and I don't like military
affairs. I work, and I work well, and nothing more. . . ."

In contrast to these hostile remarks were such noncommittal replies as a shoemaker's, "Our movies and our athletes," or a brewery worker's equivocal, "I am a peaceful
worker. I have no passionate interest in anything. After my
work, I spend my time in my house in Manacas with my
little one and my wife," or a cigarmaker's witty but equally
noncommittal, "Our women, and our cigars." There was
this rather bland response from a miner: "We do nothing
more than work. We work for these enterprises and we
worked for the other enterprises, too." Or the following,
which the worker may have meant as a positive comment
about the revolution, but which could not be clearly identified
as such: "We feel all right now. It feels good. We're working
harder, but it feels good."

Occasionally a revolutionary worker would wax poetic,
as did a copper miner in Matahambre: "Cuba is a cup of
gold to me. It is the only country in the world that is now

moving forward. . . ." A sugar worker's simple statement was more typical, however: "I earn good money now. I lack nothing. . . . All of the workers are with the revolution." A Havana brewery worker said: "I am content with the revolution in general. . . . For the first time one can do what one wants without fear." "The revolution is a correct thing, and today, frankly, it is my greatest pride," said a worker at the Nicaro nickel refinery. "I have nine sons, all of whom are working. All of my family are revolutionaries." A leather worker who came from a property-owning family spoke passionately about the past: "We lived in a state of prostitution. Peasants and workers were not valued in any way. We had *latifundias* of a thousand or more *caballerías* unsown while peasants and workers died of hunger. Therefore, I am proud of the moment in which we are living. When I was young, there were special privileges. We, for example, lived from renting houses, and it was hard to see the tears of the others when I was a child. I was in the Catholic youth movement, and I am proud of the work we did for the poor. But the clergy opposed this revolution, a just revolution, that is doing more for the poor than we ever could have hoped." Another worker in the same factory, whom we also interviewed, was a bootblack before the revolution, and a shoemaker now: "Here is a government that is giving us work as we never had before. I was left in the streets by my dad, and I grew up there. Now, I have three sons, with a future. I have had two sons since the revolution, but I wouldn't have had a child before the revolution if I could have helped it. I have an eighty-year-old grandmother who was young during the war against Spain in the 90's. She is proud of Fidel, but she was not proud of any government before this one."

One hundred and twenty-five workers replied to question (*b*) ("What sort of people govern this country now?") in terms clearly favorable to the revolution.

Given the double meaning in Spanish of the word "*clase*," which can mean "type," "sort" or "kind," as well as "class," the workers could, of course, choose to interpret the question's meaning in a number of ways. As with question (*a*), we counted as favorable to the revolution only those replies which clearly indicated a favorable attitude: "the people," "the humble," "hardworking," "good," "sincere," "moral," "honest," "defenders of the poor and humble," "the working class." Responses such as "socialists" or "revolutionaries" which did not clearly *commit* the worker, were *not* coded as favorable; neither were such equivocal replies as "Cubans," "Fidel," "Communists," nor replies which *likely* were meant to be hostile, such as "Russians," "Soviets," or *undoubtedly* meant to be, such as "shameless," or "traitors."

"To me," an opponent of the revolution working at the nationalized Texaco oil refinery in Santiago said, "they are completely Communists. All of their accomplishments have been through the work of others—including how they think. I have a sister-in-law and a brother-in-law in prison for speaking against the government—[sentenced to] seven years. . . ." "A heterogeneous mixture," said an electrical worker, "some of capacity and good intentions, and others of incapacity situated in very important places because they are old militants of the Communist Party." A sugar worker was discontent with the revolutionary leaders, but was obviously an opponent of the *ancien régime* as well: "They are men who have forgotten their ideals, and have gone toward communism—but they are far better than the lackeys of imperialism, exploiters, racketeers, and assassins who ruled this country before the revolution." Another anti-revolutionary worker said: "Socialists, they say; the kids say Communists. I don't know. Listen, if somebody comes and takes that pen of yours, and you bought it, what are you going to think?"

"Well, I've never been 'political,'" a cigarette-machine operator said. "For me, they are all right." A brewery worker's reply was equally equivocal: "My experience so far is good. I don't worry about such things—neither before the revolution nor now." A skilled electrician in Santiago committed himself only so far as to say that the men in the government are "persons with socialist ideas who, though they have good intentions, have committed many serious administrative errors." "Well, I don't know who they are, or if they are governing well or not. . . . Whoever comes, I am quiet. That's it," said a coppper miner. A sugar worker's statement indicates how even in the midst of a revolution, many workers are simply untouched: "Revolutionaries govern, but, logically, I've had no contact with the revolutionary leaders, as I had none with Batista and his *camarilla*, since I have always been working." The same is true of the words of a copper miner—a miner, it is relevant to note, who told us that he had eight children who were active revolutionaries, members of the militia, and of revolutionary organizations in Matahambre. He had a daughter on scholarship studying in Havana, and another daughter studying in a local self-improvement course; and he himself was enrolled in a course designed to teach illiterate individuals to read. Yet his response to our question as to who was ruling Cuba, was thoroughly traditionalist: "The revolutionaries are ruling. I am a worker. The Americans also ruled, and I worked for them, too."

"The truth is," a carpenter in a sugar central in Camaguey said, "that *now* those who are governing here are Cubans. They are honest and hardworking men." A former agricultural laborer, now employed at the Nicaro nickel plant, said: "Look, before I couldn't look a boss in the eye—I looked at my feet. Not now, now we have liberty and walk where we want, and nothing is prohibited to us. It is a great joy to be alive now. These men [who govern us] are one hundred percent better than before. I have known governments from [Mario García] Menocal [Cuban President 1913-

21] until Batista left three years ago, and I have never seen any like this government." Equally articulate in his support of the revolution was a 20-year-old bootmaker in a newly established factory in Guanajay: "*We* are the government, *we* run things. Go to a factory or *consolidado* anywhere, *chico*, and see: those who work govern, those who govern work, not like the capitalists who lived without working before the revolution triumphed. Now, the power of the workers and peasants has emerged." "They are people of high and untouchable morality," said a sugar worker, while an oil refinery worker described them as "products of the most sensitive and humble that our people have." And an electrical worker spoke of them as "individuals of conscience who feel a patriotism such as has never been experienced in our country before."

Two questions which posed fixed alternatives to the workers were also included in the index of attitude toward the revolution:

(*c*) Do you believe that the country ought to have elections soon?

Answer	(N)
No	136
Yes	44
No Opinion	22

(*d*) Do you think the workers have more, the same, or less influence on [*en*] the government now than before the revolution?

Answer	(N)
More Influence	170
The Same	17
Less	8
No Opinion	7

In addition, this question was included in the index as an "action criterion":[13]

[13] Whether or not the worker belongs to the militia is a *behavioral criterion* built into our "index of attitude toward the revolution." Arthur Schlesinger, Jr. has recently made an important criticism of measures of "public opinion":

> Irresponsible opinion is certainly of interest. It may well tell us a great deal about the general atmosphere of a period. But it is responsible opinion—opinion when the chips are down, opinion which issues directly in decision and action—which is relevant to the historical process and of primary interest to the historian. . . . The measure of responsible opinion is not answers but *acts*. ["The Humanist Looks at Empirical Social Research," *American Sociological Review*, XXVII, 6 (December 1962), p. 769. (My italics)]

Joining the militia when the country is under constant threat of attack—whether imagined, feigned or real—is certainly an act when "the chips are down." Some workers might have joined the militia opportunistically because they believed that they might somehow gain personally from such membership. Some might have joined out of social pressure or veiled threats from fellow workers. I think, from my own observations in Cuba within a couple of months after the invasion at Playa Girón in the summer of 1961, and during the tense summer and early fall of 1962, that such workers represent an insignificant proportion in the militia. Among nonworkers, and nonpeasants, however, this proportion might be greater. The workers we spoke to obviously respected the *milicianos*. Those who told us they were not *milicianos* often volunteered various reasons that they said prevented their joining the militia—as if not to lose the interviewers' esteem: "My feet are no good anymore—but I do guard duty whenever I can." or "I have a new baby and I can't spend the time necessary to train."

It bears emphasizing that in the various invasions of the island, and most notably in the invasion at Playa Girón, *milicianos*—not regular soldiers—were reportedly the heaviest casualties. The newspapers in Cuba had numerous reports on such militia casualties. Cubans also know that guard duty imposes a grave risk on one's personal well-being. Hit and run attacks by terrorists were frequent during the summer of our interviews. Serving in the militia also means extra hours of duty before work; the training, as I observed it, is grueling and thorough, and continues on weekends—as any *miliciano* will tell anyone who asks. So if being a *miliciano* may enhance one's prestige and bring certain possible personal benefits, it is also a good indicator that a Cuban is willing to fight with arms in hand to defend the revolution.

However, while belonging to the militia indicates active support of the revolution, not belonging does not necessarily indicate lack of

(e) Do you belong to the militia?

Answer	(N)
Member	110
Nonmember	92

Few workers were content merely with answering the forced-choice questions as stated, and their spontaneous remarks are inherently interesting as well as indicative of the meaning their answers had for them. Some workers, for example, believed the country should have elections soon because it was the principled thing to do. Thus, several workers whose responses to the other questions included in the index of attitude toward the revolution classified them as favorable to the revolution, gave such answers as these:

"No country ought to have a government without elections, whether or not it is a revolutionary government."

"We must periodically check on our leaders. After all, the people and their leaders change their ideas. One may be something entirely different after ten years."

---

support. Many personal reasons—ill health, old age, a nagging wife who wants you home, dislike of the military, fear—might intervene to prevent a Cuban worker who very much favors the revolution from, nevertheless, not joining the militia.

Finally, I should point out that the "wrong" answers to the various questions in the index, taken singly, are not necessarily indicators in themselves of lack of support for the revolution. Some workers whom I personally rated as fervent supporters of the revolution from my impression of them in the long interview, for example, answered "yes" to the question on elections. They thought national elections should be held because it was necessary to begin the institutionalization of formal democracy, or because the elections would "tell the world," as they put it, that the people of Cuba want the government they now have. Generally, though, agreeing that Cuba needed elections soon would be a vote against the regime. When the various questions are combined into one index, it serves as a reliable "operational" device for determining supporters of the revolution. The index combines features of the projective test, ordinary forced-choice indicators of attitude used in most surveys, and a criterion of action.

"Elections are necessary in a democratic and constitutional government."

A majority of the workers who wanted elections to be held simply saw it as a means of expressing their opposition—and what they believed to be the opposition of most other Cubans—to the revolution:

"They are necessary because there is no representative government here."

"We need elections because this has got to be changed."

"The country is not eating. I say, let's have elections."

"You need elections because you don't show what you think of a government with applause but with votes, and many who applaud would not vote that way."

"Elections would put an end to this government."

In contrast, many of the workers opposed holding elections at that time because they believed that they already had a representative government:

"I consider that those who are now the leaders of our country are the true representatives of the people."

"No, because the people of Cuba are living a better life, a more sane life, a more pure life now."

"Our leaders are doing sufficiently well. '*Más vale malo conocido que bueno por conocer.*'" (Roughly equivalent in meaning to "A bird in the hand is worth two in the bush.")

"We will always have faith in Fidel and the other men who govern."

"The people are electing the government now, a government that the majority agree with."

Their experience with elections in the past, and what they considered to be a democratic facade hiding an oppressive and corrupt regime was a dominant theme in the workers' comments:

"We need them like the plague. In the past, they served only to rob us."

"Elections were used precisely to sustain imperialism on the backs of the people."

"The politics in Cuba never gave anything more than benefits for a few, while with the revolution, the benefits are equal for all Cubans, whether they are reactionaries or not."

"Batista was elected, no?"

"Candidates were bought and sold in the markets. I prefer doing without them. I never sold my own vote, I always voted as I wanted, but most were forced to sell their votes for a pair of shoes."

"With elections, only two or three lived well. Now everyone does. Before, a candidate would ask you: 'Say, what kind of work do you do? A mechanic? Well, look, I'm going to be a Senator. You want your job—or the army to come? Vote for me, huh?' "

Still other workers thought elections were not advisable in the midst of the revolution:

"Our revolution is very young. Our people are not well-prepared. Let's wait until later when we can see what industry and education this government will give us. Then we can have elections."

"We are now trying to overcome and eradicate the past. In this process, elections would get in the way."

"There must be a more stable situation than now exists. Then they'll be possible. Meanwhile, the people's will is expressing itself in the process of the revolution."

"While there are convulsions in the revolution, there can be no elections, because the revolution is the source of the law and it must develop."

Finally, a few workers lacked faith in their fellow workers and their elitist views were apparent:

"The people still lack in consciousness. Many do not understand what we are doing for them. A party of the capitalists is in a sense still influential among us."

"No, because the people must acquire greater consciousness, that is to say, they must raise their cultural level. They must have a better base for interpreting things in order to be able to act with clearer judgment on the basis of the facts."

Asking the workers in our sample how they thought the collective influence of workers had changed since the revolution, also stimulated some interesting remarks:

Some saw the major change as their newly won freedom, as workers, to protest and state their grievances freely. As one put it: "The worker can now give his opinion and protest anywhere he pleases." "The coercion has ended," said another, "that means we have more freedom." A miner summed up the change in these words: "More liberty, fewer insults." To others, who believed the workers had more influence, politics was still viewed in essentially traditionalist terms, as was true of this worker: "The working class is now heard more by those above." The traditionalist workers were rare, however, and comments which indicated the workers really believed themselves to have power were quite typical: "The working class *is* the government," said a worker at the Venezuela sugar central. An old cigar worker seemed to think the anarchosyndicalist beliefs of his youth were now realized: "The working class has the power. It is we who are managing the industries." Others, while a bit leery of some aspects of the revolution, believed, as did this oil worker, that "despite the errors, the workers have more influence now. There are, of course, individuals who want to be more revolutionary than anyone, and they simply do not understand that everything has its place. But, after all, in the past our rulers had only the appearance of human beings, but the people were scorned." Some thought they had lost significantly since the revolution, not only materially but in their freedom: "There are fellows around all the time spying on you," a young paper mill worker said, "I'm afraid to speak. We have lost our rights." A cement worker lamented that "We have less influence; and we work harder and earn less."

Taken in concert, then, as the foregoing comments they stimulated should indicate, these five questions probably form a valid measure of attitude toward the revolution. Favorable responses were distributed as follows:[14]

Question	(N)
(e)	110
(a)	115
(b)	125
(c)	136
(d)	170

The index of attitude toward the revolution was constructed of the five questions taken together by coding all favorable responses as $+ 1$, and all others as 0 (zero):

Index

Points	Definition	(N)
3 - 5	"Favorable" (4-5, "very favorable")	142
2	"Indecisive"	24
0 and 1	"Hostile"	36
	Total:	202

[14] Item analysis of the workers' answers to the five questions indicates that the latter form an acceptable Guttman scale, 88 percent of the workers giving answers exactly (67 percent) or consistently (21 percent) in conformity with a Guttman model. The coefficient of reproducibility equals 0.95. See Samuel Stouffer *et al.*, *Measurement and Prediction* (Princeton: Princeton University Press, 1950), p. 117.

CHAPTER 2

Economic Insecurity and Politics

🖋 How will unemployed workers respond to their situation? Will unemployment and underemployment lead them to seek radical solutions to their common plight—or will they withdraw and become apathetic and demoralized under the impact of this experience? Under what conditions is one or the other response likely? Even given the prior presence of a significant radical political organization, is this sufficient to ensure that the unemployed workers will be more likely to support it than the employed? Social research has yet to provide coherent answers to these simple questions, although numerous students of working-class politics have focused on the relationship between economic insecurity and political radicalism. Karl Marx, for example, observed that a major consequence of recurrent unemployment would be the workers' formation of organizations "in order to destroy or to weaken the ruinous effects of this natural law of capitalist production in their class."[1] Karl Kautsky believed that economic insecurity would become sc "intolerable for the masses of the population" that they would be "forced to seek a way out of the general misery . . . [finding] it only in socialism."[2] More recently, leading social scientists who have studied the determinants of Left voting among workers have interpreted it as a consequence of, among other factors, certain central "needs" not being met, the "need for security of income" being foremost among them.[3]

[1] Marx, *Capital: A Critique of Political Economy* (New York: Modern Library edition, 1936), p. 702.

[2] Kautsky, "Krisentherien," *Die Neue Zeit*, xx (1901-1902), p. 140.

[3] Seymour Martin Lipset, *Political Man: The Social Bases of Politics* (Garden City, N.Y.: Doubleday, 1959), p. 232. The original article in which this formulation appeared was by Lipset, Paul Lazarsfeld, Allen Barton, and Juan Linz, "The Psychology of Voting: An Analysis of Political Behavior," in *The Handbook of Social Psychol-*

A good deal of comparative research has shown that the workers who have experienced relatively more unemployment or underemployment are more likely than others to be discontent with the existing order, to conceive of themselves as its "exploited victims," to be "class conscious," politically radical, "pro-Soviet," or "pro-Communist."[4] Yet,

---

ogy, ed. Gardner Lindzey, xx (Cambridge, Mass.: Addison-Wesley, 1954), I, 124-75.

[4] See Richard Centers, *The Psychology of Social Classes* (Princeton: Princeton University Press, 1949), pp. 177-79; Herbert G. Nicholas, *The British General Election of 1950* (London: Macmillan, 1951), pp. 297-98; John C. Leggett, "Economic Insecurity and Working Class Consciousness," *American Sociological Review*, XXIX (April 1964), 226-34; and Richard F. Hamilton, *Affluence and the French Worker: The Fourth Republic Experience* (Princeton: Princeton University Press, *in press*), Chapter 10. Lipset's *Political Man*, pp. 113-14, 232-37, contains an excellent summary of the literature and findings on the political effects of unemployment. For the earlier literature see Philip Eisenberg and Paul Lazarsfeld, "The Psychological Effects of Unemployment," *Psychological Bulletin*, XXXV (June 1938), 358-90. O. Milton Hall's "Attitudes and Unemployment: A Comparison of the Opinions and Attitudes of Employed and Unemployed Men," *Archives of Psychology*, CLXV (March 1954), is a monograph on the effects of unemployment on the attitudes of professional engineers during the depression of the 1930s. General economic insecurity in any form—whether because of the fear and presence of unemployment, or being in an economically vulnerable position—apparently conduces to support of radical politics. Thus, Lipset noted in *Agrarian Socialism* (Berkeley and Los Angeles: University of California Press, 1950), pp. 10-18, that: "It was the economically and climatically *vulnerable* wheat belt that formed the backbone of all protest movements from the independent parties of the 1870's down to the contemporary C.C.F. in Canada. . . . It is highly significant that the first electorally successful Socialist Party in the United States or Canada should have developed in the same Great Plains wheat belt that earlier produced the Greenbackers, the Populists, the Non-Partisans, and other agrarian upheavals." Evidence has also been adduced to show that the general insecurity of small businessmen in a large-scale corporate capitalism results in their support of so-called *right-wing* radicalism. Martin Trow, "Small Businessmen, Political Tolerance, and Support for McCarthy," *American Journal of Sociology*, LXIV (November 1958), pp. 270-81.

other (earlier) research found little or no such relationship,[5] even, indeed, that the unemployed were disoriented and politically indifferent.[6] Particularly apt to our own study is the conclusion by Zawadski and Lazarsfeld to their study of unemployed Polish workers during the depression of the thirties, that "the experiences of unemployment are a preliminary step for the revolutionary mood, but . . . they do not lead by themselves to a readiness for mass action. Metaphorically speaking, these experiences only fertilize the ground for revolution, but do not generate it."[7]

Less than a decade before the Revolutionary Government, headed by Fidel Castro, came to power in Cuba, the International Bank for Reconstruction and Development noted that "the insecurities which result from chronic unemployment and from the instability and seasonal fluctuations of the Cuban economy, continue to keep the worker in a state of anxiety."[8] That the recurrent unemployment and underemployment and the consequent "state of anxiety" of the Cuban workers in prerevolutionary Cuba later became a significant determinant of their support for the revolution and its leadership is the thesis of this chapter.

[5] Juan Linz, for example, found only a modest relationship among West German workers between unemployment and party choice (Social Democrat vs. other parties), and a reverse relationship between job security and support for the socialists. See his unpublished dissertation, "The Social Bases of West German Politics" (Columbia University, 1959), Chapter 12. See also David S. Street and John C. Leggett, "Economic Deprivation and Extremism: A Study of Unemployed Negroes," *American Journal of Sociology*, LXVII (July 1961), 53-57.

[6] Paul F. Lazarsfeld *et al.*, *Die Arbeitslosen von Marienthal* (Leipsig: S. Hirzel, 1933); E. Wight Bakke, *The Unemployed Worker* (New Haven: Yale University Press, 1940), and *Citizens Without Work* (New Haven: Yale University Press, 1940).

[7] Bohan Zawadski and Paul F. Lazarsfeld, "The Psychological Consequences of Unemployment," *Journal of Social Psychology*, VI (May 1935), 249.

[8] *Report on Cuba* (Baltimore: The Johns Hopkins Press, 1951), p. 359.

Prior to the 1959 revolution Cuba was both misdeveloped and underdeveloped. Her economy was subject to the vagaries of export demand for sugar, which created a "boom and bust" psychology affecting all strata of the population, not merely the working class, and inhibiting general economic growth. Chronic economic stagnation, a fluctuating, perhaps decreasing, per capita income,[9] and widespread unemployment, both seasonal and structural, characterized the prerevolutionary economy.

As early as the first decade of this century, Charles Magoon, Provisional Governor of Cuba during the United States occupation, reported that "practically all the sugar cane cutters are unemployed during six months of the year and by August find themselves without money and without means of maintaining themselves and their families."[10] A half century later this situation persisted without substantial change, and an authority of the United States Bureau of Commerce quipped that a Cuban worker might find it "easier to find a new wife than to find a new job."[11]

How correct this remark was, and how strategic an experience in the life of Cuban workers their ability to get work and keep it must have been, can be indicated briefly by the fact that in the two years preceding the establishment of the Revolutionary Government, *known* average unemployment and underemployment in the labor force was about 20

[9] Real per capita income in 1903-1906 averaged $203; in 1923-26, $212; in 1943-46, $211; and in 1956-59 about $200. Data for first three periods are from Julian Alienes y Urosa, *Caracteristicas fundamentales de la economía cubana* (Havana: Banco Nacional de Cuba, 1950), p. 52. He deflated his income series by means of the old United States wholesale price index, since there was no Cuban index. Money income figures for 1956-58 were adjusted by the writer, using the same set of prices.

[10] As cited in Alberto Arredondo, *Cuba: tierra indefensa* (Havana, 1945), p. 176.

[11] *Investment in Cuba: Basic Information for United States Businessmen* (Washington, D.C.: U.S. Government Printing Office, 1956), p. 21n.

percent.[12] This figure for the labor force as a whole *underestimates*, of course, the extent of unemployment and underemployment *in the working class alone*. Although there are no industry-by-industry data, we do know that in the major industry of the island, sugar, the vast majority of the workers, including perhaps two-thirds of the mill workers, were unemployed most of the year. In the sugar industry, "most of the workers were employed only during the *zafra*," which averaged about 100 days a year.[13] (Perhaps a third or so—at

[12] The 1953 Cuban census estimated 8.4 percent of the labor force was unemployed during the year's period of *fullest* employment, namely, at the height of the *zafra* (sugar harvest). (Oficina Nacional de los Censos Demográfico y Electoral, *Censos de población, viviendas y electoral* [Havana: Republica de Cuba, 1953].) Systematic data on unemployment and underemployment were not collected in Cuba until 1957. In 1957, 10.8 percent of the labor force was estimated as unemployed, on the average, during the *zafra*, with a high during the dead season of 15.1 percent. In 1958, the average unemployment in the *zafra* and dead season, respectively, was an estimated 8.4 percent and 18 percent. Year averages were 12.6 percent in 1957, and 11.8 percent in 1958. Estimated *under*employment averaged 7.6 percent in 1957, and 7.2 percent in 1958, making a combined total of known average underemployment and unemployment of 20.2 percent in 1957, and 19 percent in 1958. These figures are calculated from data in the following: *Anuario de estadisticas del trabajo, 1959* (Geneva: Oficina Internacional de Trabajo, 1959), Table 10, p. 186; Oficina Nacional de los Censos Demográfico y Electoral, Departamento de Econometría, "Cantidades e Indices de Empleo y Desempleo," *Empleo y desempleo en la fuerza trabajadora* (Havana: Consejo de Economía, June 3, 1958, mimeographed); *Encuesta sobre empleo, desempleo, y subempleo* (Havana, 1961, unpublished data made available to the author). A table showing unemployment and underemployment in the Cuban labor force 1957-58, by month, appears in the author's unpublished dissertation, "Working Class Politics in Cuba," (University of California, Berkeley, January 1964), p. 121. "Underemployment" was defined by the Department of Economic Statistics of the Cuban Government to include "persons who work less than thirty hours a week for pay, or 'on their own account' [self-employed] and those who work without pay for a relative." Departamento de Econometría, "Informe Técnico No. 7," *Empleo y desempleo en la fuerza trabajadora, julio, 1959* (Havana: Consejo Nacional de Economía, October 5, 1959, mimeographed), p. 12.

[13] *Investment in Cuba*, p. 24; *Cuba: Economic and Commercial Conditions* (London: Her Majesty's Stationery Office, 1954), p. 39.

most—of the cane cutters found not more than two months more of employment picking coffee beans.) The labor force estimates probably are themselves *under*estimates, then, since *just counting the workers in the sugar industry* (who comprised 23 percent of the labor force, and about three quarters of whom worked no more than five months a year) about 18 percent of the labor force was unemployed seven months of the year.[14] Since the volume and the value of the sugar crop profoundly affected unemployment throughout the island's industries, not only in sugar, 20 percent is an absolute minimum estimate of prerevolutionary average unemployment. The comparative prerevolutionary employment status of workers in the different industries represented in our sample is shown in Table 2.1. Obviously we cannot infer the actual prerevolutionary unemployment rates in these industries because of the small number of workers in our sample from various industries. Yet the table probably indicates the comparative interindustry rates fairly well. In any case, the data are all that are now available. Further, the data for our workers accord with prerevolutionary estimates of unemployment in the sugar industry. Thus, in our sample only 30 percent of the sugar workers were employed 10 months or more per year, on the average, before the revolution as compared with two-thirds of the workers in the

[14] Cuba Económica y Financiera, *Anuario Azucarera de Cuba, 1954* (Havana, 1954); *Investment in Cuba*, p. 23. If the 1953 census categories: "Craftsmen, foremen, operatives, and kindred workers," "Laborers, farm," are taken to constitute the working class, that class numbered 1,111,743 in 1952, or 56.3 percent of the "economically active population." There were an estimated 474,053 sugar workers, and thus they constituted about 42 percent of the manual working class, excluding private household workers, service workers, and unclassified occupations, the latter of which totalled about 10 percent of the economically active population. This means, then, that (since most workers in the sugar industry were employed only during the *zafra*) between a third and two-fifths of the working class in Cuba must have been unemployed and underemployed most of the year before the establishment of the Revolutionary Government.

other industries combined. And according to the estimate of a report written for the British government about a decade ago "Only *one-third of the millworkers* and one-twentieth of the field workers are kept fully employed during the dead season."[15]

TABLE 2.1

Prerevolutionary Employment, by Industry[a]

INDUSTRY	MONTHS WORKED PER YEAR BEFORE REVOLUTION			
	6 *or less*	7-9	10 *or more*	(N)
Sugar milling	57%	13%	30%	(30)
Beer and malt products	19	6	75	(16)
Tobacco manufactures	33	7	60	(15)
Textile mill products	33	11	56	(9)
Paper and paper products	33	33	33	(6)
Chemicals and petroleum refining	25	10	65	(20)
Leather products	40	—	60	(15)
Cement	25	—	75	(8)
Agricultural equipment	20	—	80	(5)
Nickel refining	14	19	67	(7)
Copper mining	10	10	80	(10)
Electric power	27	—	73	(11)
Total	32	9	59	(152)

[a] Those who were not workers before the revolution are excluded from this table. This and the following tables in this chapter do not include workers who did not enter the labor force before the revolution.

It scarcely seems problematic that the severe and recurrent fluctuations of the entire economy, and the widespread unemployment and underemployment in the population, were of major significance in the formation of the workers'

[15] *Cuba: Economic and Commercial Conditions*, p. 39.

political consciousness—especially given the significant influence that revolutionary socialists (first anarchosyndicalists and then Communists) had always exerted in the Cuban working class.[16]

That Fidel Castro believed unemployment politically significant is clear. For example, in his speech at his trial for leading the abortive attack on Fort Moncada on July 26, 1953, he said the revolutionaries had based "their chances for success on the social order, because we were assured of the people's support. . . ." Among "the people we count on in our struggle," he said, "are the seven hundred thousand unemployed Cubans, who want to earn their daily bread honorably without having to leave their country in search of sustenance; and the five hundred thousand rural workers who live in miserable *bohios* [huts], work four months of the year and spend the rest of it in hunger, sharing their misery with their children. . . ."[17]

And repeatedly in his speeches since coming to power, Castro has referred to the problem of unemployment, linking it with the meaning and the destiny of the revolution:

A people that produces below its capacities, and, further, where an appreciable portion of what it produces is carried off by others, is not a people enjoying the economic and social conditions that are conducive to progress and to resolving its problems. That is why our country suffered that problem of permanent unemployment; . . . that is why there was chronic unemployment in our country extending to several hundred thousand idle citizens; that

[16] "It must be remembered that nearly all the popular education of working people on how an economic system worked and what might be done to improve it came first from the anarchosyndicalists, and most recently—and most effectively—from the Communists." (*Report on Cuba*, p. 366.) On the political history of the Cuban working class, see the author's dissertation, "Working Class Politics in Cuba," Chapters 1 and 2, and the references cited therein.

[17] *Pensamiento politico, económico, y social de Fidel Castro* (Havana: Editorial Lex, 1959), p. 38.

is the reason for the ills of the Republic, which could never have been overcome if the Republic had not adopted forms of social organization and production putting human effort in harmony with the interest of the people in progress and greater production. . . . The issue became one of the revolution having to resolve the unemployment problem and, even more difficult, to resolve it under conditions of economic aggression, embargo on spare parts, raw materials and machinery, and complete suppression of the sugar quota.[18]

That such speeches as these would appeal to the workers and especially to the ones who had borne the brunt of unemployment and underemployment before the revolution, seems clear. In fact, whatever their own political persuasion, most serious observers of the revolution have argued that this vast reservoir of unemployed and underemployed workers inherited by the Revolutionary Government has been a major source of its popular support, although they were not the initiators of the struggle against the old regime.[19] Once the Revolutionary Government came to power, however, its social base was formed, in the words of Boris Goldenberg, by

[18] Speech to the workers' delegates to the Council of Technical Advisers, *El Mundo* (Havana, February 12, 1961).

[19] It should be noted, however, that the rebels emphasized that workers were well represented among them. A youthful unidentified leader of the 26th of July movement's Labor Front told an interviewer in February 1958 that he "was eager to dispel the notion . . . that the 26th of July movement headed by Señor Castro was predominantly a middle class affair. He said that although Cuban labor leaders were 'on Batista's payroll' the rank and file sympathized with Señor Castro." (*New York Times*, February 3, 1958, p. 7.) More to the point, Javier Pázos (son of Felipe Pázos, the former head of the Cuban National Bank), who was active in the anti-Batista underground, but who is now in exile from Cuba, wrote recently that "of the militants in the action groups, some were students, others were *workers* who were either *unemployed* or sick of a corrupt trade union in league with Batista." (*Cambridge Opinion*, No. 32, p. 21, as cited in Robin Blackburn, "Sociology of the Cuban Revolution," *New Left Review*, No. 21 (October 1963), 80. (My italics)

the "enormous and heterogeneous mass of the economically 'rootless,' . . . the unemployed [and] underemployed . . ." throughout the population.[20]

The general instability of the Cuban economy and, therefore, the economic insecurity of the working class must in itself have had political consequences, aside from whether or not the particular individual worker may himself have had secure employment. But while we cannot gauge this indirect impact of economic insecurity on the workers, we can examine the political consequences on the workers of their personal unemployment.

The profound significance that prerevolutionary unemployment and underemployment had for many workers was evident from the spontaneous remarks they made during our interviews. When we asked them simply: "About how many months during the year, on the average, did you work before the establishment of the Revolutionary Government?" some typical remarks were:

"If I was lucky, I worked two and a half months a year, and the rest of the time, I had to spend my time looking for work. I worked at trying to work, and I passed the time hungry the rest of the year. Now, everyone works."

"I worked when I could. Maybe I worked regularly three months a year, but I got by. I speak English, and I could work [for tourists] as an interpreter on my own account."

"Before, when the *zafra* ended, that was it. So you worked two or three months, and then if you couldn't find anything—you'd die for lack of work. Now whenever I wish, wherever I want to go, here in the mines or elsewhere, I have work."

"I fought for work, and then I got only about seven months a year."

[20] Goldenberg, "El desenvolvimiento de la revolución cubana," *Cuadernos*, XLVI (Paris: January-February 1961), 35. Theodore Draper cites Goldenberg's views with approval in *Castro's Revolution: Myths and Realities* (New York: Praeger, 1962), p. 53.

"I worked about nine, ten months a year. I was one of the more fortunate."

Thus, it is not surprising that our findings bear out our expectation that the relative security of their employment *before* the revolution would have a significant bearing on the workers' attitudes toward the revolution *now* (Table 2.2). There is a clear relationship between the number of months the workers worked during the year, on the average, before the revolution and the probability of their support for the revolution. The workers with the least prerevolutionary economic security are the ones who are most likely to support the revolution.[21]

TABLE 2.2

Attitude toward Revolution, by Prerevolutionary Employment

MONTHS WORKED PER YEAR BEFORE REVOLUTION	FAVORABLE	INDECISIVE	HOSTILE	(N)
6 or less	86%	9%	5%	(63)
7-9	74	10	16	(19)
10 or more	62	13	25	(105)

If their prerevolutionary relative economic security has had an important impact on the workers' responses to the revolution, it should certainly be true that their prerevolutionary situation significantly affected their prerevolutionary political orientations as well. We know, for example, that a major social base of the Communists in the labor movement was among the workers in the sugar industry, that is, in an

[21] It might be noted also that if we compare the proportions "very favorable," we find that among the workers who worked nine months or less before the revolution 63 percent were *very* favorable, compared to 40 percent who were *very* favorable among those who worked 10 months or more. This is essentially the same magnitude of difference (even slightly larger) between unemployed and employed as when comparing the proportions favorable to the revolution (83 percent vs. 62 percent).

industry which was economically very unstable and whose
workers suffered perhaps the greatest burden of the seasonal
unemployment cycle. We should expect, therefore, both on
historical and comparative sociological grounds that the
workers who experienced the most unemployment and underemployment before the revolution were the ones who
were most likely to support the Communists.

As a rough guide to their prerevolutionary attitude toward the Communists, we asked the following simple structural question: "How would you describe your attitude
toward the Communists before the revolution—hostile, indifferent, friendly, or supporter?"[22]

When we compare the workers' prerevolutionary views of
the Communists in accordance with their prerevolutionary
security of employment, the evidence indicates (Table 2.3)
that, indeed, the workers who experienced the most recurrent
unemployment before the revolution were the ones most
likely to be sympathetic to the Communists.[23]

[22] Answer	(N)	Percent
Hostile	(57)	28
Indifferent	(83)	41
Friendly	(49)	24
Supporter (partidario)	(10)	5
Don't know	(3)	1
Total:	(202)	99

It is relevant to note here that according to this crude measure of
their attitude toward the Communists before the revolution, 29 percent of the workers in our sample classified themselves as prerevolutionary friends or supporters of the Communists; and according to
the International Bank for Reconstruction and Development *Report*,
written after the Communists had been officially purged from the
labor movement, the Communists still had "a strong underground
influence in some unions, and some authorities estimate that perhaps
25 percent of all Cuban workers are secretly sympathetic to them."
Report on Cuba, p. 365.

[23] It may be objected that this relationship between prerevolutionary
unemployment and procommunism is an artifact of the fact that revolutionary workers are likely to "recall" a favorable attitude toward
the Communists, because of their present support for the revolution.

TABLE 2.3

Attitude toward Communists, by Prerevolutionary Employment

MONTHS WORKED PER YEAR BEFORE REVOLUTION	FRIENDLY OR SUPPORTER	INDIFFERENT[a]	HOSTILE	(N)
6 or less	35%	36%	29%	(63)
7-9	32	52	16	(19)
10 or more	26	45	29	(105)

[a] Includes three "don't knows."

Moreover, this relationship is considerably strengthened when we view it among only those workers in our sample who were also workers before the revolution. There has been a sizeable influx of formerly salaried or self-employed persons, as well as agricultural laborers and peasants, into the working class since the revolution—which is reflected in our sample: and these nonworkers were less likely to support the Communists before the revolution than the workers. Thus, when we exclude those who were not workers before the revolution, we find that the gap in prerevolutionary support for the Communists widens between the prerevolutionary unemployed and employed workers (Table 2.4). There is also a slight strengthening of the relationship between prerevolutionary employment insecurity and support for the revolution when viewed among only those who were workers before the revolution (Table 2.5).[24]

The fact that the proportion favoring the revolution exceeds the proportion who favored the Communists before the revolution by more than twice casts doubt on the validity of this objection. Moreover, when we view the relationship between prerevolutionary employment status and pro-Communist attitudes *among revolutionary workers only*, the same relationship holds: 44 percent of the recurrently unemployed (N = 68) supported the Communists before the revolution compared to 35 percent of the regularly employed (N = 65).

[24] It might be suggested, though, that this is a spurious relationship, that, for example, it is simply that the younger workers are less likely

TABLE 2.4

Attitude toward Communists, by Prerevolutionary Employment

MONTHS WORKED PER YEAR BEFORE THE REVOLUTION	FRIENDLY OR SUPPORTER	INDIFFERENT	HOSTILE	(N)
9 or less	40%	32%	29%	(63)
10 or more	27	46	27	(89)

TABLE 2.5

Attitude toward Revolution, by Prerevolutionary Employment

MONTHS WORKED PER YEAR BEFORE THE REVOLUTION	FAVORABLE	INDECISIVE	HOSTILE	(N)
9 or less	87%	6%	6%	(63)
10 or more	62	13	25	(89)

So far, I have referred only to the workers' prerevolutionary economic security, but, to be sure, there has been a significant change in the economic security of many workers since the establishment of the Revolutionary Government. Among our respondents, for example, more than three

---

to have secure employment than the older workers and that since the young are generally more amenable to radical appeals than the old, the relationship between unemployment and radicalism merely reflects an age differential among the workers. As we shall see in our discussion of political generations, however, this is quite incorrect. Within each age category, the workers who were least secure economically were most likely to support the revolution.

We also explored the possibility that the unemployed were differentially located in large plants and, therefore, subject to radicalizing pressures and organizational drives to which the more secure workers were not. Our data indicate, however, no systematic relationship between the size of plant and the unemployment rate among the workers; and a control for size of plant shows that the workers who had the most unemployment experience were most likely to support the Communists before the revolution irrespective of the size of the plant in which they worked (See Table 7.5).

quarters (79 percent) of those who had worked six months or less before the revolution, reported that they were working 10 months or more on the average since the revolution, and 19 percent said they now worked between seven and nine months a year. Thus, fully 98 percent of the previously most underemployed workers said they were working more regularly than they had been before the Revolutionary Government came to power. Thus, it would seem quite likely (to say the least) that these changes have had consequences for their response to the revolution. To test this assumption that the workers whose economic security has been most enhanced since the revolution would be the most likely to support it, we would have to look simultaneously at their prerevolutionary and present employment status.

Optimum test of the hypothesis concerning the relationship between change in employment status since the revolution and attitude toward the revolution would require us to relate *decreased* economic security, as well as maintenance of *the same level* of security, to the workers' attitudes. However, as is obvious from inspection of Table 2.6, not all the necessary types of change in employment status are represented among the workers in our sample. We can, nevertheless, make some useful inferences concerning the consequences of relative change in economic security on the workers' attitudes by comparing the available groups of workers.

Now, as can be seen from Table 2.6, our expectation is confirmed that those workers whose economic security is greater than it was in prerevolutionary years are more likely than other workers to support the revolution—in this case, than those workers who were employed regularly before and have continued to be since the revolution. (Again, this relationship is strengthened slightly among only those who were workers before the revolution.)

It might be suggested that unemployment is merely one

TABLE 2.6

Support for Revolution, by Employment

MONTHS WORKED PER YEAR BEFORE REVOLUTION	MONTHS WORKED PER YEAR SINCE REVOLUTION		
	10 or more	7-9	6 or less
10 or more	62% (101)	(4)	(0)
7-9	78 (18)[a]	(1)	(0)
6 or less	86 (50)[a]	82 (11)[a]	(1)

[a] Of these 79 workers whose economic security is greater since the revolution, 83 percent support the revolution.

road to poverty for the worker, and poor workers "obviously" are more likely than more well off workers to support radical or revolutionary parties. Hendrik de Man, for example, in his essay on the appeals of socialism, argued that "Such improvements as are affected tend to bring the workers more and more under the cultural influence of the bourgeois and capitalist environment, and this counteracts the tendency towards the formation of a socialist mentality."[25] But this "hypothesis" is fundamentally wrong, both as a theoretical assumption about the sources of political radicalism and as to the specifics of our own and others' findings. There is poverty and there is poverty. Whether or not poverty will be (a) felt as a deprivation and (b) lead to discontent with the social order, is conditioned by a variety of social and historical circumstances. For example, peasants in a traditional society whose structure of social relations is stable and hierarchical and buttressed by traditional and religious beliefs, who seldom find themselves in close and constant contact with each other, seldom, that is, communicate with each other, or see anything but the local, narrow, provincial way of life with which they are familiar, and who may be attached to a particular landowner and a

[25] *The Psychology of Socialism* (London: George Allen and Unwin, 1928, Eden and Cedar Paul, translators), p. 242.

piece of land to which their family have owed obligations for generations, are not likely to be amenable to radical appeals. (Nor are workers reared in such an agrarian setting.) On the contrary, as we know, the peasants often form the backbone of conservative parties in Europe and Asia and Latin America, despite their poverty and deprivation— though, as China and Viet Nam show, once activated and organized, their exploitation serves as a powerful spur to revolutionary action. The deprived poor whites and Negroes of the American South have hardly been exemplary of poverty impelling people to radical action—although this deprivation may be *made* politically relevant by "outside agitators." Within the working class, certainly, income is by no means necessarily indicative of the worker's social position. It, in itself, tells us nothing about the range of his social contacts, and the types of social pressures to which he may be subject.[26] Of course, in an industrial capitalist society in which income roughly corresponds, at the extremes, to social class boundaries,[27] it is scarcely surprising if we find that the lower income groups, namely the workers, are more likely than higher income groups to support a variety of policies such as social security, publicly financed medical care, unemployment compensation, etc., and the party or parties advancing such policies. Yet even here research has found nothing like an invariant relationship between income and

[26] Cf. Richard F. Hamilton, *Affluence and the French Worker*, *passim*; and Lloyd Warner and J. O. Low, *The Social System of the Modern Factory* (New Haven: Yale University Press, 1947), Chapter 6. In *The Social Bases of West German Politics*, pp. 323-28, Juan Linz has critically reviewed the findings on income and politics in various countries. Also relevant is William Foote Whyte *et al.*, *Money and Motivation* (New York: Harper and Bros., 1955).

[27] See Richard F. Hamilton, "The Income Difference between Skilled and White Collar Workers," *British Journal of Sociology*, XIV (December 1963), 363-72, and his "Income, Class, and Reference Groups," *American Sociological Review*, XXIX (August 1964), 576-79; Gabriel Kolko, *Wealth and Power in America: An Analysis of Social Class and Income Distribution* (New York: Praeger, 1962).

politics. In the United States, for example, in the 1948 presidential elections, as Richard Hamilton has brought to my attention, the lower income groups were more likely to vote Democrat than upper income groups, while almost the reverse occurred in 1952, when the proportion Democrat increased with income until the $5,000-plus annual income level which had the same percentage in both elections.[28] Heinz Eulau threw out income as a component of his class index in his study of the politics of the Eisenhower years because, as he put it, "between 1952 and 1956 it proved so variable as an indicator that it seriously undermined the stability of the index and interfered with the comparability of the results."[29]

Richard Hamilton has devoted an entire book to exploring this "more wealth, more conservatism" hypothesis as it applies to the French workers, and found it seriously wanting in explanatory value. He concludes that:

> What we can say with a high level of confidence is that the low stability of the relationship between income and radicalism and the correlated high fluctuation with changes in the social pressures make it clear that income is a variable of only minimal "independence." This should come as no surprise since income changes *per se* clearly exert no pressure or influence on the income recipient. The pay check, after all, is an inert object.[30]

In some countries, as we shall discuss in greater detail below, such as Germany and Sweden, it has been the *higher* income strata of the working class which have been the most likely to support the political left, while the poorer ones have been most conservative. In others, it has been the reverse, as seems to be the situation in the United States and Eng-

[28] *Affluence and the French Worker*, Chapter 8.
[29] Heinz Eulau, *Class and Party in the Eisenhower Years* (Glencoe, Ill.: The Free Press, 1962), p. 45.
[30] *Affluence and the French Worker*, Chapter 8.

land—although here too there is some question about the validity of previous claims.[31]

Now, if we simply look at the relationship between wage and politics among Cuban workers, we find nothing like a systematic relationship either to prerevolutionary support for the Communists or to support for the revolution. (Table 2.7) The problem is that what this means is not entirely clear. For one thing, there have been significant changes in wage rates since the revolution, changes which may merely have obscured the original relationship. Secondly, we are here looking not at the *annual* income of the worker but at his *weekly* wage—which may not be indicative of his actual relative income position compared to other workers. Some workers, for example, in the docks, or in the sugar mills were receiving relatively high hourly wages, but their employment was erratic and irregular, and their annual incomes may thus have been lower than that of workers whose hourly wages were lower than theirs but who were working regularly.

TABLE 2.7

Wage and Political Attitudes[a]

| | SUPPORTING | | |
WEEKLY WAGE	Revolution	Communists	(N)
$30 or less	71%	26%	(31)
$31-40	80	44	(25)
$41-50	67	33	(27)
$51-60	72	25	(36)
$61 or more	73	36	(33)

[a] Those who were not workers before the revolution are excluded from this table and the remaining tables in this chapter.

When we look at the relationship between wages and politics among only those workers who say that their hourly wage is the same as it was before the revolution we find the following: It is, in fact, the *higher income* workers who are

[31] These findings are reviewed in Chapter 4, "Skill and Politics."

more likely to have supported the Communists before the revolution (Table 2.8), while there is no significant difference in the proportion favoring the revolution in the different income brackets (Table 2.9).

TABLE 2.8

Wages and Prerevolutionary Attitude toward Communists among only Workers Whose Hourly Wage Reportedly Has Not Changed since Revolution

WEEKLY WAGE	FRIENDLY OR SUPPORTER	INDIFFERENT	HOSTILE	*(N)*
$50 or less	28%	42%	31%	(36)
$50-60	35	23	41	(17)
$60 or more	44	56	0	(9)

TABLE 2.9

Wages and Attitude toward Revolution among only Workers Whose Hourly Wage Reportedly Has Not Changed since Revolution

WEEKLY WAGE	FAVORABLE	INDECISIVE	HOSTILE	*(N)*
$50 or less	69%	8%	22%	(36)
$50-60	65	12	23	(17)
$60 or more	67	22	11	(9)

If we control for their prerevolutionary employment status we find that (*a*) the prerevolutionary unemployed both in the higher and lower income brackets are more likely to support the revolution, and to have supported the Communists, than the employed, and (*b*) if anything, the workers with the *higher* wages again show up as the more radical ones (Table 2.10).

Three conclusions emerge from these findings: First, that the "lesson" of unemployment, once learned, stays with the workers, and high wages does not suffice to make them forget it. Second, the conventional assumption that the low

TABLE 2.10

Support for Revolution or Communists, by Prerevolutionary
Employment and Wage

WEEKLY WAGE	UNDER- AND UNEMPLOYED[a]			REGULARLY EMPLOYED		
	Revolution	Communists	(N)	Revolution	Communists	(N)
$40 or less	88%	37%	(33)	56%	22%	(23)
$40 or more	87	42	(30)	64	29	(66)

[a] "Under- and unemployed" refers to workers who worked, on the average, nine months or less per year before the revolution, while "regularly employed" refers to those who worked more than nine months.

income workers inevitably will be the more radical ones is not supported by our findings; on the contrary, the Communists and the revolution secured solid support both among the low *and* the high income workers. Our findings support neither the assumption that material deprivation in itself radicalizes the workers, nor the assumption that well-being necessarily makes them conservative. And this conclusion is further strengthened, and will become especially clear, when we turn to the question of skill and politics.

Third, even comparing workers in the same income bracket, those who were underemployed and unemployed before the revolution are still more likely to be revolutionaries and to have been Communists than those who were employed regularly. It follows, then, that there is something about the experience of unemployment, apart from the experience of economic deprivation, that is responsible for making the workers more amenable to radical politics. I want to turn to this question in the next chapter, after first taking a look at the consequences of economic insecurity from a different vantage point.

CHAPTER 3

Race Relations and Politics

▶ ETHNIC and racial divisions have been among the most significant sources of internal political cleavage within the working classes of a number of countries. The heterogeneous ethnic composition of the working classes of Europe often made class politics difficult, and posed a major obstacle to the development of class consciousness. Not only are there simple obstacles to organization along class lines, such as the variety of languages spoken, but such differences are often exploited to create or heighten ethnic and racial antagonisms, thereby splitting the working class into warring factions. In his analysis of the German revolution of 1848, Marx singled out the ethnic division of Germany along the frontier of ancient Poland, and in Bohemia and Moravia, into German and Slavonic populations, as a blow against revolutionary solidarity.[1] Otto Bauer pointed out over half a century later that these same divisions continued to undermine working-class solidarity, Czech workers often acting as strike breakers when the German workers went out on strike.[2] Engels regarded the ethnic heterogeneity of the American working class as one of the "very great and peculiar difficulties for a steady development of a worker's party. . . . The bourgeois need only wait passively and the dissimilar elements of the working class fall apart again."[3] Gunnar Myrdal also has observed that "The huge immigration [into the U.S.] through the decades has constantly held the lower

[1] *Revolution and Counter-Revolution* (Chicago: Charles H. Kerr and Co., 1919), Chapters 8 and 9. These articles were written in 1851-52, perhaps by Engels.

[2] *Die Nationalitätenfrage und die Sozialdemocratie*, Vol. I (Vienna: Brand, 1907), 187-234.

[3] Letter to Friedrich A. Sorge, London, December 2, 1893, in *Marx and Engels: Basic Writings on Politics and Philosophy*, ed. Lewis Feuer (Garden City, N.Y.: Anchor Books, 1959), p. 458.

classes in a state of cultural fragmentation. They have been split in national, linguistic and religious sub-groups, which has hampered class solidarity and prevented effective mass organization."[4]

The only significant ethnic or racial difference in the Cuban working class is that between whites and Negroes. The first Negroes were brought to Cuba in chains in the early sixteenth century, and although the slave trade was legally

[4] *An American Dilemma* (New York: Harper and Bros., 1944), p. 714. The racial issue in our country has, of course, been of profound political significance. Seymour Lipset and Reinhard Bendix have written, for instance, that "today there are two working classes in America, a white one and a Negro, Mexican, and Puerto Rican one. A real social and economic cleavage is created by widespread discrimination against these minority groups, and this diminishes the chance for the development of solidarity along class lines. . . . *This continued splintering of the working class is a major element in the preservation of the stability of the American social structure.*" (Seymour Martin Lipset and Reinhard Bendix, *Social Mobility in Industrial Society* [Berkeley and Los Angeles: University of California Press, 1959], p. 106 [My italics].) Division between Negroes and the so-called poor whites and workers of the South, of course, made the "Solid South" possible, which in turn, as E. E. Schattschneider has put it, "made impossible a combination of the southern and western radicals," and

> turned the country over to two powerful national minorities: (1) the northern sectional business-Republican minority and (2) its Southern Bourbon Democratic sectional counterpart. The establishment of a one-party system in the South simplified tremendously the task of the conservative business Republicans in getting a stranglehold on the Republican Party in the North, because *it isolated the western radicals*. Thereafter, the western insurgents had no place to go; unable to make any combination able to win a national election, they were reduced to launching a succession of futile sectional parties. . . . The southern Bourbons and the northern Republican conservatives . . . shared a strong antagonism to the agrarian radicals everywhere. The establishment of the sectional alignment is the best example in American history of the successful substitution of one conflict for another. . . . The conservatives won power because they were able to impose on the country the conflict which divided the people as they wanted them to be divided.

Modern Political Parties, ed. Sigmund Neumann (Chicago: University of Chicago Press, 1956), pp. 202-203.

abolished in 1820, Negroes were illegally imported into Cuba as slaves for another half century, until slavery itself was abolished. Another major wave of Negro immigration came during the early twentieth century when workers from Haiti and Jamaica were imported for the sugar harvests, many of whom settled permanently in Cuba. Thus, from the early twentieth century, the Negro population has been about a third of the total Cuban population.

Few of the Indians indigenous to Cuba survived the Spaniards' exploitation of them beyond the end of the sixteenth century, and the presence of a few known Indian families in an isolated part of Oriente Province has had no political significance.[5] Thus, unlike most other Latin American countries, Cuba has no *mestizo*[6] population, nor especially a large unassimilated and culturally isolated Indian nation similar to those in Guatemala, Mexico, and Bolivia. In Bolivia, for example, few (about six percent according to the 1950 Census) Indians can speak Spanish, and few white Bolivians can speak either of the two Indian languages—Quechua and Aymara. The Indians are a majority of the population, and this fundamental barrier between Bolivians has posed a major obstacle to the development of Bolivian national consciousness since the 1952 Bolivian revolution.[7]

The position of the Negro worker vis-à-vis his white fellows in prerevolutionary Cuba is not easily delineated. From what we know, it is probably correct to say that Negro workers were subject to relatively greater economic insecurity and deprivation. While Negroes were distributed

[5] Antonio Nuñez Jimenez, a Cuban geographer and a prominent leader of the revolution, discovered a few families of Indians in remote regions of Oriente during an expedition in the 1950s.

[6] When Cubans use the term *mestizo*, they usually have in mind what we in the U.S. mean by mulatto.

[7] The cultural barrier, of course, is enhanced by class differences and the nature of the tenure system in Bolivia, not to speak of the fact that the vast majority of the Indians are illiterate in their own language besides not being able to speak Spanish.

throughout the occupational structure, they were disproportionately concentrated in the poorest income groups and
the most menial jobs. They were, as Lowry Nelson put it,
"predominantly the 'hewers of wood and drawers of
water.' "[8] Apparently, there also was a tendency for Negroes working at the same jobs as whites to receive less pay,[9]
although this was primarily true of the workers in the weakest
unions and least organized industries. Further, in the urban
slums, or *solares*, Negroes predominated and the better
rooms commonly were rented only to whites. To the extent
to which our own data (Table 3.1) indicate the relative

TABLE 3.1

"Life Chances," by Race[a]

	EMPLOYED 9 MONTHS OR LESS BEFORE REVOLU- TION	PRESENT WEEKLY WAGE $40 OR LESS	SKILLED WORKERS	EDUCA- TION THIRD GRADE OR LESS	(N)
Negroes	47%	46%	28%	39%	(36)
Whites	40	34	37	28	(116)

[a] Those who were not workers before the revolution are excluded
from this table.

material insecurity and deprivation of Negro and white workers, it is clear that proportionately more Negro than white
workers were unemployed, received low wages, and had only
minimal schooling before the revolution, while fewer of them
were able to become skilled workers.[10] Insofar as such sys-

[8] *Rural Cuba* (Minneapolis: University of Minnesota Press, 1950),
pp. 157ff. Also cf. Dirección General de Censo, *Censo de 1943*
(Havana: Republica de Cuba, 1945); and *Censos de población,
vivienda y electoral* (Havana: Republica de Cuba, 1953).

[9] Nelson, p. 156.

[10] While fewer Negro workers apparently were able to become
skilled workers, our data do *not* indicate them to be more concen-

tematic disadvantages as these could become politically relevant, then, it might be expected that Negro workers would be more amenable to the appeals of radical agitation and more likely to be revolutionaries than white workers.

In fact, some of the most prominent left-wing leaders in Cuba were Negroes, and among leaders of the Communist Party, as well as of the non-Communist labor unions, Negroes were well represented, perhaps disproportionately so. During the revolution of the 1930s the "soviet" of workers and peasants which withstood the military forces of Batista the longest, *Realengo 18*, right into the early months of 1934, was led by a Negro Communist, León Álvarez. Perhaps the most revered labor leader was the martyred Jesús Menéndez, the Negro head of the sugar workers' union, who was murdered in 1947 by cohorts of the notorious Eusebio Mujal. Of note also, is the fact that Oriente Province, the province with the highest concentration of Negroes in the population—perhaps twice the proportion of other provinces—was the rebel stronghold[11] during the guerrilla struggle against Batista; and Santiago, the province's capital, was the one major city in which the otherwise abortive general strike of April 1958 was fully supported by the workers, and the entire city shut down.

However, it must also be emphasized that the social status of the Negro in prerevolutionary Cuba differed markedly from the status of the Negro in our own country. Largely as a result of social processes characteristic of Negro slavery and of the slaves' emancipation in Cuba, in contrast to slavery's development in the United States, the barriers

---

trated in unskilled jobs than the white workers. On the contrary, there are proportionately more whites in our sample who were workers before the revolution who are unskilled than Negroes (26 percent of the white workers vs. 19 percent of the Negro workers).

[11] *Investment in Cuba*, p. 179. Forty percent of the population of Oriente was estimated to be Negro or *mestizo*, compared to 20 percent or less in the other five provinces.

to social intercourse between Negroes and whites—well before the revolution—were not as strong as those in the United States. While these early developments are too complex to explore here,[12] it is important to emphasize that Jim Crow laws comparable to our own have never existed in Cuba; nor were there legal, political, and social supports to Negro exploitation after emancipation from slavery like those in force in the United States. Compared to the United States, at least, the social history of Cuba involved a relatively high degree of racial integration and intermarriage, especially in the working class. Nevertheless, racial discrimination *was* socially and politically enforced to a certain extent. "Before 1959, Negroes were excluded from most of the better hotels, beaches, and places of entertainment patronized by Americans and upper class Cubans."[13] While not a common practice, in some cities the public squares and parks in which Cubans congregate in the evenings had a promenade plaza reserved for whites which was a step higher than the one reserved for Negroes. As the Cuba Survey of the Human Relations Area Files (HRAF) states:

> Opponents of Castro maintain that he invented the racial issue. It is, however, an old problem which has always become more serious in times of political crisis. . . . Many wry Negro proverbs commenting on the relations between Negroes and whites refer unmistakably to home grown attitudes of long standing: "The black fought the war, the white enjoys the peace"; "If you see a black and a white together, either the white man needs the black, or else the black has won a lottery."[14]

[12] See Frank Tannenbaum, *Slave and Citizen* (New York: Alfred Knopf, 1948); and Stanley Elkins, *Slavery* (Chicago: University of Chicago Press, 1959).

[13] Wyatt MacGaffey and Clifford R. Barnett, *Twentieth Century Cuba* (Garden City, N.Y.: Anchor Books, 1965), p. 39 (originally published as *Cuba: Its People, Its Society, Its Culture*, by the Human Relations Area Files Press, 1962).

[14] *Ibid.*

That many Negroes recognized their disadvantaged social status as a problem is indicated by the fact that a Negro national federation was organized against racial discrimination.

One further element of importance in the formation of the Negroes' attitudes toward the revolution is the fact that they had a history of broken promises before the revolution and, for that reason, were not likely to take too seriously mere assertions by the Revolutionary Government that it would eliminate discrimination. "Before 1959" as the HRAF survey notes,

> various political leaders gained electoral support by promising to uphold Negro rights but subsequently failed to carry out these promises. The legislative initiative gradually fell to the Communists and to the *Frente Cívico contra la Discriminación Racial*, sponsored by the CTC [Confederation of Cuban Workers] and incorporated in Batista's patronage system. Many Negroes resented left-wing efforts to capitalize on the issue, and pointed to progress made by the United States in racial matters as a commendable example. Others saw signs of a deliberate imperialist effort to weaken Cuba by depriving it of part of the resources of its population.[15]

Thus, given this complex mix of relative Negro economic insecurity, a rebel tradition, the presence of discriminatory practices and yet a relatively high level of social integration, and the probability of disillusionment with political programs, prediction of the differential response to the revolution of Negro and white workers is not without difficulty—although one would probably surmise that Negroes would be more likely than whites to support the revolution. It is particularly interesting, therefore, as Table 3.2 shows, that, taken as a whole, the Negro workers in our sample were not more

[15] *Ibid.*, p. 337.

likely than white workers to sympathize with the Communists in prerevolutionary Cuba, while even slightly more likely to be hostile to them. If we look at the same relationship, among only those who were workers before the revolution, there was a slightly greater likelihood for the Negro workers to have been pro-Communist before the revolution (Table 3.3).[16] We shall take a closer look at this relationship a bit later, after we complete our discussion of the differential response of Negro and white workers to the revolution.

TABLE 3.2

Prerevolutionary Attitude toward Communists, by Race

	FRIENDLY OR SUPPORTER	INDIFFERENT	HOSTILE	(N)
Negroes	28%	36%	36%	(50)
Whites	29	45	26	(152)

TABLE 3.3

Prerevolutionary Attitude toward Communists, by Race[a]

	FRIENDLY OR SUPPORTER	INDIFFERENT	HOSTILE	(N)
Negroes	36%	30%	33%	(36)
Whites	31	41	26	(116)

a Those who were not workers before the revolution are excluded from this table.

Since the revolution the Revolutionary Government has conducted a propaganda campaign in behalf of racial equality, and also has opened all hotels, beaches, and resorts

[16] While we cannot make much of this, given the size of the bases, it seems worthwhile to note, at least, that among the workers who were in nonmanual occupations before the revolution or who had not yet entered the labor force, only 10 percent of the Negroes (N:10) were pro-Communist compared to 28 percent of the whites (N:29).

(previously almost entirely privately owned and closed to the public) to all Cubans, regardless of color. "In the larger cities conspicuous desegregation was accomplished although the familiar patterns were to be observed in provincial towns in 1961."[17] Fidel Castro has sprinkled his speeches with allusions to the past exploitation and revolutionary traditions of the Negro, a typical example of which comes from a speech the writer attended at the 26th of July anniversary celebration in 1962 in Santiago: "In the past when voices were raised in favor of liberation for the slaves, the bourgeoisie would say 'impossible, it will ruin the country' and to instill fear, they spoke of the 'black terror.' Today they speak of the 'red terror.' In other words, in their fight against liberty they spread fear of the Negro; today they spread fear of socialism and communism."

From what we know, it seems likely that the social barriers between members of the races were least among workers and, consequently, the impact on them of nondiscriminatory policies alone should be least, although not insignificant for that reason. Most beaches, resorts, hotels, were closed to the *poor* of Cuba—black and white alike. As a *white* cigarette-machine operator put it to us:

> This is now a socialist country—everybody is valued the same and considered equal. Before, I couldn't have gone into the Havana Hilton; now, on Sunday, I was at the Riviera—a magnificent building. But *it was not for the poor before*. Now, there are social circles and you can go to Varadero, the best resort in Cuba.

Thus, it is possible that the Negro worker felt the impact of *class* more than of *racial* membership.

As to the economic policies of the regime, it is not clear whether or not these have differentially benefited Negro workers. The fact, for instance, that as of the summer of

[17] MacGaffey and Barnett, *Cuba*, p. 338.

1962 when we gathered our data, proportionately more of the Negro workers in our sample were still receiving lower wages than white workers, indicates, at least, that the wage inequalities that existed between white and Negro before the revolution were yet to be eliminated (although we know nothing of the improvement of the relative wage position of the Negro worker that may have already occurred since the revolution).

Thus, while it is probable that Negroes feel their status has improved, the complex events since the revolution make it difficult to predict the Negro workers' responses.

Many of the workers alluded spontaneously to the question of Negro-white relations when we spoke with them—although, unfortunately, there was no specific question on the subject in our interview schedule. A Negro electrical worker said:

> The ideals of the revolution, as far as I understand them, are: to bring equality of rights to both the Negro and the white worker—indeed, that all of us will live in the same society, and that the workers and the peasants, the working masses of the country—and even the reactionary elements—will become integrated into the revolution. . . .

A Negro worker at the Uruguay sugar central claimed that "special privileges" had ceased to exist: "Here," he said, "there's not a place which my child can't enter, or anyone else's—whether he's poor, or Negro, or whoever."

In response to our question as to what aspects of Cuba he was proud of, another said, too, that he was proud "of the way we are living now. We can frequent any place we want, beaches, hotels, movies. This was not possible for us before."

A shoemaker in Guanajay—a white worker married to a Negro woman—was especially emphatic in his opinion of the impact of the revolution:

Look, *chico*, this is many times better than we had before the revolution when our women slept on the floor in the midst of roaches and rats, and so they never wanted to come home. Negroes had to go to a different beach, they couldn't even buy refreshments in some places in the same store with white American tourists who came here only to take pictures of pleasure and not of the misery that we were living in. At least, now we have three big rooms, and three small ones, for our family [seven children, a brother-in-law, and a grandfather]. We have no running water yet, or gas, or electricity that we can count on; we still carry our water home in pails, but at least now we are alive.

One Negro worker, at the former Texaco oil refinery, took the opportunity, when asked what sort of people he thought were now governing Cuba, to take a swipe at the Communists, while endorsing the revolution for its action in race relations:

Fidel is out front. Not the Communists, they don't sacrifice for the revolution as he does. They were with Batista. They criticized Fidel when he was at Moncada [the fort against which Castro led an attack on July 26, 1953 to launch the anti-Batista struggle]. The revolution did away with discrimination, and it has done other great things. But not the Communists. Not men like [Lazaro] Peña and [Blas] Roca who were with Batista.

There were, of course, also Negro workers who made their discontent with the revolution quite clear, as did a worker whose father had left the island:

My father, all my family, has left Cuba. My father had a job in the other government, and now nobody would let him work, so they're in Miami. My father was secretary-general of the bus drivers' union local—and now what is he?

While many Negro and white workers spoke of the gains made by the Negro since the revolution, not one in our sample *said* the Negroes as a group had been adversely affected, or offered this as a reason for his disaffection with the revolution. (This includes opponents of the revolution, such as the sugar worker who told us that "My sons were militiamen. But they resigned because of communism, and, too, they weren't happy because there were many Negroes in the battalion who thought they were better than others.")

What, then, do our quantitative data indicate about the differential response of Negro and white workers to the revolution? Taken as a whole, the Negro workers in our sample are more likely to favor the revolution than the white workers (Table 3.4), and the relationship is essentially the same when viewed among only those who were workers before the revolution.[18]

TABLE 3.4

Attitude toward Revolution, by Race

	FAVORABLE	INDECISIVE	HOSTILE	(N)
Negroes	80%	8%	12%	(50)
Whites	67	13	20	(152)

In the preceding discussion we mentioned both economic and status considerations as relevant to predicting the differential appeals of the revolution to Negro and white workers. It is possible that our findings that Negro workers are more

[18] The gap between the proportions *very* favorable among Negro and white workers who were workers before the revolution is essentially the same (even slightly larger); 61 percent of the Negroes vs. 46 percent of the whites were very favorable to the revolution. It might be worth noting that whereas the prerevolutionary nonworking-class Negroes in our sample were less likely than their white counterparts to be pro-Communist, they are quite as likely to support the revolution: 60 percent of the Negroes vs. 62 percent of the whites who were not workers before the revolution support the revolution.

likely to support the revolution than white workers indicates only the relatively less secure position of Negro workers as a group before the revolution and that control for prerevolutionary employment status would eliminate the Negro-white difference. However, this reasoning is not supported by our evidence. As Table 3.5 indicates, both among the workers who were recurrently unemployed before the revolution, and those who were regularly employed, Negroes are more likely to support the revolution than whites. It is also true, looking at the tables differently, that the original relationship between prerevolutionary employment status and attitude toward the revolution holds both among Negro and white workers.

TABLE 3.5

Percent Pro-Revolution, by Race and Prerevolutionary Employment[a]

| | MONTHS WORKED PER YEAR BEFORE REVOLUTION | |
	9 or less	10 or more
Negroes	91% (22)	73% (22)
Whites	80 (60)	59 (83)

[a] It might be noted that the relationship between employment and attitude is strengthened in each racial group if those who were not workers before the revolution are excluded from this table.

Indeed, if we look at the effect of change in employment status since the revolution on Negro and white workers (Table 3.6), the results are essentially the same as when we looked at prerevolutionary employment status alone. Both among the workers who are working more regularly and those who worked regularly before and since the revolution, Negroes are more likely than whites to favor the revolution. Of course, employment security is not the only aspect of economic security, but it is certainly among the most significant, and we might infer that the social status of the Negro racial group accounts for the Negro-white differences.

TABLE 3.6

Percent Pro-Revolution, by Race and Change in Employment

	EMPLOYED REGULARLY BEFORE AND SINCE REVOLUTION	UNDER- AND UNEMPLOYED BEFORE, EMPLOYED MORE REGULARLY SINCE REVOLUTION
Negroes	71% (21)	90% (21)
Whites	60 (80)	81 (58)

Now, in contrast to our findings that the Negro unemployed are more likely to support the revolution than regularly employed Negro workers, is our finding when we compare these workers' *prerevolutionary* attitudes toward the Communists (Table 3.7). It is a finding which is especially interesting in the light of some other research reported recently, to be discussed below. Among white workers, we find the expected relationship, namely, that the workers who experienced the most prerevolutionary unemployment were the most likely to support the Communists. However, among Negro workers, the difference between the unemployed and the regularly employed in their prerevolutionary attitudes toward the Communists is slight—and even in the opposite direction. Further, looking at the same tables differently, among the prerevolutionary employed workers, Negroes were more likely to favor the Communists, while among the unemployed the reverse is true.

Two fundamental questions about our findings in this and the preceding chapter are now relevant:

TABLE 3.7

Percent Pro-Communist, by Race and Prerevolutionary Employment

| | MONTHS WORKED PER YEAR BEFORE REVOLUTION | |
	9 or less	*10 or more*
Negroes	27% (22)	32% (22)
Whites	37 (60)	24 (83)

1. Why are the prerevolutionary unemployed and under-employed workers more likely than the regularly employed to favor the revolution, and to have had pro-Communist political orientations before the revolution? Indeed, the general theoretical question of the reasons for the increased probability of political radicalism among the unemployed workers is at issue.

2. Why are the Negro prerevolutionary unemployed more likely to support the revolution than the regularly employed Negro workers, though they were not any more likely (and even less likely) to be pro-Communist before the revolution?

Radical politics and "leftist voting," as Seymour Lipset has pointed out, are "generally interpreted as an expression of discontent, an indication that needs are not being met." He suggests, as has already been noted, that one such central "need" is the "need for security of income. This is quite closely related to the desire for higher income as such; how-ever, the effect of periodic unemployment or a collapse of produce prices, for example, seems to be important in it-self."[19] Positing such a "need" is not, however, a particularly fruitful formulation, especially as it stands. We know, for instance, that stable poverty, accompanied by social isola-tion, such as that of subsistence peasantry, tends to be a source of political conservatism rather than radicalism. We know that low income per se does not lead to worker radi-calism. Yet their "need" for security of income obviously is not being met either. One crucial factor, as Lipset himself indicates in another discussion, is whether or not individuals are exposed somehow to possibilities for a life better than their present one.[20] In fact, of course, disemployed workers have had a better life and lost it.

The question remains, nonetheless, whether such an inter-pretation is sufficient to explain what makes unemployed

---

[19] *Political Man*, p. 232.   [20] *Ibid.*, p. 63.

workers more likely to perceive a connection between their private troubles and the economic structure, and to perceive it in class conscious or politically radical terms, than simply to blame themselves and look inward for the source of their troubles. The answer, I would suggest, is that—aside from the effects of political agitation on them—their radical response, "is especially linked," in Max Weber's phrase, "to the *transparency* of the connections between the causes and the consequences" of their situation as unemployed workers. It is not only the contrast between their situation and that of employed workers, which makes them amenable to the appeals of radical politics, but also (perhaps primarily) the fact that they can so easily recognize the source of their situation to be in the "concrete economic order." "For however different life chances may be," as Weber put it, "this fact in itself, according to all experience, by no means gives birth to 'class action'. . . . *The fact of being conditioned and the results of the class situation must be distinctly recognizable. For only then the contrast of life chances can be felt not as an absolutely given fact to be accepted*, but as a resultant from either (1) the given distribution of property, or (2) the structure of the concrete economic order."[21] This reasoning, which Weber applied to "the class situation of the modern proletariat," is particularly appropriate to the situation of those who are unemployed and underemployed.

Especially in Cuba was the connection transparent between the "concrete economic order" and the situation of the unemployed. For it was precisely from *recurrent dis*employment that the unemployed suffered. The relationship between the seasonal nature of their unemployment, and the misdevelopment of the economy was certainly "distinctly recognizable." Either the perceptual obstacles to

[21] Hans Gerth and C. Wright Mills, eds., *From Max Weber: Essays in Sociology* (New York: Oxford University Press, 1946), p. 184. Except for italicization of "transparent," italics are not in the original.

class consciousness were gradually eroded away by the workers' underemployment or abruptly torn away by their *dis*employment: recurrent disemployment repeatedly exposed to view the interconnection between their class situation and the irrationalities of Cuban capitalism as a whole. It is understandable, then, that they should be more likely than employed workers to want to alter radically an economic order which they perceived as the source of their collective troubles, and be more amenable to the appeals of Communist political agitation.

This same line of interpretation applies, I think, to our contrasting findings on the Negro unemployed and their political attitudes. Let us compare, first, what John Leggett reported recently concerning his research into sources of class consciousness of Negro and white workers in Detroit. Having found a general relationship between unemployment and class consciousness, he noted that it might be expected that "unemployed Negro workers should be more class conscious than their employed counterparts." His evidence, however, failed "to support this hypothesis. If anything, the Negro unemployed are slightly *less* class conscious than the employed, while the whites are distributed as expected. Clearly, unemployment, considered by itself, is not a source of class consciousness among Negroes."[22] He did find, however, that among *unionized* Negro workers unemployment is related to class consciousness as expected, and that unionized unemployed Negro workers are far more likely than their nonunion counterparts to be militantly class conscious. His interpretation of the effects of union membership on Negro workers was, in brief, that the impact of unions is partly to make Negroes more likely "to develop and use a class frame of reference to appraise their circumstances," and "partly because of the behavior of these

[22] Leggett, "Economic Insecurity and Working Class Consciousness," *American Sociological Review*, XXIX (April 1964), 230.

unions on class and race questions such as unemployment. ... "[23]

Now, while it is true that class consciousness and left-wing political orientation are not precisely the same, they certainly are similar phenomena, and their determinants have been found consistently to be similar. There is, in fact, a parallel worth speculating about between Leggett's findings and mine.

Leggett found that "the combination of unemployment and union membership clearly heightens class consciousness." Although on the basis of my data, it was not possible to gauge the effect of union membership on the worker's prerevolutionary political orientations, it will be remembered that we found that the combination of unemployment and their experience since the revolution apparently heightened the probability of revolutionary political orientations among Negro workers who were unemployed before the revolution. We might speculate, then, that the experience of living through the revolution has been an experience for Negro unemployed workers equivalent in significant respects to the experience of union participation for unemployed Negro workers in Detroit. That is, the revolution may have had an impact on the Negro unemployed in three relevant ways:

First, since the revolution they have been reached effectively by an ideology which certainly stresses, as Leggett said regarding industrial unions, "a class frame of reference to appraise their circumstances."

Second, the Revolutionary Government's "behavior on class and race questions" has emphasized racial equality both in propaganda and in deed.

Third, to the extent to which revolutionary propaganda and deed have, in fact, altered the social status of the Negro racial group and of the unemployed, the connection between

[23] *Ibid.*, pp. 233-34.

the racial situation and the prerevolutionary class structure and economic order which the revolution destroyed becomes distinctly recognizable. This process may also be likened to the impact of unionization on unemployed Negroes who may recognize that their unemployment cannot now be "explained" by (be attributed to) only their racial membership, but is also a condition affecting members of the working class be they white or Negro.

This third point may deserve amplification, especially since it relates to our earlier interpretation of the radicalizing effects of unemployment.

Class consciousness and political radicalism may not be meaningful responses for unemployed, nonunionized Negroes, because the fact of *being Negroes* is the significant aspect of their lives, to which they probably attribute their situation as unemployed workers. They do not see the interests of organized workers as relevant to their lives because, indeed, in a significant respect those interests are *not* relevant to them, so long as their *racial group* does not necessarily benefit from the furthering of those interests. *Class* issues become relevant to Negro workers when, as members of the organized working class, *they* benefit as their *class* benefits. A class conscious perspective or radical political orientation can then be meaningful to them.

The same reasoning may apply to the impact of the revolution on unemployed Negroes. That is, their response to the revolution may have its source in the transparency of the connections between the causes and the consequences of their prerevolutionary situation and that of unemployed white workers. The connection between the prerevolutionary racial situation, the prerevolutionary class structure and economic order, and the new structure of social relations formed since the revolution, may now be recognizable. To Negroes who were unemployed before the revolution, however, the connection between their situation and that of white unemployed workers was not obvious. It is, we may surmise, the revolution which has made the fact that they were conditioned by the prerevolutionary economic order, and not only by membership in the Negro racial group, "distinctly recognizable" to Negro workers who were unemployed before the revolution.

Particularly apt here are the remarks of a Negro worker at the Nicaro nickel refinery in Oriente, when he was asked what he was most proud of in Cuba. Implicit in his words is the recognition of a connection between the fate of Negroes who were unemployed before the revolution and the prerevolutionary economic order, yet with emphasis on their racial membership as the significant reason for their situation:

> I am most proud of what the revolution has done for the workers and the *campesinos*—and not only at work. For example, Negroes couldn't go to a beach or to a good hotel, or be *jefes* in industry, or work on the railroads or in public transportation in Santiago. *This was because of their color!* They couldn't go to school or be in political office, or have a good position in the economy either. They would wander in the streets without bread. They went out to look for work and couldn't get it. But now, no—all of us—we're equal: the white, the Negro, the mulatto. . . .[24]

[24] Optimum test of this interpretation of our findings on the politics of the Negro unemployed in terms of the parallel effects of unionization and the revolutionary experience would involve comparing (a) Negro and white workers who were union members before the revolution with those who were not, and (b) unemployed Negro union members with unemployed white union members. If our speculations are correct, then the Negro workers who were unionized should have been more likely than the unionized white workers to be pro-Communist, while among the nonunionized workers, the Negro workers should not have been more likely (and even less likely) than the white workers to be pro-Communist. Secondly, among the unionized workers, the Negro unemployed should have been more likely than the employed to be pro-Communist, just as among the white workers. Thirdly, of course, unionized workers, Negro and white, should have

A final point: perhaps one of the most important findings of this chapter is that the revolution is supported by a majority of the workers in each subgroup—even among those who were neither black nor unemployed or under-

---

been more likely to be pro-Communist than the nonunionized. Unfortunately, neither of these tests is possible with our data. We do not have information on the workers' past union membership (alas), and even if we did, the bases would be far too small for reliable percentages, given our sample size.

However, it is possible to make an indirect test of our interpretation. This would be to compare Negro and white workers while controlling for skill level—using skill level as a crude and indirect indicator of unionization. Our reasoning is as follows: While there are no reliable statistics on the comparative unionization of the different skill levels of the working class in prerevolutionary Cuba, it seems likely from what we know of the pattern of union development elsewhere, and from the historic information available on Cuban labor development, that the skilled and semiskilled workers were more likely to be unionized than the unskilled—or, at least, for their unions, in fact, to have been functioning and meaningful organizations for the workers.

The Truslow Mission to Cuba described the general prerevolutionary situation in the unions as follows:

A weakness of Cuban unions is the wide gap which often exists between the leadership and the rank and file. *Membership is too frequently more nominal than real* (in the sense of an active, informed participation). [*Report on Cuba*, p. 364.]

Another close student of prerevolutionary Cuban labor reported, after a study of a sugar workers' union at one of the larger centrals in 1950 (which nominally had 800 members) that the union's secretary-general lived in Havana and made only occasional visits to the central. For this purpose, the national labor federation provided

him with a car and a chauffeur. In the 1950 elections his slate was uncontested. At a general assembly attended by the writer, there was a quorum of the Executive Committee present, but not one single member [of the union rank and file]. The members of this pocket [union] . . . which looks impressive on paper, do not pay dues, do not participate in general assemblies, show no interest in elections. . . . The union does not function. It is merely the instrument of a politically ambitious "little *cacique*." [Charles A. Page, "The Development of Organized Labor in Cuba," unpublished dissertation (University of California, Berkeley, 1952), p. 212.]

employed before the revolution. Though they were, in this sense, an exceptionally *un*deprived subgroup of the working class, the majority of the regularly employed white workers favor the revolution. Moreover, a fourth of these same workers also were Communist supporters before the revolution. No conventional theory of political radicalism can account for such "deviant cases."

This situation, of course, did not exist in all unions. Some—especially unions of skilled workers—were actively involved in protecting and advancing their members' interests—and had comparatively high membership participation. The skilled workers were the first to organize historically, and were the so-called cradle of the labor movement. Their conditions of work in part contributed to their high level of literacy, and to their greater familiarity with contemporary knowledge and competing visions of the role of the workers in society. The most militant workers in the early development of the Cuban labor movement were cigar workers and other artisans such as the cobblers, bakers, carpenters, cabinet makers, and bricklayers. And apparently the skilled workers continued to maintain a position of political and organizational leadership right up to the revolution, as we shall see presently.

In any case, it seems clear, as the HRAF study of Cuba put it, that "the unions with the most active membership and with leaders most responsive to their followers" were those of the skilled workers. "Their bargaining power in the labor market was greater than that of unions comprised of unskilled or semiskilled manual workers, and their leaders depended less on political connections and support in bargaining with employers. . . . These same workers, by virtue of their social background, tended to be deeply involved in political activity and were often in the forefront of political strikes." [MacGaffey and Barnett, *Cuba*, p. 181.]

Now, if it is permissible to assume that skill level is crudely and indirectly indicative of the workers' likely unionization, then we should expect to find, as we suggested above, that among these "unionized workers," namely, the skilled and semiskilled, the Negroes would be more likely than the white workers to be pro-Communist, while among the unskilled (or "*un*-unionized") they would not be. This (admitting the small size of the relevant base) is, in fact, what the following table shows. Thus, if this admittedly very indirect way of approaching the question is valid, unionization apparently brought the Negro worker in prerevolutionary Cuba a class perspective and made him more amenable to the appeals of radical class-based political appeals, which lends further credence to our interpretation of our

In the course of their lives as workers in the employ of the owning classes, even the most secure, least deprived, highly paid workers may decide that their interests would best be served by a socialist revolution. Their position in the social structure, under certain circumstances, may indeed be such that they are even more likely than less well-off workers to come to this political conclusion. Apparently, as we shall see, this was true of the skilled workers in prerevolutionary Cuba.

findings on the difference between the response of the Negro unemployed to the revolution, and to the Communists before the revolution.

TABLE 3.8

Percent Pro-Communist, by Skill Level and Race[a]

	NEGROES		WHITES	
Skilled	50%	(10)	42%	(43)
Semiskilled	35	(17)	22	(41)
Unskilled	29	(7)	27	(30)

[a] Those who were not workers before the revolution are excluded from this table.

CHAPTER 4

Skill and Politics

🖋 THE old and enduring economic cleavage between skilled workers and semiskilled and unskilled workers has often been reflected in their differing roles within the labor movement. Not only did the skilled workers dominate the labor movement of many countries in their early periods of industrialization but, in fact, their craft unions and mutual aid associations were usually the sum and substance of these movements. Not until the growth of mass industrial unions, cutting across craft lines and organizing whole industries, did the dominant position of the skilled workers in many labor movements begin to weaken; and even today in the United States, the most developed industrial capitalist nation on earth, the merged central labor federation of craft and industrial unions apparently continues to be dominated by the former craft union leaders. Many observers of working-class politics, whatever their own political views, have thought of the skilled workers as alleged "natural" conservatives within the working class, since the skilled are so much better off economically than their lesser skilled, working-class peers. The term "working-class aristocracy" was often (and still is) used as a term of opprobrium by many political radicals and union militants to refer to the workers who have allegedly sold their "true" interests for a mess of pottage— and it is usually the skilled workers they mean when they say "aristocrats" or "privileged." Lenin was particularly vehement in his denunciation of "the craft union, narrow-minded, selfish, hard-hearted, covetous and petty bourgeois 'labor aristocracy,' imperialistically minded, bribed and corrupted by imperialism," who, he said, served "as the principal bulwark of the Second International."[1] In his political evalu-

[1] *Selected Works*, x (New York: International Publishers, 1943) 92.

ation of the skilled workers, however, if not in his vituperation, Lenin had ample precedent and company.

His contemporary, Roberto Michels, had similar reservations about the militancy of the skilled workers. "As time passes," he said, the difference in the economic position and working conditions of the skilled and unskilled workers "becomes transformed into a veritable class distinction. The skilled and better paid workers hold aloof from the unskilled and worse paid labourers." He continued:

> Within the *quatrième état* we see already the movements of the embryonic *cinquième état*. One of the greatest dangers to the socialist movement, and one which must not be lightly disregarded as impossible, is that gradually there may come into existence a number of different strata of workers . . . in conjunction with the efforts made by the workers themselves to elevate their standard of life; this may in many cases enable them to secure a position in which . . . they will become so far personally satisfied as to be gradually estranged from the ardent revolutionary aspirations of the masses. . . .[2]

Some two decades earlier, Engels noted that the militant "New Unionism" in England was based on "the organization of the great mass of 'unskilled' workers," whose "founders and promoters were Socialists either consciously or by feeling; the masses, whose adhesion gave them strength, were rough, neglected, looked down upon by the working-class aristocracy. . . ." The skilled workers, he claimed, had "succeeded in enforcing for themselves a relatively comfortable position, and they accept it as final." Thus, they were "model working men," and "very nice people nowadays to deal with, for any sensible capitalist in particular and for the whole capitalist class in general."[3]

[2] *Political Parties* (Glencoe, Ill.: The Free Press, 1949), pp. 292-95.
[3] *The Condition of the Working Class in England*, ed. and trans.

Contemporary political sociologists have largely followed in this tradition and have assumed, likewise (though not deploring it), that the skilled workers, being in general the least deprived and economically most well off of the workers, are the least likely to be political "extremists" or left-wing supporters. Survey research evidence from Britain, Australia, France, the U.S., and Italy has been adduced to support the thesis that the skilled workers are the base of "moderate" and of conservative politics in the working class. In general such findings have usually been presented without further discussion or analysis as confirming the more conservative propensities of the higher economic strata of the working class. Recent findings in West Germany and Sweden, however, have called this "explanation" into question, since in these countries the skilled workers are *more* likely to be *radical* than the semi- and unskilled. Yet while these findings provoked some speculation, the basic assumption continued at least implicitly, that their relative well being *should* lead the skilled to be conservative and only where they are proportionately more radical is there need for "further research" toward explaining these deviations. Thus, Seymour Lipset and Reinhard Bendix, for example, concentrated their speculations on the supposed sources in the social structures of Germany and Sweden of their skilled workers' comparative radicalism, but ignored the possible sources—other than relative economic well-being or greater work satisfaction—of the comparative conservatism of skilled workers revealed elsewhere.[4] In fact, as Richard Hamilton points out, the

---

W. O. Henderson and W. H. Chaloner (New York: Macmillan, 1958), pp. 370-71, 368.

[4] *Social Mobility in Industrial Society* (Berkeley: University of California Press, 1959), pp. 67-68; Lipset, *Political Man* (Garden City, N.Y.: Doubleday, 1960), pp. 240-42. The relationship between skill and conservative political attitudes even in the United States is far from being definitively established. Inspection of the following table, for example, from a source (Richard Centers, *The Psychology of Social Classes* [Princeton: Princeton University Press, 1949], p. 60)

explanation "of what is probably one of the most important sources of [political] cleavage within the working class remains for the most part unresearched."[5] Hamilton, who also found that the skilled in France were less likely than other French workers to be "Pro-Soviet" or revolutionary, *did* systematically explore a number of hypotheses concerning the bases of their comparative conservatism. He found, however, that neither differences in income nor in work satisfaction could explain their political differences; "no matter what indicator of reward and deprivation or of work satisfaction was controlled for, the unskilled still were the more extremist."[6]

Now it will be remembered that in Cuba historic sources indicate that the skilled workers not only initiated and led the organized labor movement but also apparently formed the early secure base of revolutionary anarchosyndicalist ideology in the working class. Unlike skilled workers in the United States, for example, business unionism seems to have had little early appeal to the skilled in Cuba. If Sam Gompers, cigarmaker, epitomized the early craft ideology's apolitical

---

often cited to indicate the relative conservatism of American workers, indicates that the relationship, even without controls, is not firm: when asked whether the "working people" should be given more power and influence in government, a cross-section of the adult white male manual worker population in the U.S. in 1949 responded:

	PERCENT		
	Agree	*Disagree*	*Don't Know*
Unskilled	54.5	28.6	16.9
Semiskilled	65.5	25.3	9.2
Skilled	59.3	31.5	9.2

Richard Hamilton has analyzed the relationship between skill and politics in detail in "Skill Level and Politics," *Public Opinion Quarterly*, XXIX (Fall 1965), pp. 390-99. Using national public opinion data, he shows that when the relationship is examined, excluding Southern workers and removing foremen from the skilled category, that there is no difference in either Republican voting or identification between the skill levels.

[5] *Affluence and the French Worker*, Chapter 7.
[6] *Ibid.*

bread and butter unionism in our own country, Emilio Sánchez, Vicente Tejera, and Carlos Baliño, cigarmakers,
epitomized the early political unionism and revolutionary
socialism in the Cuban working class. Leadership of the
workers shifted in the thirties, however, as we know, from
the anarchosyndicalists to the Communists, and with the
latter's emphasis on industrial unionism and the consolidation of their major base in the sugar industry they may
not have maintained the differential support that the anarchosyndicalists had among the skilled workers.

The HRAF report on Cuba states in this connection that
"Permanently employed skilled and semi-skilled workers
tended to develop into exclusive, privileged, and conservative groups with a stake in the existing political and economic order."[7]

The skilled workers in our sample do not appear, however, to have any pronounced conception of themselves as
more privileged, at least so far as their wages are concerned,
than semiskilled and unskilled workers. Rather, for instance,
the proportion of the skilled who believe that their wages are
higher than those of other workers scarcely differs from the
proportion of semiskilled and unskilled workers with the same
belief. Neither was the proportion who perceived themselves
as earning about the same wage as others markedly different among skilled and semiskilled workers, though both
were more likely than the unskilled to think their wages were
on a par with other workers. It is only in the comparative
proportions in each skill level who thought their wages *lower*
than those of other workers that the skilled clearly differ
from workers on lower skill levels (Table 4.1), and are less
likely to think their wages lower.

In reality, however, our data (Table 4.2) indicate that the
skilled workers *were* in a better wage position as a whole
than were the less skilled. Proportionately almost three times

[7] Wyatt MacGaffey and Clifford Barnett, *Twentieth Century Cuba*
(Garden City, N.Y.: Anchor Books, 1965), p. 172.

TABLE 4.1

Skill[a] and Perceived Relative Wage

	HIGHER	SAME	LOWER	DON'T KNOW	(N)
Skilled	31%	55%	5%	9%	(65)
Semiskilled	32	52	13	3	(75)
Unskilled	29	41	16	14	(56)

[a] We ascertained the skill level of the workers from the descriptions of their work given us by the workers, and by classifying them in accordance with the job definitions and descriptions contained in *Dictionary of Occupational Titles*, 2nd ed., Vols. I and II (Washington, D.C.: U.S. Government Printing Office, 1949). The descriptions of their work given us by six workers during their interviews turned out to be insufficient to allow their classification, and they are not included here or in other tables in which skill appears as an *independent* variable.

as many of them were in the highest wage bracket, for instance, as the semiskilled. It is also quite clear that they had proportionately far more formal schooling than the semiskilled and unskilled. In contrast, their relative prerevolutionary economic security was apparently no greater than that enjoyed by the semiskilled workers—though both upper skill levels suffered much less proportionately from unemployment than the unskilled workers.

One of the most characteristic features of the skilled workers, of course, is precisely the fact that they are "skilled"—that they are considered, and consider themselves, to be equipped with special skills which required study and training to develop—and they can thus have a "pride of craft" denied to other workers. Their skills characteristically allow them a great deal of control over their tools, materials, and pace of work—and their work discipline is essentially self-discipline, which particularly sets them off from other workers. They "command," as Blauner puts it, "a variety and degree of freedom [at work] unrivaled in the blue-collar

TABLE 4.2
"Life Chances," by Skill Level[a]

	EMPLOYED 10 MONTHS OR MORE BEFORE REVOLUTION	PRESENT WEEKLY WAGE OVER $60	EDUCATION OVER SIXTH GRADE	(N)
Skilled	64%	43%	30%	(53)
Semiskilled	64	15	15	(58)
Unskilled	40	3	6	(37)

[a] This table excludes those who were not workers before the revolution; thus, our view of the differences between the "life chances" of workers in different skill levels is not distorted by the fact that there has been an influx into the working class of former nonworking-class individuals since the revolution.

world."[8] It is hardly surprising, therefore, that studies indicate that whatever index is used to measure work attitudes the skilled are consistently more likely to be content with their work than workers on lower skill levels.

The same is true of our own findings. Using the simple question "What do you think of your particular work? Would you say you like it a lot, more or less, or a little?" and defining "a lot" as a positive work attitude, we found that the skilled were consistently more likely to have positive work attitudes than the semiskilled and unskilled.[9] This was true if we took (a) all the workers in our sample, (b) only those who were workers before the revolution, or (c) only those who were workers before the revolution and whose attitudes toward their work are the same as they were before the nationalization of industries—as far as they are concerned. Many workers had obviously changed their attitudes toward their work since nationalization, as we discuss in detail in Chapter 8, and for reasons extraneous to their

[8] Robert Blauner, *Alienation and Freedom* (Chicago: University of Chicago Press, 1964), p. 170.
[9] See Chapter 8, note 21.

skill level. So if we exclude those whose attitudes had
changed, insofar as they themselves perceived a basic change,
it is among the nonchangers that the workers on different skill
levels should be most distinct in their work attitudes, as indeed they are (Table 4.3). It is among the latter workers
(column *C*) that the impact of skill on work attitude can be
most clearly seen, and among whom the gap in work satisfaction is widest from one skill level to another. In sum,
our data indicate that the skilled workers earned proportionately higher wages, received more schooling, and were
more content with their work than semi- and unskilled
workers, while their margin of economic security was far
greater than that of the unskilled, although only equal to
that of the semiskilled.

TABLE 4.3

Percent with Positive Attitude toward Work, by Skill Level

	(A)		(B)		(C)	
Skilled	83%	(65)	87%	(53)	87%	(30)
Semiskilled	80	(75)	81	(58)	76	(25)
Unskilled	64	(56)	60	(37)	38	(21)

[A]Among all workers in sample.

[B]Among those who were workers before the revolution.

[C]Among those who were workers before the revolution whose attitudes toward work have not changed since nationalization.

Given these objective and subjective advantages over their
less skilled working-class peers, it should be expected, in
accord with the hypothesis that greater rewards lead
to greater working-class conservatism, that the skilled would
be least likely to be revolutionaries and least likely to have
sympathized with the Communists before the revolution. The
fact is, however, that our data do not support these sup-
positions. As Table 4.4 indicates, there are identical numbers,
proportionately, of workers favorable to the revolution on

each level of skill; and the number of pro-Communist workers before the revolution was proportionately *greater* on each higher level of skill. The *skilled* workers were *most* likely to be pro-Communist.

Why, however, should the skill levels have differed clearly in their prerevolutionary support for the Communists but not in their view of the revolution?

TABLE 4.4

Support for Revolution or Communists,
by Skill Level

	REVOLUTION	COMMUNISTS	*(N)*
Skilled	71%	38%	(65)
Semiskilled	71	25	(75)
Unskilled	71	21	(56)

The process apparently was as follows: among the workers who were not Communist supporters before the revolution it is the unskilled who are most likely to be revolutionaries while the skilled are least likely to be revolutionaries (Table 4.5). This, in turn, apparently resulted from the fact that the non-Communist workers were responding to the revolution not because of anything directly to do with their skill differences, but because of differences in their prerevolutionary unemployment experience. Since the lower skill levels among them were more likely to have suffered unemployment before the revolution than the skilled workers, and since unemployment experience made the workers more likely to respond favorably to the revolution, the unskilled workers among the prerevolutionary non-Communists were, therefore, more likely to support the revolution. As Table 4.6 indicates, when their prerevolutionary employment status is controlled, the differences in attitudes toward the revolution of workers on the different skill levels who were not Communists before the revolution tend to disappear.

TABLE 4.5

Percent Pro-Revolution, by Prerevolutionary Attitude
toward Communists and by Skill Level

	FRIENDLY OR SUPPORTER		INDIFFERENT OR HOSTILE	
Skilled	100%	(25)	55%	(40)
Semiskilled	94	(19)	62	(56)
Unskilled	83	(12)	68	(44)

TABLE 4.6

Percent Pro-Revolution among Prerevolutionary Non-Communists,
by Employment and Skill Level[a]

	MONTHS WORKED PER YEAR BEFORE REVOLUTION			
	9 or less		10 or more	
Skilled	70%	(10)	50%	(28)
Semiskilled	71	(21)	57	(33)
Unskilled	73	(22)	57	(14)

[a] This table excludes workers who had not yet entered the labor
force before the revolution.

The Search for An Explanation

The singularly important theoretical question, however,
concerning the causes of the skilled workers' greater propensity to support the Communists before the revolution—
despite their materially and psychologically advantageous
position over the lesser skilled—is not so easily resolved.
This relationship between skill and prerevolutionary support
of the Communists, it should be remembered, holds both
among white and Negro workers. (See Table 3.8.) The
question, then, is what processes were responsible for the
disproportionate number of pro-Communists in the ranks
of the skilled workers?

Size of Plant and Community

The first possibility, of course, is that the skilled workers
were somehow exposed to social pressures which other

workers were not as likely to experience. The structure of the labor market, for instance, may have made it more likely that jobs for skilled workers would be available in the bigger cities and factories. Industries requiring their skills may well have been disproportionately located, that is, precisely in the social situations most likely to bring them into contact with Communist ideas and to make those ideas more persuasive to them. In France, for example, skilled workers are found more often than the unskilled in the bigger plants and communities.[10] Our own data, however, indicate no systematic relationship between skill and size of plant; and, as we shall see later (Table 7.6), in each category of plant size (with the exception noted) the skilled were more likely than the semi- and unskilled to have been pro-Communist; and the bigger the plant, the bigger also was the proportion of pro-Communist skilled workers. Plant size, therefore, cannot account for the greater radicalization of the skilled workers. Neither, in fact, can the size of the community. We do find that proportionately fewer of the skilled workers lived in the smallest communities of less than 5,000 population, while there were proportionately more workers on each of the lower skill levels who lived in them. The skilled were more likely to live in the larger communities of over 25,000 population than were the less skilled workers (Table 4.7). However, when we control for community size, we find that in both small and large communities the skilled workers were still more likely than the semiskilled and unskilled to have supported the Communists before the revolution (Table 4.8).

Selection and Recruitment

There is another quite similar possibility, namely, that the skilled workers in the course of acquiring their work skills acquired their political training as well. While prerevolutionary Cuba had a relatively high ratio of skilled workers in the labor force (in 1953 23 percent of the Cuban labor force were classified as skilled workers), re-

[10] *Affluence and the French Worker,* Chapter 4.

TABLE 4.7

Skill and Size of Community[a]

	LESS THAN 5,000	5,000-25,000	25,000 OR MORE	(N)
Skilled	40%	19%	42%	(53)
Semiskilled	48	15	36	(58)
Unskilled	51	19	29	(37)

[a] This and table 4.8 exclude those who were not workers before the revolution.

TABLE 4.8

Percent Pro-Communist, by Skill Level and Community Size

	COMMUNITY OF	
	Less than 5,000	5,000 or more
Skilled	43% (21)	44% (32)
Semiskilled	14 (28)	37 (30)
Unskilled	26 (19)	23 (18)

cruitment and training of skilled workers still presented a problem. Opposition to vocational training and apprenticeship by organized skilled workers, and the almost guild nature of many skilled occupations, led to a shortage of certain skills. With neither formal training nor apprenticeship, however, many workers managed to develop the necessary skills to get jobs as skilled workers, and a major center in which this sort of self-training, especially in the more mechanized skilled jobs, could be acquired was in the mills of the sugar industry. Apparently the sugar industry was a major recruiting ground, that is, from which skilled workers could be drawn into other industries. Many were hired by other industries on the basis of the skills they had developed in the course of their work in the relatively mechanized shops of the sugar mills.[11]

[11] MacGaffey and Barnett, *Twentieth Century Cuba*, p. 169. Apropos of this, David Chaplin has pointed out that "in Peru, textiles was

Thus, distributed throughout the skilled industrial stratum were workers who had lived, worked, formed friendships, and *gained their political "education"* in the industry which formed the major social base of the Communists before the revolution. In other words, it is possible the sugar industry served as a major political training ground for a disproportionate number of skilled workers and that this accounts for the proportionately greater number of pro-Communist workers among them. Unfortunately, while this appears to be a reasonable hypothesis, there is no way we can directly test it on the basis of our data. Legitimate test of this hypothesis would require work histories or, at the least, data on the simple fact of whether or not a worker had ever been employed, and for how long, in the sugar mills, and we simply do not have such data.

Still another related possibility is that sugar workers' sons, since they grew up in an occupational community, were therefore provided with greater opportunities to learn specialized skills than the workers who grew up in the cities and towns. As they entered the skilled working-class stratum, therefore, they were, in effect, also filling it disproportionately with workers who were politically socialized in a strongly pro-Communist milieu. It seems likely, certainly, that they tended to inherit their fathers' political views (and as we show below, sugar workers' sons were more likely than urban workers' sons to support the Communists), and that they also reinforced these views in the course of their own early working lives in the mills. Thus, if they migrated into the urban working-class sector, they had good reason to bring already developed pro-Communist views with them. Our data indicate, however, that there are *not* proportionately more sugar central workers' sons in the skilled stratum

---

the 'escuela tecnica' for the rest of Lima's manufacturing sector, hence the 'unduly' long persistence of a skilled craft mentality in other branches of industry." (Personal communication)

than in the other strata of the working class. On the contrary, 20 percent of the unskilled workers in our sample are the sons of sugar workers compared to only nine and eight percent of the skilled and semiskilled workers, respectively.

Further, while our data indicate that on each level of skill (despite the very small bases for our computations), the sons of sugar mill workers were more likely than urban workers' sons to support the Communists, the original relationship between skill and politics *holds in both of these subgroups* (Table 4.9). The differences, in fact, not only do not diminish between the skill levels *among the sons of urban workers* but even increase slightly. The differences are even wider between the skill levels among sugar workers' sons (though this may well be a statistical artifact resulting from the very small bases). In any case, it seems clear that the hypothesis that the relative procommunism of the skilled workers might be accounted for by their differential recruitment from a particularly radicalized sector of the working class such as the sugar central workers is not supported by our findings.

TABLE 4.9

Pro-Communist Attitude before Revolution among
Sons of Sugar Central and Urban Workers,
by Skill Level

| | SONS OF | |
	Sugar Central Workers	*Urban Workers*
Skilled	67% (6)	36% (25)
Semiskilled	33 (6)	25 (32)
Unskilled	18 (11)	12 (17)

It is relevant to note here that support for a similar hypothesis concerning the differences between the political attitudes of workers on the different skill levels *was* found in France by Richard Hamilton. He suggests that the unskilled workers in France, who are the most "revolutionary" and pro-Soviet, were more likely than skilled workers to be migrants from rural areas which are themselves already centers of "extremism," and therefore "were predisposed toward extremist solutions before they entered the industrial labor force." When he compared skilled and unskilled workers in eastern France, a region he believes is characterized by a relatively conservative peasantry, Hamilton found that the skilled workers in this region are more likely to be pro-Soviet and revolutionary than the unskilled. Unfortunately, since his study was a secondary analysis, Hamilton had to infer the workers' social origins from the region they lived in, so his test of the hypothesis was not a direct one.[12]

As for the Cuban scene, Hamilton's hypothesis would not seem to be relevant. The sons of agricultural laborers and peasants do constitute a somewhat greater proportion of the semi- and unskilled workers in our sample than of the skilled workers: only 19 percent of the latter workers are the sons of agricultural laborers or peasants, compared to 24 and 25 percent, respectively, of the semiskilled and unskilled. But, as will be seen (in Chapter 6) the workers whose fathers were agricultural laborers or peasants were as likely to support the Communists before the revolution as were the urban workers. So though they probably constituted a steady radical source for the industrial working class, it was as a source of radicalism in the unskilled and semiskilled strata, rather than in the skilled stratum, to which the sons of agricultural laborers and peasants should have been flowing disproportionately, were this hypothesis correct. Moreover, the skilled workers were recruited less often proportionately from the comparatively radical peasants and agricultural laborers, and also were recruited proportionately *more frequently* from the comparatively conservative petite bourgeoisie than were the lower skill levels; 23 percent of the skilled workers are from petite bourgeoisie fami-

[12] *Affluence and the French Worker*, Chapter 7.

lies compared to only 13 percent in each of the lower
skilled strata (though the proportion of salaried employees'
sons is roughly the same in all three skill levels, eight percent of the skilled, and seven of the semi- and unskilled).
Thus, there is nothing about the recruitment pattern of the
different skill strata, insofar as class origins is concerned,
that suggests that this is the explanation of the greater prerevolutionary pro-Communist propensity of the skilled
workers. This was already clear, of course, from Table 4.9,
since the original relationship between skill and politics
continued to hold, as we saw, even when all but workers'
sons were excluded from the table.

Political Generations

So far, we have looked at a number of social sources of
differential political socialization and patterns of recruitment that might have accounted for the skilled workers' relatively greater political support of the Communists before the revolution. Now, as we shall see in detail in
Chapter 9, one major source of working-class political
socialization comes from their collective historical experiences
in the labor movement. Workers entering the labor force
when the labor movement is relatively secure and its leadership largely reformist, are likely to develop political outlooks
quite different, say, from those developed by workers whose
decisive politically relevant experiences come during a period
of heightened social struggle, and whose outstanding leaders
proclaim themselves to be revolutionary socialists or Communists. The significant political role of the anarchosyndicalists was coming to an end and Communist influence was at
its maximum in the working class at a time when many
of the workers in our sample had not even been born and
most were still children. Some workers, however, were
young men during the anti-Machado struggles and the subsequent abortive social revolution of the thirties; these experiences apparently so decisively affected their political

views that three decades or so later they were still more likely to be pro-Communist than younger workers.

Thus, if there is an age bias associated with getting into and staying in the skilled level of the working class, the apparent pro-Communist propensity of the skilled workers as a whole might be explainable simply by the fact that proportionately more of them lived through the struggles of the thirties and received the major impulse to the development of their pro-Communist views during this turbulent political period of their youth. It certainly seems reasonable to assume that the almost guild-like restrictions surrounding entry into skilled positions, coupled with the fact that acquisition of skills required time and usually periods of working as an apprentice and a journeyman before full status as a skilled worker could be attained, would tend to increase the average age of the skilled workers as compared to that of semi- and unskilled workers. Given the especially tight restrictions on entry into the skilled level that was true of Cuban workers, openings in skilled jobs for workers who already had the appropriate skills but were forced to work below their skill capacities might not come until they were already well into middle age. Our data, in any case, are consistent with the suggestion that the skilled level tended to recruit older workers. Thirty-one percent of the skilled workers in our sample were 44 years or older in 1962 at the time of our interviews, for instance, compared to 24 and 18 percent, respectively, of the semiskilled and unskilled workers who fell in this age group.

It is not true, however, that the comparative procommunism of the skilled workers is explainable by the disproportionate number of them who were old enough to have experienced and to have been decisively affected politically by the profound working-class struggles of the thirties. As Table 4.10 indicates, in each age category, the skilled are more likely to have been Communist supporters than the semi- or unskilled workers. It should be noted, further, that while the semiskilled and unskilled workers of the generation of the thirties were not more likely to have been Communist supporters than younger workers, the skilled of this generation (*i.e.*, the oldest skilled workers) were, in fact, the most likely of the workers in all the subgroups to have been supporters of the Communists. This is perfectly consistent with our other findings presented in Chapter 9, since, as we shall see, it was precisely among the workers with the least objective economic reasons for procommunism that the impact of their youthful historical experiences proved to be most important in their ideological development.

TABLE 4.10

Pro-Communist Attitude before Revolution, by Skill Level
and Political Generation

| | AGE CATEGORY AT TIME OF STUDY (1962)[a] | | |
	28-35	36-43	44 plus
Skilled	42% (19)	42% (12)	55% (20)
Semiskilled	28 (18)	29 (21)	28 (18)
Unskilled	15 (13)	23 (17)	20 (10)

[a] As in Chapter 9 on political generations, the youngest generation (21-27 in 1962) is excluded here since the question about their prerevolutionary attitudes toward the Communists refers to an attitude held before they were adults.

Relative Deprivation

Several studies have found, as I mentioned earlier, that in Germany and Sweden, in contrast to the apparent situation in other countries studied, the skilled and higher income workers are more likely to support the left-wing political parties—the Socialists and Communists—than are the semiskilled and unskilled workers. Lipset and Bendix, who first presented this data to American readers, suggested the skilled workers in these Northern European countries might experience more "status-rejection" than the skilled in the United States, Britain or Australia; their higher economic status might actually result in greater frustrations than is true for the less skilled workers, or for the well-paid skilled workers in other countries where there may be more real opportunities for them to aspire to middle class status. Germany and Sweden, Lipset argues, are "among the most status-differentiated countries in the Western world," since the nobility still had major power and influence there well into this century. Thus, with superiority and inferiority in status emphasized in formal and informal interpersonal relations, the skilled workers are more likely than their less economically "successful" fellow workers to actually experience rejection by middle class individuals, to feel that rejection sharply, and to resent it—much like American middle class Negroes may be more likely than working-class Negroes to feel status deprivation per se because of their more frequent association with middle class whites. Lipset tentatively hypothesizes, then, "that the more open the status-linked social relations of a given society, the more likely well-paid [and skilled] workers are to become conservatives politically. In an 'open' society, relative economic deprivation will differentiate among the workers as it has traditionally done in the United States and Australia. In a more 'closed' society, the upper level of the workers will feel deprived and hence support left-wing parties."[13]

Now a similar argument obviously can be offered concerning the situation of the Cuban workers. Prerevolutionary Cuba was hardly an "open" society—except perhaps, for grafters, racketeers, corrupt politicians, and military officers. While perhaps less so than in other countries of Latin America, social relations, and patterns of personal interaction between members of the same or of different social strata, still bore the heavy imprint of the Spanish colonial heritage. Cuba was, in fact, the next to the last of the former Spanish colonies to gain her formal independence,

[13] *Political Man*, pp. 241-42.

only some six decades before the present revolution. The Spanish feudal tradition had, according to many observers, continued to have a significant bearing on certain aspects of social interaction. Lowry Nelson, in his study of Cuban social structure less than 10 years before the Revolutionary Government came to power, emphasized the lingering "psychological barriers" that existed "between those who work with their hands and those who work with their heads." For this reason, he believed that although on the basis of economic criteria "one might be justified in postulating a middle class in Cuba, . . . in the more subtle psychological sense it is very doubtful that the classification would be valid."[14] The status barriers and social distinctions between manual workers and those in nonmanual occupations in pre-revolutionary Cuba were probably, then, at least as difficult to overcome as they are for German or Swedish workers. Thus, the upper or skilled stratum of the Cuban working class may have felt an even more heightened sense of social rejection and social resentment than the lower strata, and may consequently have been more disposed to accept the Communist view of the class structure, and of class conflict. Unfortunately, while this is a reasonable and interesting interpretation of the relative pro-Communist orientations of the skilled workers, there is no way we can directly test it with our data.

There are a number of reasons, moreover, why I do not think this hypothesis would be borne out were it possible to test it directly.

First, Lipset and Bendix make an unsupported and perhaps unwarranted assumption concerning the status aspirations of workers in general and the better-off workers in particular. They assume the skilled workers want middle class social status and acceptance, an assumption that re-

[14] *Rural Cuba* (Minneapolis: University of Minnesota Press, 1950), p. 161.

mains to be proven. Given what we are beginning to learn, and the little we know already, about differences in aspirations between working-class and middle-class individuals even in the so-called middle-class haven of the United States, this may be quite wrong. Even the subculture of the American working class, which is far from homogeneous and probably much less distinct from the subculture of the middle classes than in other major capitalist countries, has its own "design for living" and value system, as recent studies indicate.[15] "On an a priori basis," therefore, as Richard Hamilton points out, "it seems just as reasonable to assume that [skilled workers] . . . desire status among their peers in the working class,"[16] as to assume that they desire middle-class social recognition.

I suggest, moreover, that in certain types of underdeveloped countries, rather than skilled workers striving to get middle-class jobs, the process might very well be the reverse—in particular among the probably very insecure lower rungs of the petite bourgeoisie. The latter might very well look upon the skilled workers as their reference group, and strive to enter or at least have their sons enter skilled working-class jobs. And our findings indicate (Table 6.3) that workers from petite bourgeoisie families are more likely to be in skilled positions than workers of other class origins. Thus, the assumption that the Cuban skilled desired social recognition, but failed to receive it from individuals in nonmanual occupations with whom they were likely to have much social contact (namely, those in lower petite bourgeoisie occupations), hardly seems correct.

[15] Herbert Gans, *Urban Villagers* (Glencoe, Ill.: The Free Press, 1962); S. Michael Miller and Frank Riessman, "Are Workers Middle Class?" *Dissent* (Autumn 1961), pp. 507-16, and "The Working Class Sub-Culture: A New View," *Social Problems*, IX (Summer 1961), 86-97; David Lockwood, "The 'New Working Class,'" *European Journal of Sociology*, I (1960), 248-59; Ferdinand Zweig, *The British Worker* (Harmondsworth: Penguin Books, 1952).

[16] *Affluence and the French Worker*, Chapter 7.

Second, one of the most important indices to the social barriers between classes is probably the rate of intermarriage between their members. Where marriage across class lines is approved, it should be more likely to occur than where social distance and a host of social pressures make such marriage difficult. Lipset and Bendix themselves indicate, as Hamilton has brought to our attention, that "the barriers to marriage across the manual-nonmanual class lines are equally strong . . . in Germany and America."[17] Therefore, their assumption that German workers experience comparatively greater status-rejection in interpersonal relations with those in non-manual occupations than do their American counterparts, does not seem to be correct. In Cuba, it seems quite likely that marriage between the offspring of well-off and established middle-class families and those of working-class families was exceedingly rare. But since the workers' contact was more likely to be with the poorer representatives of the "middle class," namely, small traders and artisans, and since their homes were more often than not in the same areas of the big cities, association and intermarriage between their children may well have been a not unusual occurrence. Unfortunately, there are no such data available on inter-marriage rates across manual-nonmanual class lines in prerevolutionary Cuba; so while objection to the Lipset-Bendix hypothesis' applicability to Cuba seems reasonable on the grounds I have sketched, the objection is not subject to proof.

Third, we know (see Chapter 7) that it is precisely in the industries where regular interaction is possible between workers and nonworkers, and, in fact, is required by the production process (in the "high" A/P ratio industries), that support for the Communists was weakest. Presumably, however, if Lipset's and Bendix's reasoning was correct, since the workers in these industries were more likely than other

---

[17] *Social Mobility*, p. 34.

workers to come into informal contact with white collar employees, they supposedly should have experienced relatively greater status-deprivation than other workers. That is, since marked differences in status would be expressed in these relations, the workers would be rejected by the very individuals they were seeking to emulate. On this account, then, because of their heightened social resentment, these workers presumably should have been ripe for Communist agitation, and should have been more likely than other workers to support the Communists. As we shall see, however, this is not so.

Fourth, Lipset and Bendix assume that the skilled workers in status-differentiated or "closed" societies experience status-frustration in contact with middle class individuals because of their objectively higher economic status in the working class. It would, therefore, seem to follow that those workers who think of themselves (subjectively perceive themselves) as enjoying a relatively higher economic position in the working class, should experience more status-frustration than those who think their position generally is on a par with other workers. After all, the fact that they think they are better off than other workers and still get rejected by midd!e-class individuals ought to be particularly galling to them, whatever their actual objective economic position. They should, therefore, if the Lipset-Bendix hypothesis was correct, be more likely to develop social resentment and consequent pro-Communist views than other workers. Now, it will be remembered that we asked the workers to compare their own wage to that earned by other workers generally. And we find that, contrary to what we should expect on the basis of the assumptions of the Lipset-Bendix hypothesis (if I have followed their reasoning correctly), the workers who think their wage is "higher" than that of other workers are less likely to have supported the Communists than those who think their wage is the "same" as that earned by other workers (Table 4.11). Moreover, this is true within both higher skill levels. The skilled workers who subjectively perceived themselves to be better off than other workers were not most likely to support the Communists—contrary to what we should expect on the basis of the Lipset-Bendix hypothesis. Thus, this particular formulation of the relative deprivation hypothesis gains little credence on inferential grounds.

TABLE 4.11

Percent Pro-Communist before Revolution, by Skill Level and Perceived Relative Wage

	HIGHER WAGE		SAME		LOWER	
Skilled	35%	(20)	47%	(36)	0%	(3)
Semiskilled	21	(24)	31	(39)	10	(10)
Unskilled	25	(16)	26	(23)	11	(9)

There is another possible formulation of a relative deprivation hypothesis, however, that makes a great deal of sense in the Cuban context—a hypothesis suggested by the findings in Table 4.11. Skilled workers should have the right to expect that their wages would generally be higher than those of lesser skilled workers. It was a common belief in pre-revolutionary Cuba that comparative wages crisscrossed skill lines erratically and arbitrarily, and that workers doing the same skilled work often were receiving vastly different wages. The HRAF report notes in this connection that "considerable disparity existed between the [wage] rates received by workers in similar occupations but employed by different firms, and more skilled workers did not necessarily receive higher wages."[18] Our data indicate a closer fit between skill and wage than such a widespread belief would lead us to anticipate, but they also indicate the big grain of truth in the belief since many skilled workers were earning lower wages

[18] *Twentieth Century Cuba*, p. 178.

than many unskilled workers. Thus, for example, if some 36 percent of the *unskilled* in our sample were earning over $40 per week, there were 22 percent of the *skilled* who were earning *less* than that figure. What this means is if workers in these categories chanced to discuss their respective earnings, which there is no reason to assume was a rare occurrence, the skilled would be quite likely to resent what they found to be were their lower wages, to see this as an injustice attributable to the existing social system, and, therefore, be disposed to make radical changes in that system.

Semiskilled or unskilled workers who thought they were earning about the same as other workers would have had no particular reason to be discontent on this score; but skilled workers who thought other workers were earning just as much as they were should have been discontent—to the extent, of course, to which they believed that their special skills deserved better pay. Thus, the latter workers ought to have been most discontent and most amenable to Communist agitation against the irrationalities of the capitalist wage system. Therefore, in the subgroup of workers who thought their wages were on a par with others, the skilled should have been far more likely than the lesser skilled to support the Communists. In contrast, of course, the skilled workers who thought they were getting higher wages than other workers would have had no cause for discontent (on this score at least) nor especially should the semi- and unskilled workers in this subgroup have had cause for discontent. In this subgroup, therefore, the political differences between workers on the different skill levels should have been relatively small. Put differently, to the extent to which the skilled workers' *belief in their relative wage deprivation* was a major intervening variable in the development of their comparatively greater support for the Communists, where the belief was *not* present, the differences between the skilled and the less skilled should have tended to disappear; where the belief *was* present, the differences between the skill levels ought to have tended to *increase*; and the skilled in this subgroup should have been the most likely of all the workers to have supported the Communists.

The findings presented in Table 4.11 do indicate a tendency in the direction anticipated in accord with this hypothesis of relative deprivation. However, it is also quite clear that the skilled workers in the subgroup of those who believed they were earning higher wages than other workers, still had about the same likelihood of supporting the Communists compared to the less skilled as in the original relationship we found. There appears to be little reason, then, to think that this interpretation of the reasons for the skilled workers' comparative procommunism is any more valid than the others we have discussed. It is possible, however, that our test of the general hypothesis is inadequate.

The hypothesis, stated more generally, might be put as follows: where the skilled workers have a conception of themselves as the particularly exploited stratum of the working class, because (*a*) not only are they exploited like other workers but, in fact, (*b*) they receive even fewer relative "rewards" for their labor power than other workers (since their labor power while more valuable than lesser skilled is nonetheless "rewarded" at the same rate), they will be more amenable to Communist ideology and leadership. Where they conceive of themselves as "privileged" in comparison to other workers, on the other hand, the chance for the penetration of Communist ideology will be relatively small. This means enlarging our conception of "reward for labor" to include not only the workers' conception of their wage position, but also of their general economic security, working conditions, chances for promotion and upward mobility, and so on. Unfortunately, I never asked the workers how they evaluated their general situation, taking all things into account, compared to the situation of other workers. So this direct test of the hypothesis is not possible.

However, it became clear in the course of our interviews that many workers had pronounced conceptions of themselves as generally more "privileged" than other workers—while many, in turn, agreed that there was a distinct group of "privileged workers."

A brewery worker told us, for instance, when we asked if there were any groups who earn "too much money or who have special privileges," that "there are still some workers whose wages haven't been equalized with others. We, for example, are very fortunate and earn very good money—and I think the cigarette workers do, too."

A nickel refinery worker said: "Before, workers like Bacardi [rum] made much more money than the other workers." An equipment repairing and manufacturing worker thought that "electrical and telephone workers earn more than we do," and a worker at the former Texaco oil refinery said rather defensively: "They say in the street that we're 'privileged' workers. I don't think so. After all, we studied. And the work here in the refineries is dangerous—though, of course, not like at Matahambre [the copper mine in Pinar del Río]. But still it's very dangerous and hard work. Many of us do more than our share of volunteer work." An *unskilled* revolutionary worker in the major mechanized cigarette factory in Havana told us: "We are in the privileged sector—just as before the revolution. Of course, none of us are rich. The workers, after all, produced capital, and were exploited. I never expected to be a capitalist. I knew Martí's words: *Cuando se nace pobre y es honrado, nunca se llega a ser rico.* [If one is born poor and is honorable, he will never become rich.]"

Long before the revolutionary leadership first referred to workers in such industries as communications, electric power, oil refining, tourism, cigarette manufacturing, and beer and malt brewing as privileged, the term "aristocrats" had already been pinned on those workers. Because of their fortunate industrial situation, militancy, and successful union struggles, they had managed to achieve relatively greater material security, and better working conditions than other workers, but had now allegedly forgotten their bonds to the rest of the working class. Speaking of these workers, the authors of the HRAF report note, for instance, that

> The middle-class character of these groups, especially in the Havana unions, and their exclusive concern with their own interests and habit of achieving their ends through political contacts and compromise, disqualified them in the eyes of the Castro regime for leadership of the labor movement as a whole. Extreme examples were the electrical workers, who were singled out for criticism by the government, and the restaurant workers, who by the end of the Batista regime were sufficiently wealthy to own part of the luxurious Havana Hilton Hotel.[19]

While we have no direct systematic evidence, then, on whether or not the workers in these industries conceived of themselves as "privileged," the impressionistic evidence from the spontaneous remarks of many workers, and the descriptions of certain workers as "privileged" by responsible students of Cuban society, allow us, at least, to tentatively categorize certain workers in our sample as "privileged": electrical, oil refining, brewery, and cigarette manufacturing workers. If our speculations have any basis in reality, that is, that these workers did think of themselves as "privileged," then, according to our hypothesis, not only would they be less likely than other workers to have been supporters of the Communists, but, in fact, the skilled among them, having no reason to resent their relative situation, would not be more likely than the less skilled to have pro-Communist views. The political differences between skilled, semiskilled, and unskilled "privileged" workers should tend to disappear. On the other hand, among the rest of the urban

19 *Ibid.*, p. 172.

workers and among the sugar central workers, neither of which groups were privileged nor thought of themselves as privileged, the political differences between skilled, semiskilled, and unskilled workers should persist, and even increase. The skilled workers in the more typical industries should have been even more likely than their fellow, less skilled, workers to resent their situation, for the reasons discussed above, and, therefore, to have responded more favorably to the political appeals of the Communists. As Table 4.12 indicates, this long chain of interpretation seems to be borne out by our findings.

TABLE 4.12

Percent Pro-Communist before Revolution, Among "Privileged" and Ordinary Workers, by Skill Level

	"PRIVILEGED"		OTHER URBAN		SUGAR CENTRAL	
Skilled	24%	(25)	42%	(26)	57%	(14)
Semiskilled	27	(26)	21	(39)	40	(10)
Unskilled	25	(12)	21	(28)	25	(16)

It is well to emphasize that the chain of interpretation and inference has, indeed, been long. I have assumed (a) that the "privileged" workers had a self-conception of themselves as such, and were considered as such by other workers; (b) that the reference group of the skilled workers would not be primarily the less skilled workers in their own industries, but rather their fellow skilled in other industries—industries in which the workers were especially well situated economically; (c) that the skilled in the ordinary industries would resent the fact that not only their fellow skilled but even workers with less skill and training were in a more favorable material situation than themselves if they were in the privileged sector; and (d) that they would turn their resentment not primarily toward their more fortunate fellow workers but at the capitalist system itself, and thus find

Communist ideology appealing. None of these assumptions, while reasonable, is proven; and each of them may be wrong.

I myself am frankly ill at ease with this interpretation and find it intellectually unsatisfying, for reasons probably having to do in part with the number of undemonstrated assumptions on which the interpretation rests and in part with my theoretical preference for explanation of political behavior in terms of differential political socialization in varying types of social contexts. In our search for an explanation of the relatively greater support which the skilled workers gave the Communists before the revolution, however, none of the possible explanations in terms of differential political socialization suggested were substantiated. Neither possible differences in the size of the plant in which they typically worked, nor of the community they lived in, accounted for the political differences we found. While we could not test the hypothesis that they received their political "education" disproportionately in the sugar mills, which seem to have been major training grounds for skilled workers, the possibility that the skilled might have been disproportionately recruited from a particularly radicalized sector of the working class, such as the sugar mill workers, or from radicalized agricultural laborers or peasants' families, *was* tested but found wanting. We also were compelled to reject the possibility that the age composition of the skilled, and consequent greater likelihood that they experienced the revolutionary events of the thirties, could account for the skilled workers' politics. As to the hypothesis of status-deprivation suggested by Lipset and Bendix to account for findings similar to our own in Germany and Sweden, I rejected it on a number of inferential grounds. For the present, then, we are left with our indirectly supported hypothesis that the explanation for the skilled workers' relative pre-revolutionary procommunism lies in the possibility that they conceived of themselves as, paradoxically, the particularly exploited stratum of the working class.[20]

One stratum—of a rather special kind—that objectively was the most exploited, or at least whose material situation was the poorest in prerevolutionary Cuba, was that composed of women workers. In the following chapter, here again we shall see that material deprivation and political attitudes are not related in accordance with conventional assumptions.

[20] One possible explanation for the skilled workers' greater support for the Communists before the revolution is the following: We have reason to believe (see Chapter 3, note 24) that the skilled stratum was the most unionized—that is, that proportionately more skilled workers were in active, functioning, meaningful unions than was true of semiskilled and unskilled workers. Since the unions were in most instances dominated by Communist militants and run by Communist officials, the skilled would, therefore, have been more likely than other workers to be subject to Communist "political education," and, therefore, more likely to become supporters of the Communists than other workers. This is a simple, economical, and enticing explanation which, unfortunately, we have no way of testing with our data since while I asked the workers whether they were union members at the time of our interview (which turned out to be a useless question since all the workers were), I failed to ask about their prerevolutionary union experience.

CHAPTER 5

Sex and the Single Worker

⚜ WOMEN won political suffrage (where they have it) only after considerable struggle, and usually with the decisive support of the Left. So far, however, the Left probably has only reason to regret its principled support of the emancipation of the second sex; for from what we know about the differences between the voting behavior of men and women in such diverse countries as Norway, West Germany, Chile, Italy, and France, women are far more likely to vote for the clerical and conservative political parties than men, and less likely to support the electoral ambitions of the socialists and Communists.[1] The slimmer the difference between support of the different political parties, of course, the more decisive the women's vote, since it takes only a slight shift in votes to give a party victory at the polls. In such circumstances, "women may thus really be the arbiters in deciding the government."[2] This seems to have happened in France in 1946, when the women's vote in the national referendum probably was responsible for the rejection of the draft constitution backed by the Left. Some two-thirds of the women apparently voted against the new democratic constitution largely because they opposed its lack of guarantees to private religious schools. Women played a crucial role, there-

---

[1] Maurice Duverge, *The Political Role of Women* (Paris: UNESCO, 1955); Herbert Tingsten, *Political Behavior* (London: P. S. King and Sons, 1937); Mattei Dogan, "Le comportement politique des femmes dans les pays de l'Europe occidentale," in *La condition sociale de la femme* (Brussels: Cahiers de l'Institut de Sociologie, Solvay, 1956); Gabriele Bremme, *Die Politische Rolle der Frau in Deutschland* (Göttingen: Vandenhoeck and Ruprecht, 1956); Juan Linz, "The Social Bases of West German Politics," unpublished dissertation, Columbia University, 1959, Chapter 6; Brunilda Vélez, "Women's Political Behavior in Chile," unpublished thesis, University of California, Berkeley, 1963.

[2] Duverge, *Political Role of Women*, p. 72.

fore, at a major turning point in postwar French politics that "marked the beginning of a new trend, and a departure from the alliance of the Left policy followed since 1944."[3] The decisive importance of women in a political struggle, at least one fought by ballots, was also shown recently in the elections in Chile in September 1958, only three months before the Cuban revolution began to set the continent on revolutionary edge. Voting in their second presidential election, having gotten the vote largely as the result of the parliamentary Left's backing, the women turned out to be the chief obstacle to the establishment there of the first socialist government to gain power through elections in a capitalist political democracy. The Socialist-Communist coalition (FRAP) candidate, Dr. Salvador Allende, lost the elections by a margin of less than three percent of the total vote. Among the women, he lost by almost 12 percent, but among the men, he actually won a majority by about the same margin by which he lost the election in the electorate as a whole.[4]

It is no small irony, then, that the possible model for other Latin American leftists of a "peaceful path to socialism" through the decision of the ballot box was rejected only a few months before the Cuban revolution was to become the symbol in Latin America of the conquest of power through armed struggle. The women of Chile may, therefore, be credited not only with having had a decisive influence in 1958 on the future of their country, but also on the future of the entire hemisphere.

Women voted in Cuba for the first time in the presidential "elections" of January 1936, after the working-class insurrection was crushed by Batista; thus, women's suffrage was gained as a direct consequence of a Communist-led abortive

[3] *Ibid.*, p. 73.
[4] Dirección del Registro Electoral, *Resultado Elección Presidencial, 4 de Septiembre de 1958* (Santiago, Chile, 1958), mimeographed.

revolution; and in the 1940 Constitution, which the Communists played a leading role in drafting, women were for the first time specifically guaranteed equality of rights and married women were granted the right to control over their own property and wages (a provision renewed by the Revolutionary Government in the Fundamental Law of 1959). Once women got the vote, however, they probably did as members of their sex do elsewhere, continuing their support of the conservative forces of Cuban society. It is interesting to note, for instance, that from the moment of the women's entry into the electoral arena in 1936, parties began to make use of "religious appeals in their slogans and posters aimed at the women's vote."[5] The fact that only the most conservative political parties spoke of "Christian principles" in their programs probably contributed to their differential support by women—though, unfortunately, we shall probably never know, since there are no data available on the comparative voting patterns of men and women in prerevolutionary Cuba. Certainly, the women seem to have been the major base of the Church before the revolution. Men had a general scorn for priests, tinged with their particular conception of *Machismo.* "Church congregations were made up largely of women from the middle class. The general male attitude was that religion was women's business and that the woman of the house was sufficient representative for the whole family."[6]

The women of Cuba, much like women throughout the Hispanic world, were pampered, sheltered, and subordinate to the men; and while this was more characteristic of the upper classes, perhaps, it was also true, to an extent, of the working classes and the peasantry; one could often see, especially in rural areas, the woman of the house serving the meal to the men and then retiring to the kitchen to eat by

[5] Wyatt MacGaffey and Clifford Barnett, *Twentieth Century Cuba* (Garden City: N.Y., 1965), p. 165.

[6] *Ibid.*, p. 243.

herself; working-class bars rarely if ever were frequented by "respectable" women; they were reserved for men alone; marital infidelity by the man, lovers, mistresses, and frequent trips to the house of prostitution were accepted and expected behavior. The woman, of course, was supposed to be faithful and subservient to the man, attend church, and uphold the values of family life. These circumstances, it hardly seems doubtful, nurtured the comparative political conservatism of the women, even after they were ostensibly emancipated politically. Relegated to the home, fettered in their freedom of movement and rarely participating in the same social activities as men, taught to respect male (and paternal) authority, and loyal to the Church, they were hardly likely to suddenly break with their traditional values upon getting the vote.

Yet from the 1930s onward in Cuba, women increasingly entered the labor force, especially in commercial and industrial employment, and this must have had considerable consequence for their self-conceptions and the definition of their role in the society, probably weakening the hold of traditionalist values. To the extent women take on jobs once exclusively reserved to men, become exposed to new ideas, interact with men on a different level at work than at home, their protected, subservient, and tradition-bound position ought to be undermined. Especially among women industrial workers, who are members of the same unions as their fellow male workers, subjected to the same sorts of agitational appeals, privy to the frustrations as well as the satisfactions of the work-place, doing the same work and having the same (if not greater) grievances—in short, to the extent to which they are subject to the same experiences and social pressures as men, the political differences between them ought to be reduced, if not eliminated. In fact, if material deprivation were the crucial source in itself of a radical political ideology, the employed women should very soon in all countries become a major revolutionary force, since they are generally paid less for the same work, relegated to the less skilled jobs, and laid off sooner and more often than male workers. The greater exploitation of women workers, however, so far has failed to lead them to revolutionary action anywhere. Even when they themselves become industrial workers, they apparently continue to be relatively more conservative than men, although this is far from well established. There has yet to be a systematic analysis published of the weight of different factors in the formation of the political views of men and women workers. Hamilton found in his study of French workers that the woman worker was less likely than the man to be "Pro-Soviet" or "revolutionary," but his sample of women workers was too small to allow systematic analysis.[7]

Before the revolution, an estimated 11.8 percent of the employed miners, craftsmen, and industrial workers in Cuba were women. But they were concentrated in a few industries, especially the textile industry, where some 46 percent of them were employed, and which—apart from the major textile center at Ariguanabo—was predominantly made up of unmechanized small shops. Another 37 percent of them were in the food and tobacco industries, and the rest were thinly distributed in other industrial occupations.[8] As to their relative "life chances" compared to the men, our own data indicate that the women workers in our sample who were workers before the revolution earned lower wages than their fellow male workers, and were less likely to have secure prerevolutionary employment, or to have skilled work; also proportionately fewer of them managed to get more than a sixth grade education (Table 5.1).

While what we know would probably lead us to predict

[7] Richard F. Hamilton, *Affluence and the French Worker*, Chapter 5.

[8] Computed from Republic of Cuba, *Censos de población, viviendas, y electoral* (Havana: Oficina Nacional de los Censos Demográfico y Electoral, 1955), pp. 204-205.

TABLE 5.1

Life Chances and Sex[a]

	EMPLOYED 6 MONTHS OR LESS BEFORE REVOLUTION	PRESENT WEEKLY WAGE $40 or LESS	SKILLED WORKERS	EDUCATION OVER SIXTH GRADE	(N)
Women	44%	50%	19%	12%	(16)
Men	31	36	37	19	(136)

[a] This and tables 5.2 and 5.3 exclude those who were not workers before the revolution so that our view of the impact of the "sexual divison of labor" in the working class is not distorted by the fact that there has been an influx of former nonworking-class individuals into the working class.

that the women employed in the mines, mills, and factories of Cuba were less likely to have supported the Communists before the revolution than the men, their response to the revolution is somewhat more knotty to predict, since Castro's personal appeal may be a significant factor, especially for women. Some comparative data indicate, for example, that charismatic figures are more likely to receive the support of women.[9] Moreover—perhaps paradoxically—the revolution has been exceptionally conservative in some ways that are most likely to appeal to the women.

Aside from putting an end to the thriving, police-protected prostitution of prerevolutionary Cuba, the Revolutionary Government "has reaffirmed the value of the ideals of family life [ostensibly] upheld by its predecessors and has shown itself conservative in its policies toward family life. . . ."[10] The government has also encouraged the vast numbers of

[9] See Elizabeth Noelle and Erich Neumann, eds., *Jahrbuch der Offentlichen Meinung: 1947-1955* (Allensbach: Verlag für Demoskopie, 1956), p. 132; and Luzzatto Fegiz, *Il Volto Sconosciuto dell' Italia* (Milano: Dott. A. Guiffre, 1956), p. 412.

[10] *Twentieth Century Cuba*, p. 62.

common-law couples to be formally married, and has even held mass marriage ceremonies in the countryside. An estimated 400,000 couples were married as the result of the government's encouragement within the first two years of the revolution. On the other hand, the government has also "championed women's rights, and has taken many women into the militia; it has also encouraged women to take jobs," and established child centers to care for the children of working mothers.[11] These policies might serve as a further basis of female support for the revolution. For these reasons, we might expect the women workers to be even more likely than the men to support the revolution, though they may have been less likely than the men to support the Communists before the revolution. The fact is, however, that despite the reasonableness of this assumption, it appears that the hold of conservative values prevented as many of them from being pro-Communist as their male counterparts, and also from being revolutionary. As Table 5.2 indicates, significantly fewer women workers were pro-Communist before the revolution, and the difference between them and the men is even more pronounced in the number who were anti-Communist. Proportionately fewer of the women workers support the revolution; and the contrast in the percentage of "very revolutionary" workers among the sexes is even greater, 51 percent of the men being very revolutionary, compared to only 37 percent of the women.

If sex has its effect on politics so, too, does marriage. Marriage brings with it a host of responsibilities, especially once children arrive, that might be expected to exercise a conservative influence on the politics of married individuals. They are no longer as free to act politically as they were when they were single, for fear of jeopardizing not only their own but also their family's security. The mere pressures of

[11] *Ibid.*

TABLE 5.2

Prerevolutionary Attitude toward Communists, by Sex

	FRIENDLY OR SUPPORTER	INDIFFERENT	HOSTILE	(N)
Men	33%	41%	26%	(136)
Women	25	31	44	(16)

TABLE 5.3

Attitude toward Revolution, by Sex

	FAVORABLE	INDECISIVE	HOSTILE	(N)
Men	73%	10%	16%	(136)
Women	62	12	25	(16)

earning a living, caring for children, and running the home might be sufficient to prevent even those who would like to maintain an interest in politics from doing so. Moreover, it might be expected that new responsibilities, the concern of establishing oneself in the community, the very act of acquiring a variety of possessions, house, furniture, appliances, would contribute to a more "responsible," more "moderate," and, finally, more conservative political outlook, as well as a diminished interest in politics. This might be especially true in the working class where the young unmarried worker, having less to lose, may be more willing to engage in strikes, and to support militant political action than his married fellows. Married workers may be less able to stand the immediate economic loss involved in striking, or to withstand the ire of their wives who are likely to be relatively more subject to the anti-labor opinions promulgated in the mass media. Torn between the loyalty he feels to his fellows at work and to his family, between his class consciousness and his wife's relative conservatism, the married

worker might be more prone to accept his situation than the
single worker, and to go along with less militant and less
radical leaders.

Interestingly enough, however, these speculations appear
to be contradicted by the available evidence. Married men
and women are consistently more likely to vote and be
interested in politics than are single individuals.[12] This is
true in all countries studied and the relationship holds even
when other variables are controlled. While there is less evidence concerning the effect marriage has on support for the
Left, it is consistent with the relationship between marriage and
political participation. In the French working class, for instance, Hamilton found greater conservatism among single
than among married women, even with age controlled; married
housewives and married women working outside the home
were both more likely to support the Communists than were
single women.[13] And our findings also show that married workers are more likely to be revolutionary than the single workers,
with divorced and widowed workers about midway between
them (Table 5.4). What is more, this is not a spurious
finding, resulting from age or sex differences. As will be
seen in Chapter 9, the older workers lived through experiences as young men which apparently resulted in their greater
propensity to support the Communists and the revolution.
Yet with age controlled, married workers are still more likely
than their single counterparts to support the revolution
(Table 5.5). Nor can the finding be explained by a possible
over-representation of women among the married workers,
since the relationship holds equally among men only (Table
5.6). Why should this be so? What is it about marriage that,
contrary to what "common sense" would predict, makes

[12] Tingsten, *Political Behavior*, p. 229; Seymour Lipset, *Political
Man* (Garden City, N.Y.: 1960), p. 212.
[13] *Affluence and the French Worker*, Chapter 5.

TABLE 5.4

Attitude toward Revolution, by Marital Status

	FAVORABLE	INDECISIVE	HOSTILE	*(N)*
Married	73%	8%	18%	(155)
Divorced or spouse deceased	64	18	18	(11)
Single	58	25	17	(36)

TABLE 5.5

Percent Pro-Revolution, by Marital Status and Age

	UNDER 30		30 AND OVER	
Married	69%	(32)	75%	(123)
Single, divorced or spouse deceased	61	(23)	58	(24)

TABLE 5.6

Men's Attitude toward Revolution, by Marital Status

	FAVORABLE	INDECISIVE	HOSTILE	*(N)*
Married	73%	9%	18%	(143)
Divorced or spouse deceased	67	11	22	(9)
Single	58	23	19	(31)

married workers more likely to be politically interested, to vote, and, apparently, to support the Left and revolution than single workers?[14]

It might be suggested that (despite the old adage that "two can live as cheaply as one") since married workers

[14] The apparently greater propensity of married *women* workers to support the Left, and to be interested in politics, as Hamilton has shown, for instance, might be attributed to the political influence of their husbands. This "explanation" seems to me to lack plausibility, however, since marriage has the same apparent politicizing effect on men.

are supporting at least one or more individuals than single workers, and thus really living on half or less the wage, it is actually greater material deprivation that is the basis of their greater support for the revolution. As we have already seen, however, our findings contradict this "more wealth, more conservatism" hypothesis. In general, the relationship between material deprivation and political radicalism is far more complex and less easily predicted than is often assumed.

Maurice Duverge has suggested that "the single person, whether man or woman, probably feels less closely integrated into the society than the married couple."[15] Marriage objectively may bring more integration into the class community; single workers may be more mobile, more frequently changing jobs and even communities than married workers, and thus less subject to homogeneous social pressures than those who have "settled down" in a community of their fellow workers.[16]

Moreover, single workers may be less responsive to the very same social pressures that are directed at married workers because they subjectively are not ready to feel them. Their dominant concerns in life may still be part of what we might call the premarital syndrome of looking for sex, fun, and games. Their class situation as workers may not seem relevant to them since they do not yet *see themselves* as members of the class community. Marital responsibilities, once assumed, will alter their perspective and alert them to aspects of their lives they had not yet perceived as part of them. Politics simply does not yet interest them; they have other things to think about, and even the concrete and immediate economic demands that are dominant concerns of their fellow married workers may seem secondary.[17]

[15] *The Political Role of Women*, p. 44.

[16] Cf. Lipset, *Political Man*, p. 212.

[17] Apropos of this, my colleague, Marion Brown, has suggested that the fact that single men are less likely than married men to support the revolution may be explained by the Revolutionary Government's elimination of institutionalized prostitution.

That it is the proportion of individuals *indecisive* in their attitudes toward the revolution that varies with marital status, rather than the proportion hostile, lends support to this idea. Less integrated into the community, objectively and subjectively, and, therefore, subject to more numerous cross-pressures than the married worker, the single worker responds not with hostility but by wavering and being unable to develop a coherent attitude toward the revolution.

The effect of cross-pressures, differential political socialization, and integration into the working-class community on the development of political attitudes among workers is the principal focus of the following two chapters.

CHAPTER 6

Social Mobility and Politics

⚒ THE working class is recruited from all strata and classes of the population. In every country, there is a continuous shift of population across the line separating the working class from other classes;[1] new members are drawn into it not only from the strata closest to it, but also—especially in times of social upheaval or economic crisis—from the heights of power and privilege. What are the political responses of individuals who "fall" within the class structure, brought up as they were in homes with greater material comfort and higher social status, likely to be when circumstances compel them to become manual workers? Are they likely to be embittered and hostile to a society which has effectively thwarted their fulfillment of the aspirations they acquired in their middle class homes? Is it likely that they will now see their society in a different perspective, that their discontent, resulting from their loss of status, will make them amenable to the appeals of a radical political ideology? Will they, as Karl Marx apparently believed, now "supply the proletariat with fresh elements of enlightenment and progress"?[2]

The comparative evidence, on the contrary, indicates that such *arriviste* workers are, from a Marxist's point of view, more likely to supply the working class with fresh elements of obscurantism and reaction. Such first-generation workers apparently bring with them into the working class the motives, ideas, and aspirations they acquired in their class of origin and are, therefore, a constant source of new political values which contradict or modify in one way or

[1] Seymour Lipset and Reinhard Bendix, *Social Mobility in Industrial Society* (Berkeley and Los Angeles: University of California Press, 1959), *passim*.

[2] "The Manifesto of the Communist Party," in *Karl Marx and Friedrich Engels: Basic Writings on Politics and Philosophy*, ed. Lewis Feuer (Garden City, N.Y.: Anchor Books), p. 17.

another the extant values of the working-class political culture. The middle class origins of such individuals makes them less likely to identify with the Left than their fellow workers who were born into the working class. "Thus," as Lipset and Bendix have put it, "the process of social interchange through which some men rise in status and others fall weakens the solidarity and the political and economic strength of the working class."[3] In the United States, for example, a study of the determinants of voting found that "most of the deviants in class voting can be explained in terms of father's traditional vote." Lower socio-economic status Republicans were largely voting as their fathers had before them, and the same was true of Democrats of upper socio-economic status.[4] Another American study found that, whatever their present occupation, individuals from business, professional or white-collar homes were more likely to identify themselves with the upper classes and be politically conservative than those whose fathers were manual workers.[5] Similar findings have been reported for every country studied. In Germany, England, Norway, Sweden, and Finland the workers of working-class origin are more likely than those of the middle class to support the leftist (Social Democratic or Communist) political parties. The longer the worker's genealogy in the working class, in fact, the greater apparently, is the likelihood of his being a radical. In Germany and Finland, for instance, studies have found that those workers whose grandfathers were also workers were more likely to support the Left than those who had working-class fathers but farmer or middle-class grandfathers.[6]

Even if they may not continue to support the conservative

[3] *Social Mobility*, p. 69.

[4] Bernard Berelson, Paul F. Lazarsfeld, and William McPhee, *Voting* (Chicago: University of Chicago Press, 1954), p. 90.

[5] Richard Centers, *The Psychology of Social Classes* (Princeton: Princeton University Press, 1949), pp. 179-80.

[6] *Social Mobility*, p. 69.

politics of their class of origin, downward mobile individuals are more likely to vacillate politically and be indecisive in their allegiances than their fellow workers. They are subject to cross-pressures between their old political values and social ties and the new ones they are acquiring as workers. Therefore, much of their political behavior probably is explainable not by their present situation but by their early political socialization in a nonworking-class milieu. Thus, whom the worker feels are his own kind, whom he has been taught to respect and whom to deprecate, can be crucial in determining his political views and affiliations. "It may be said," as Talcott Parsons has put it, "that the question is not so much for *what* he is voting as it is *with whom* he is associating himself in voting."[7]

Migration from the countryside and urbanization are also major sources of social mobility, and new workers are almost continuously drawn into the industrial working class as a result of these related processes. Depending on the specific historical situation, such social transplantations will undoubtedly have different consequences. (For example, whether they occur during the earliest and most tumultuous periods of a country's industrial revolution that results in the dispossession and expropriation of masses of small holders and their involuntary entrance into the working class, or through rather gradual additions to the working class from the rural population as a result of the sometimes coerced, sometimes voluntary abandonment of the land by peasants and farmers and/or their sons.)

Writing of the profound impact early capitalist development in England was having through "the destruction of the old isolation and with it the destruction of the political insignificance of the small peasants," Friedrich Engels observed that "the extension of the industrial revolution over the

---

[7] " 'Voting' and the Equilibrium of the American Political System," in *American Voting Behavior*, ed. Eugene Burdick and Arthur J. Brodbeck (Glencoe, Ill.: The Free Press, 1959), p. 96.

rural areas" was resulting in "the transformation of the most stable and conservative class of the population into a revolutionary hotbed."[8] Leon Trotsky, analyzing the causes of the Soviet revolution, also pointed to Russia's "uneven development" which resulted in the vast removal of masses of peasants to gigantic factories in a few rapidly burgeoning industrial and urban centers, and their consequent radicalization.[9] And recently a contemporary student of Communist revolutions has argued that it is precisely their so-called "unerased peasant background" that makes industrial workers likely to accept Marxism as an explanation of the human condition. "One of the most potent spurs to revolutionary feeling," writes Adam B. Ulam, "is the loss of 'property'—hence, status—which the peasant or small craftsman experiences in becoming a proletarian." Marxism, he argues, is able to explain and to apportion blame "for the destruction of a world which, as it recedes into the past, looks all the more—and unrealistically—stable and uncomplicated," thereby transmuting anti-industrialism into anticapitalism.[10] Similarly, the contrasting ideological histories of the labor movements of Norway, Sweden, and Denmark—which share a common cultural heritage—have been attributed largely to differences in the agrarian economies from which the original recruits to the industrial labor forces of these countries came.[11] Survey research studies in a number of countries have found that workers of rural origin respond to the appeals of leftist politics differently than

[8] Preface to the Second German Edition, 1887, *The Housing Question* (New York: International Publishers, n.d.), pp. 17-18.

[9] Leon Trotsky, *History of the Russian Revolution* (New York: Simon and Schuster, 1937), pp. 33-51.

[10] *The Unfinished Revolution* (New York: Random House, 1960), pp. 69 and 62.

[11] Edvard Bull, "Die Entwicklung der Arbeiterbewegung in den drei Scandinavischen Ländern," *Archiv für Geschichte des Sozialismus und der Arbeiterbewegung*, Vol. x (1922). Also see Walter Galenson, "Scandinavia," in *Comparative Labor Movements*, ed. Galenson, (New York: Prentice-Hall, 1952), esp. pp. 109-11 and 148-49.

second generation workers; in turn, the type of rural origin will have different consequences. Juan Linz has shown, for example, that the sons of farmers in the working class of West Germany are more conservative not only than the sons of workers but even than the sons of middle-class fathers. They are less likely than other workers to be union members or to support the Social Democrats.[12] In France, Richard Hamilton found that workers coming from regions where aristocratic and clerical influence was strong and independent farming predominant are less likely to be Communist supporters than workers from regions characterized by sharecropping and tenant farming. Particularly relevant to our own study, as we shall see, is the finding that in France agricultural workers, along with industrial workers, are more likely than individuals in other strata to be revolutionaries and pro-Soviet.[13] Similarly, Braga found that the Communists and Left-Socialists in Italy receive greater support from agricultural laborers than do other parties.[14]

The two social strata that were the major sources of recruits into the working class in prerevolutionary Cuba were probably (a) the lower salaried employees and lower petite bourgeoisie and (b) the peasantry and agricultural laborers. In our sample, for instance, seven percent of the workers had fathers who were salaried employees, and another 18 percent who were petite bourgeoisie; 23 percent were from peasant or agricultural laborer families. Thus, close to half of the workers were not of working-class origin, and the relative social position in prerevolutionary Cuba of the strata from which these workers came may have significantly affected their political development.

[12] "The Social Bases of West German Politics" (Unpublished dissertation, Columbia University, 1959), Chapter 23 and pp. 439-50.

[13] *Affluence and the French Worker: The Fourth Republic Experience* (Princeton: Princeton University Press, *in press*), Chapter 3.

[14] Georgio Braga, *il comunismo fra gli italiani; saggio di sociologia* (Milan: Edizioni di Comunitiá, 1956).

The Petite Bourgeoisie and Salaried Employees

The studies which have documented the rather consistent political differences between workers who are the sons of workers and those who are the sons of middle-class fathers were done in capitalist countries that are relatively industrialized. The question is whether or not such differences are also present in underdeveloped countries. If so, in what direction are the differences likely to be? It might be suggested, for instance, that the marginal small trader, the street vendor or peddler or the "self-employed" craftsman or artisan occupying either a shack on an otherwise vacant lot, or a tiny nook on a main street, may have even greater economic insecurity or be more subject to police harassment than organized industrial workers—especially in a country ruled by a corrupt military dictatorship, as was pre-revolutionary Cuba. For many of them, and for their sons, entrance into industrial work might well mean economic (even social) improvement. Many such "petite bourgeoisie" live in the very same neighborhoods as the workers and associate informally with them; their children probably intermarry. Moreover, in such countries many workers themselves are vendors of odd items and services during their intervals of industrial unemployment. This was especially true of the poorest and most irregularly employed (nonindustrial) workers in Havana, Santiago, and other Cuban cities. Many of them "lived in poor sections of the city, in slum communities on the outskirts of Havana, or on vacant lots next to residences of the wealthy for whom they performed services."[15] They divided the city into territories, where they "guarded" parked cars, washed them, ran errands, shined shoes, carried packages, and did a multiplicity of other such services which allowed them to survive only because Havana was the center of the tourist industry

[15] Wyatt MacGaffey and Clifford R. Barnett, *Twentieth Century Cuba* (Garden City, N.Y.: Anchor Books, 1965), p. 172.

and of upper class society. Some of the more fortunate workers were able to sell fruits, souvenirs, knick-knacks, ices or lottery tickets when they were not working elsewhere. As one worker (in a brewery) told us during our interview: "I always had work before the revolution—but only because I could work at everything and anything. I hawked all kinds of goods on a street corner, like juices and pastries. I did anything I could and I got along. Or I shouldn't say *anything!* but most kinds of things. I even interpreted and acted as a guide for American tourists."

The lowest rung of the petite bourgeoisie and the working class in underdeveloped countries may, then, be very close if not identical as *social* classes—because of their members' intermarriage and regular association as equals. The political differences between them may, therefore, be minimal or nonexistent and perhaps, even the reverse of those in developed capitalist countries. The fact that the workers would be "targets" of Communist and other revolutionary political agitation at their plants and factories, however, while the lower petite bourgeoisie would still be comparatively less accessible to such agitation might be a relevant factor in determining their politics. Finally, it should be mentioned that one impulse to "rising" out of the working class may come from the "black listing" and dismissal from work of some of the most politically active and militant workers. As Roberto Michels, writing of Germany, reminded us: "It is impossible to determine with any accuracy the number of individuals who have become independent petty bourgeois as the outcome of the struggles of the workers and the political reprisals of the employers."[16] Probably of only minor social significance, this fact is worth mentioning, nonetheless, if only as one more reminder that "upward social mobility" may be neither defined as "upward," nor aspired to by workers; and in particular periods in a country's develop-

---

[16] *Political Parties* (Glencoe, Ill.: The Free Press, 1949), p. 286.

ment, especially during the early phases of working-class political and economic organization, the workers who are forced into the lower petite bourgeoisie may be precisely those who think in terms of the collective interests and advance of the working class (with which they still identify), rather than in terms of individual success.

On the other hand, it is precisely in the underdeveloped countries of Latin America, as in prerevolutionary Cuba, that such members of the "middle sectors" as salaried white-collar employees, independent small business men, professionals, and lower civil servants are most likely to look with extreme disdain on the workers, and on manual labor in general. They try to strengthen the social barriers separating them from the workers, and erect whatever social edifices they find possible in order to sustain their social status; they measure themselves by the standards of the ruling class, and accept what they believe to be the ruling values as their own. Thus, it is problematical whether even the widespread economic insecurity to which the lower white-collar workers are subject in many underdeveloped countries, as they were in prerevolutionary Cuba,[17] is sufficient to shake their general political conservatism.[18]

[17] "White-collar workers shared many of the general characteristics of permanent industrial workers; they faced job insecurity and underemployment, and relied on political and personal ties for placement and promotion." *Twentieth Century Cuba*, pp. 175-76.

[18] At the least, this discussion makes clear why we have to make finer distinctions for political analysis than the simple dichotomy of sons of manual and of nonmanual families. I have therefore separated the workers whose fathers were petite bourgeoisie from those whose fathers were nonmanual salaried employees. This still leaves difficulties, since, for example, there are obviously wide social gaps between such self-employed individuals as street vendors and small shopkeepers. This is an analytic difficulty which is insurmountable with our own data. However, since the vast majority of workers whose fathers were petite bourgeoisie probably came from the poorest and smallest in this stratum, this is probably of only minor consequence in our analysis.

The revolution, of course, shook the class structure profoundly, causing an influx into the ranks of the working class of former peasants, agricultural laborers, and especially lower, petite bourgeoisie and salaried employees. The latter strata were probably on the fringes of the working class before the revolution both in terms of their material conditions of existence and their social interaction; this must have been especially true of individuals from these strata who have found industrial employment since the revolution. Nonetheless, we find that on the available evidence (Tables 6.1 and 6.2) they enjoyed distinct advantages over the workers in terms of "life chances." Their educational advantage is especially clear. About one quarter of them, for instance, had completed secondary or technical school compared to only a tenth of the urban workers and three percent of the sugar central workers. The petite bourgeoisie-salaried employees group had something of an advantage over the workers as a whole in employment security before the revolution, but the difference is not marked. Fifty-nine percent of the latter worked ten months or more before the revolution, compared to 64 percent of the former. However, when compared only to the urban workers not only did the petite bourgeoisie and salaried employees not have the advantage but the workers had a very slight edge in regular work; 67 percent of the latter having worked regularly (10 months or more) before the revolution. We know from other sources that the agricultural laborers and peasants bore the greatest brunt of unemployment and underemployment before the revolution (see Chapter 2), and our own findings also indicate their disproportionate share of economic insecurity. Not one of the 10 workers in our sample who worked on the land before the revolution was regularly employed, and seven out of 10 of them worked only six months or less.

Of greater theoretical interest is the extent to which workers whose fathers were in nonmanual occupations have been helped or hindered as a result "in acquiring vocational

TABLE 6.1

Prerevolutionary Formal Education, by
Prerevolutionary Occupational Status[a]

| | GRADE COMPLETED | | | | | |
	None[d]	1-3	4-6	7-8	Secondary or technical	(N)
Agricultural laborers and peasants[b]	30%	10%	50%	0%	10%	(10)
Workers	5	25	5 i	9	9	(152)
sugar central	3	35	50	9	3	(34)
urban	7	22	52	9	10	(118)
Petite bourgeoisie[c] and salaried (non-manual) employees	8	20	36	12	24	(25)

[a] This and table 6.2 exclude those who had not yet entered the labor force before the revolution.

[b] "Peasants" includes tenants, subtenants, and independent small farmers (colonos).

[c] "Petite bourgeoisie" includes self-employed individuals, such as street vendors, small traders, artisans, and craftsmen.

[d] Includes two workers who "couldn't remember" the grades they completed in school.

TABLE 6.2

Prerevolutionary Employment, by Prerevolutionary
Occupational Status

| | MONTHS WORKED PER YEAR BEFORE REVOLUTION | | | |
	6 or less	7-9	10 or more	(N)
Agricultural laborers and peasants	70%	30%	0%	(10)
Workers	32	9	59	(152)
sugar central	59	12	29	(34)
urban	25	9	67	(118)
Petite bourgeoisie and salaried (nonmanual) employees	28	8	64	(25)

skill and motivation for achievement" before starting their work careers. That is, we want to know the relationship, as Lipset and Bendix put it, "between social inheritance (or starting position) and the means of mobility. Here we may be concerned with the degree to which given backgrounds determine the level of education, the acquisition of skills, access to people at different levels in the social structure, intelligence, and motivation to seek higher positions."[19]

Earlier, for instance, I pointed out that lower petite bourgeoisie fathers might very well aspire to get their sons into secure industrial employment, if possible into skilled working-class jobs, rather than having them follow their own occupations. Their sons might be better equipped to acquire the necessary education, skills, and social contacts for such upper working-class jobs than workers' sons; a process we might call "reverse upward mobility" [sic] may occur which allows them to outstrip workers' sons for the best working-class jobs. Whether this interpretation is correct or not, our own data indicate that it is precisely the sons of petite bourgeoisie families who are most likely to be found in the skilled stratum of workers. Forty-six percent of them are skilled workers, compared to 34 percent of the workers' sons (Table 6.3). Of course, it might simply be, thinking in terms of mobility patterns in developed countries, that those who fall socially are more likely to drop only one rung than many on the social ladder. Therefore, they are more likely to be found in the skilled stratum than workers' sons.

Yet this interpretation seems to have less merit since, for instance, on every *other* measure of social and economic advantage available to us, the sons of salaried employees have advantages equal to or greater than the sons of the petite bourgeoisie. Petite bourgeoisie sons outnumber the salaried employees' sons proportionately *only* in the skilled stratum.

[19] Lipset and Bendix, *Social Mobility*, pp. 5-6.

TABLE 6.3

Worker's "Life Chances" and Father's Occupational Status[a]

	EMPLOYED 10 MONTHS OR MORE BEFORE REVOLUTION	PRESENT WEEKLY WAGE $60 OR MORE	SKILLED WORKERS	EDUCATION MORE THAN SIXTH GRADE	(N)
Agricultural laborers or peasants	61%	17%	33%	6%	(36)
Workers	52	22	34	18	(71)
Petite bourgeoisie	69	31	46	30	(26)
Salaried (nonmanual) employees	100	30	30	30	(10)

[a] Nine workers who did not know their fathers' occupations are not included in this table or in others in which father's occupation is an independent variable.

This table, as usual, excludes those in our sample who were not workers before the revolution, so that the relationship between father's occupation and life chances is not distorted. However, the relationship was found to be essentially the same when these workers are also included in the computations.

Whatever the case, one thing seems quite clear from our findings, namely, that the workers whose fathers are salaried employees or petite bourgeoisie have had considerable advantages over their peers who were born into the working class (Table 6.3). In education their differential advantages are especially clear. The percentage who received secondary or technical educations sharpens the contrast: 20 percent among the sons of salaried employees, and 15 percent among the petite bourgeoisie sons, compared to only 10 percent of the workers' sons, and not one of the sons of agricultural laborers or peasants. In their relative wage position and pre-revolutionary employment status, the advantage of the workers from nonworking class families over workers', peasants', and agricultural laborers' sons, respectively, is also quite clear. They had better paying jobs with greater economic security. In fact, every single one of the salaried employees' sons was regularly employed before the revolution, compared to only half of the workers' sons. The only surprising finding is the comparatively high proportion of sons of agricultural laborers and peasants who had secure employment before the revolution. On inspection, these turn out to be primarily workers in the Matahambre copper mine and the Nicaro nickel refinery, two of Cuba's largest plants, both of which are located in the countryside providing a comparatively secure source of employment for men leaving the land.

The Peasantry

The peasantry was an important source, as we know, of new industrial workers in Cuba, and this process of industrial recruitment probably had significant political consequences. The Cuban "peasantry" differed in certain very important respects, for example, from peasantry in other parts of Latin America, such as those practicing intensive cultivation primarily for subsistence, or whose production flows into a system of marginal village "markets," as in Mexico or Peru. Many Cuban peasants were probably more akin to the peasantry cultivating sugar cane in parts of Colombia, Costa Rica, and Guatemala, who regularly sell a cash crop of half or more of their production. Distinguishing between types of peasantry or "peasant segments"[20] is of the utmost importance in any political sociological analysis since the extent to which different types of peasantry have become integrated into a capitalist market economy, or have remained parts of essentially marginal subsistence and village economies may in turn affect the extent of their development of "modern" rather than traditional and patriarchal

---

[20] Eric R. Wolf, "Types of Latin American Peasantry: A Preliminary Discussion," *American Anthropologist*, LVII (June 1955), 452-71.

attitudes toward their place in the world, and the possibilities of changing it. The Cuban peasants, insofar as they could be distinguished from the agricultural workers (since a majority of them and/or their sons also probably worked as wage laborers sometime during the year), typically were *not* subsistence agriculturalists. This was especially true of the peasants, or *colonos*, raising sugar cane. They were dependent on the huge sugar mill complexes or (*centrales*) for marketing, credit, fertilizer, etc., and were usually in debt to them, and independent in name only. In areas dominated by these *latifundios*, the peasants were dependent almost entirely on the company store for their provisions. They were an integral part of the monocultural export economy and subject to its recurrent fluctuations. They were not shielded, as was generally true of the prerevolutionary Mexican and Bolivian peasantry, for instance, from the forces of the market economy, nor were they integrated into a traditional communal social structure.

Cuba, along with several other Caribbean states, had a predominantly *plantación* or wage-labor agrarian economy before the revolution, whereas prerevolutionary Bolivia and Mexico had essentially *hacienda* economies. In Bolivia the use of wage labor had replaced the quasi-feudal peasant cultivator only in the eastern part of the country, and wage workers made up less than three percent of the entire agrarian labor force. In Cuba, by contrast, wage workers constituted an estimated 72 percent of the agricultural labor force; most were employed on the *centrales*. Of the total number of agricultural units, owned or rented, eight percent employed two-thirds of the permanent wage labor.[21] The sugar *centrales* brought agricultural laborers and industrial

---

[21] *La revolución nacional a traves de sus decretos mas importantes* (La Paz, 1955), p. 44; Lowry Nelson, *Rural Cuba* (Minneapolis: University of Minnesota Press, 1950), pp. 114ff., 166; International Bank for Reconstruction and Development, *Report on Cuba* (Baltimore: The Johns Hopkins Press, 1951), p. 71.

workers into close contact. The agricultural laborers often lived near the outlying cane fields surrounding the *batey*, or industrial workers' community in the *central*, and there was probably a great deal of interaction and mobility between them. This may have been of importance in the development of the agricultural laborers' political consciousness, since the sugar mill workers were a major radical social base. Whereas the *hacienda* of prerevolutionary Bolivia and Mexico was integrated into a traditional social structure, the Cuban *central* was a modern capitalist enterprise and the agricultural workers' community formed around it tended to be "a class isolate," as Sydney Mintz has put it. Its existence, to paraphrase his description of the "rural proletarian community" in Puerto Rico, was predicated on the existence of another class that owned the instruments of production, provided the work opportunities, paid the wages, and sold the commodities to be bought.[22] In contrast, the *hacienda* was usually managed by the *hacendado* himself, required little capital (which was usually local in origin), and employed land, labor, and capital in traditional ways. It was, moreover, a major fount of social status for the *hacendado* and established paternalistic and particularistic relations existed between him and his peasants. In the Cuban *central*, on the other hand, relations between management, often foreign (*i.e.*, American), were largely impersonal and tended to be based on universalistic norms. The *central* was managed to make profit and to provide for further investment. Agricultural workers, therefore, developed essentially secular norms and a consumption ethos that measured their wages in terms of buying power, with little or none of the status concerns typical of the traditional peasant producer's relationship with his *hacendado*. The agricultural laborers were, therefore, more likely to compare their lot with that

---

[22] "The Folk-Urban Continuum and the Rural Proletarian Community," *American Journal of Sociology*, LIX (September 1953), 136-43.

of other classes, to develop class consciousness and to organize, and to associate themselves with the struggles of the mill workers. Moreover, because a significant proportion of sugar production was owned and/or controlled by United States corporations, class consciousness and nationalism (that is, "anti-imperialism") reinforced and strengthened each other. In the 1930s first anarchosyndicalists and then Communists already had begun to penetrate the ranks of the agricultural workers and organize them; in the following years they became a major and durable political base of the Communists.

The differential susceptibility of the agricultural laborers to revolutionary agitation, as compared to other groups in the rural population, was pointed out long ago by an early student of the appeals of communism, Friedrich Engels himself. In 1844 he wrote:

> Soon after the appearance of the agricultural proletariat the old patriarchal relationships began to break down in the countryside—as they were already breaking down in the urban factories. . . . [As in the industrial economy, we find] large units of production, the disappearance of the old patriarchal relationship between masters and men —which is particularly significant in agriculture—[and] the introduction of machinery and steam-power. . . . Thus, what was once the most stable working-class group has now been drawn into the revolutionary movement. The very fact that the relationship between masters and men had so long been a stable one on the land has made it all the more difficult for the modern farm labourer to shoulder the burden that he has to bear. In the country-side (even more than in the factory districts) we see the complete dissolution of old-established social relation-ships. . . . In this way the working-class movement is spreading to remote and stable agricultural districts which from the point of view of the new ideas have long been

dead. Although the farm labourers have more contacts with religion than the factory workers, nevertheless, they have, to a great extent, broken with the Church.[23]

The Cuban revolutionary leaders were fortunate also that the Church was not a significant obstacle either to the implementation of the agrarian reform or to the securing of the political allegiance of the peasantry and agricultural workers. Aside from the secularization of norms that resulted from the penetration into the countryside of the market economy and large-scale, wage-labor units of production, the Church itself had never established ideological dominion in the rural population. The Mexican revolution, for example, was forced to encounter and overcome in violent conflict the landed economic, political, and ideological might of the Church. A major reform of the Mexican revolution (though not of the Bolivian) *had to be* to nationalize the landed wealth of the Church, while trying to break the Church's hold on the popular imagination. In Cuba, the separation of Church and state had occurred 60 years earlier with the founding of the Republic—under American aegis separation was written into the Constitution. The Cuban Church possessed no significant landed property and little political power. The rural interior of Cuba had few parishes. Chapels were located, with only a few exceptions, in cities and towns; yet the rural population lived generally in the open country. The peasants' contact with the Church was therefore minimal and their attitudes suggested to observers a condition of "general indifference" to the Church. A study of the church attendance practices of the rural population completed in 1958, just before the establishment of the Revolutionary Government, found that 91 percent of the population studied did not attend church, although they professed

[23] *The Condition of the Working Class in England*, ed. and trans. W. O. Henderson and W. H. Chaloner (New York: The Macmillan Company, 1958), pp. 296-97, 303.

to be adherents of the Catholic religion.[24] Only in the wealthy areas of urban Cuba, such as the Miramar suburb of Havana, did families regularly attend church together. The Church was, with little exception, essentially an urban and upper class-based institution. In a sense it was not even Cuban, since of the several hundred priests in Cuba at the time of the revolution, not more than a fifth were Cuban nationals, most of the remaining four-fifths being Spanish.[25]

Social Mobility and Politics

In sum, a combination of circumstances that included the integration of agriculture into the market economy, the predominance in the agrarian social structure of wage laborers and large units of agricultural production employing industrial workers and owned by foreign and absentee corporations, and the relative absence either of a landed ruling group in the countryside proper or the ideological influence and economic power of the Church—all this probably combined to create a situation favorable to the organization and radicalization of the peasants and agricultural workers. The agricultural workers, of course, or members of their families, having already been secularized (if not radicalized) by their experiences on the land, would be more easily organized and radicalized once they entered the urban working class. On the other hand, even those peasants coming from somewhat traditionalistic environments had little basis in their experience from which to develop a genuinely conservative ideology or loyalty to a paternalistic class. For that reason, once in a politicized working-class atmosphere in the city, they were probably easily convinced of a radical political perspective. They or their sons, therefore, would probably be at

[24] *La Educación Rural en Las Villas* (Las Villas: Universidad Central "Marta Abreu" de Las Villas, 1959), p. 31. See also Maurice Zeitlin, "Revolutionary Consciousness and Religion," a review article of Leslie Dewart, *Christianity and Revolution*, in *Liberation*, IX (April 1964), 27-29.

[25] MacGaffey and Barnett, *Twentieth Century Cuba*, p. 243.

least as likely as urban workers' sons to support a radical political movement.

As for the lower petite bourgeoisie and the lower white-collar workers, and/or their sons, who became industrial workers, they brought a mixed social inheritance into the working class with them. On the one hand, the lower petite bourgeoisie, as we have seen, were in some ways probably quite close to the industrial workers both socially and in their living conditions; many of the salaried employees also led a precarious economic existence. On the other hand, neither the petite bourgeoisie nor the white-collar workers, especially the more advantaged ones, were likely to be targets of Communist agitation and organization; they probably had an ideology of individual success rather than collective economic struggle, and a disdain for manual labor; and they had a higher standard of living than the industrial workers, this being especially true of the white-collar employees. The latter were also quite likely to identify with their employers and to consider themselves part of the privileged strata. Even when their sons became industrial workers, petite bourgeoisie and white-collar fathers (again, especially, the latter) were able to pass on greater social advantages to them than could working-class fathers. Coming into the working class, therefore, they and/or their sons were probably less responsive even to union organizational drives, let alone class-based political agitation and revolutionary propaganda, than their fellow workers who were of working-class origin. Moreover, since the revolution, it is probable that members of the lower middle strata have been more likely than workers to be antirevolutionary.[26] Since these

[26] An analysis of the Cuban refugees living in Florida who had registered with the Cuban Refugee Emergency Center found that comparing the occupational distribution of Cubans from the 1953 Census with the occupational distribution among the refugees, professional and semiprofessional persons in the refugee community were over-represented by a factor of more than five. This understated the disproportion since the more wealthy Cubans did not register

individuals would tend to exert antirevolutionary influence on their friends and relatives, the workers in our sample who are of petite bourgeoisie or white-collar origins probably have been more likely than other workers to be subject to such influences. Therefore, their prerevolutionary political socialization and the pressures to which they have been subject since the revolution have probably disposed them to be more likely to oppose the revolution than their fellow workers.

Our data, in any case, lend support to this analysis. First, as Table 6.4 and 6.5 indicate, among the workers in our sample, precisely those who had been in petite bourgeoisie or white-collar occupations before the revolution are the ones least likely to have been prerevolutionary Communist supporters and least likely to favor the revolution. Their greatest political distance, moreover, is not from the urban but from the sugar central workers who stand out as the base both of the revolution and of the Communists. The ex-agricultural laborers and peasants are, as we expected, as likely as the "veteran" urban workers to be revolutionaries. On the other hand, not one of the ex-agricultural laborers and peasants supported the Communists before the revolution—a surprising finding, given the reported prerevolutionary strength of the Communists among the agricultural laborers. This may be the result of sampling error; or, while this is a guess we cannot verify, it is possible that most of these workers had been independent peasants, ten-

with the center. (Richard R. Fagen and Richard A. Brody, "A Sociological Analysis of the Cuban Refugees," mimeographed paper, Department of Political Science, Stanford University.) Lloyd Free and Hadley Cantril found in their study of public opinion in Cuba during April and May 1960 that the "oppositionists" came disproportionately from the higher income and status groups in the population. "Attitudes of the Cuban People toward the Castro Regime in the late Spring of 1960," Institute for International Social Research, Princeton, New Jersey, 1960.

ants, or sub-tenants, rather than agricultural laborers, and thus relatively unexposed to Communist agitation.[27]

TABLE 6.4

Prerevolutionary Attitude toward Communists, by
Prerevolutionary Occupational Status

	FRIENDLY OR SUPPORTER	INDIFFERENT	HOSTILE	(N)
Agricultural laborers and peasants	0%	80%	20%	(10)
Sugar central workers	41	38	21	(34)
Urban workers	30	41	30	(118)
Petite bourgeoisie and salaried (nonmanual) employees	24	44	32	(25)

TABLE 6.5

Attitude toward Revolution, by Prerevolutionary
Occupational Status

	FAVORABLE	INDECISIVE	HOSTILE	(N)
Agricultural laborers and peasants	70%	20%	10%	(10)
Sugar central workers	76	6	18	(34)
Urban workers	71	12	17	(118)
Petite bourgeoisie and salaried (nonmanual) employees	64	16	20	(25)

[27] Unfortunately, the descriptions the workers gave us of their prerevolutionary position in the agricultural structure were often ambiguous and unclear, as were their descriptions of their fathers' positions. To a great extent this probably reflects the fact that the line in the social structure itself was not very clear between the poor peasantry and agricultural laborers. Our inability to distinguish the two groups is particularly unfortunate since it would have been of the utmost theoretical interest to be able to test the political differences between them. We could have, for instance, looked at the hypotheses of Edvard Bull or Walter Galenson concerning the difference between the response of peasants and agricultural laborers' sons in the working class to revolutionary ideology, and of Adam Ulam's emphasis on the peasant's loss of "property" on coming into the working class.

Second, looking at the workers by their social origins (Tables 6.6 and 6.7) further supports our analysis. Our data here allow us to separate the sons of white-collar employees from those of petite bourgeoisie; and we find that —quite in keeping with our expectations—the sons of the white-collar employees are least likely to have been pro-Communist before the revolution, and are least likely to support the revolution. Peasants' and agricultural laborers' sons are even somewhat more likely than urban workers' sons to be revolutionaries.

Again, the sons of sugar central workers are the most likely to support the revolution and to have supported the Communists before the revolution. This finding concerning the sugar workers makes sense both in historical and comparative terms. They were, as we know, the major base of the revolutionary insurrections of the thirties, which spread through almost all the sugar centrals, even the most remote ones; the young Communist Party of the period found that the strikes and seizures of the mills broke out so rapidly that Communists could not send organizers "capable of orienting and directing the movement in each place."[28] Taken by surprise by the depth of the sugar workers' offensive, the Communists nonetheless apparently led most of the strikes and occupations of sugar mills. The insurrectionary period, as we shall see in Chapter 9, was a decisive influence on the political consciousness of its working class participants. From the insurrectionary period forward, with little interruption, the Communists continued to be the major leaders of the sugar mill workers—who maintained their insurrectionary tradition. In the major strike in the sugar industry in December 1955, for example, the workers violently clashed with the police, shut down the mills,

[28] IV Congreso Nacional Obrero de Unidad Sindical, *Resoluciones y acuerdos sobre la estructura organica de la CNOC* (Havana, 1934), pp. 17-19; Raymond Leslie Buell *et al.*, *Problems of the New Cuba* (New York: Foreign Policy Association, 1935), p. 185.

blocked traffic in Santa Clara on the main highway, took control of some sugar towns in Camaguey and Havana provinces, and raised political slogans denouncing the regime. The Communists, outlawed a year earlier, had continued their agitation and organization and reportedly still led the more militant workers, "particularly among the sugar workers of the eastern provinces."[29] That our own data indicate the sons of sugar mill workers are most likely to support the revolution and to have been pro-Communist is, therefore, quite expected. We know also that workers in socially and/or regionally "isolated" industries living in communities predominantly inhabited by other workers in the same occupations, as was true of Cuban sugar mill workers, are often radicals. Not likely to have much informal contact with nonworkers, and not subject, therefore, to many political cross-pressures, once they are organized by the Left the workers in these communities usually give it overwhelming support. Such working-class "occupational communities" usually vote Communist or Socialist by large majorities.[30] These findings on the sons of sugar workers are, therefore, also consistent with the comparative evidence available on working-class politics.

Conclusions

It should be emphasized that the political differences between workers of different social origins in our sample are not large. Only sugar workers' sons, or workers who had been sugar workers, stand out as a distinct group in their prerevolutionary attitudes toward the Communists and their attitudes toward the revolution. This may indicate that especially in a society in which the *clase popular* tends to in-

[29] Charles A. Page, "Communism and the Labor Movements of Latin America," *Virginia Quarterly Review*, XXXI (Summer 1955), 379.

[30] Seymour Lipset, *Political Man: The Social Bases of Politics* (Garden City, N.Y.: Doubleday, 1959), p. 248.

TABLE 6.6

Worker's Prerevolutionary Attitude toward Communists,
by Father's Occupational Status

	FRIENDLY OR SUPPORTER	INDIFFERENT	HOSTILE	(N)
Agricultural laborer or peasant	24%	44%	31%	(45)
Sugar central worker	35	43	22	(23)
Urban worker	26	42	32	(76)
Petite bourgeoisie	26	46	29	(35)
Salaried (nonmanual) employee	21	57	21	(14)

TABLE 6.7

Worker's Attitude toward the Revolution,
by Father's Occupational Status

	FAVORABLE	INDECISIVE	HOSTILE	(N)
Agricultural laborer or peasant	73%	13%	13%	(45)
Sugar central worker	78	9	13	(23)
Urban worker	67	13	20	(76)
Petite bourgeoisie	66	11	23	(35)
Salaried (nonmanual) employee	57	14	28	(14)

clude all families whose heads are in a great variety of poorly paid occupations, be they "manual" or not, and between whom social intercourse is probably frequent and regular, the political differences will be small. Thus, the "downward mobile," or "skidders,"[31] probably more easily assimilate the political values of their new working-class milieu. They may be less likely in such a society to exert a politically conservative influence on the workers than to be influenced

[31] See Harold Wilensky and Hugh Edwards, "The Skidder: Ideological Adjustments of Downward Mobile Workers," *American Sociological Review*, 24 (April 1959), pp. 215-31.

themselves and convert politically, thus providing the radical movement with new supporters.

The process of political influence and political conversion varies, then, in accordance with the types and the extent of politically relevant social contacts one has. In the next chapter we are concerned with how the varying milieu in the plant itself effects such interaction.

CHAPTER 7
Social Relations in the Plant and in Politics

⚑ THE revolutionary potential of the workers, indeed, their very emergence as a distinct class, depended to a great extent on the growth of large-scale industry and great cities. This was the view of such diverse observers of early capitalist industrialization as Tocqueville, Disraeli, Marx, Engels, and John Stuart Mill. All of them believed, as Disraeli had put it, that large-scale industry had split the people of the advanced countries of Europe into two nations. Mill wrote that the "large industrial enterprises" that brought the workers "together in numbers, to work socially under the same roof" were making it "certain that the patriarchal or paternal system of government is one to which [the workers] . . . will not again be subject." The great problem of the age, Mill believed, was "to obtain the efficiency and economy of production on a large scale, without dividing the producers into two parties with hostile interests, employers and employed, the many who do the work being mere servants under the command of the one who supplies the funds, and having no interest of their own in the enterprise, except to fulfill their contract and earn their wages."[1] To Marx and Engels it seemed clear that "only the proletariat created by modern large-scale industry, liberated from all inherited fetters, including those which chained it to the land, and driven in herds into the big towns, is in a position to accomplish the great social transformation which will put an end to all class

[1] *Principles of Political Economy, with Some of Their Applications to Social Philosophy*, II (Boston: Charles C. Little and James Brown, 1848), 322, 329. See also Alexis de Tocqueville's comments on "the development of districts of the city [Paris] inhabited almost exclusively by the working class" and their significance in the outbreak of the French Revolution, in *The Old Regime and the French Revolution* (Garden City, N.Y.: Doubleday, 1955), pp. 75-76; see also *Democracy in America*, I (New York: Vintage, 1945), 299-300.

exploitation and all class rule."[2] If rural small-scale production had produced only "servile souls,"[3] they believed, then the concentration of the workers in industrial towns and large factories was destroying the "last vestiges of the old system of benevolent paternalism between masters and men." The development of industry increased the absolute and relative size of the working class, separated the workers in dense working-class areas, and created a "compact group with its own ways of life and thought and its own outlook on society."[4] Workers of different localities were brought into contact with one another within the huge plants and industrial towns, and communication between them was facilitated. Thus, "the numerous local struggles, all of the same character," became transformed "into one national struggle between classes."[5]

Later social theorists and political activists concerned with working-class politics, among them Karl Kautsky and Roberto Michels, also argued that the bigger plants were more likely to be centers of working-class consciousness than the smaller ones.[6] And in his recent study of the appeals of Marxism, Adam Ulam has written that

[2] Friedrich Engels, *The Housing Question*, ed. C. P. Dutt (New York: International Publishers, n.d., from 2nd German Edition of 1887), p. 29.

[3] *Ibid.*

[4] Engels, *The Condition of the Working Class in England*, ed. and trans. W. O. Henderson and W. H. Chaloner (New York: Macmillan, 1958), pp. 137-38. The importance of great cities in the development of the working-class movement is a recurrent theme in this first major work by Engels, written before his collaboration with Marx. See especially pp. 27-33, 51, and 86.

[5] *Marx and Engels: Basic Writings on Politics and Philosophy*, "The Manifesto," ed. Lewis Feuer (Garden City, N.Y.: Anchor Books, 1959), p. 16.

[6] Karl Kautsky, *The Social Revolution* (Chicago: Charles H. Kerr, 1903), p. 60. Roberto Michels reviews the speculative literature on size in "Psychologie der antikapitalistischen Massenbewegungen," *Grundriss der Sozialökonomik*, IX, Abteilung "Das Soziale System des Kapitalismus" (Tübingen: J. C. B. Mohr and Paul Siebeck, 1926), especially pp. 244-49.

The city is the symbol and the reality of modern industrial civilization. It concentrates people joined by nothing other than the accidents of employment and the necessity of earning a livelihood in industry or service. It is a visible demonstration of the soullessness and alienation of the machine age. . . . Its crowded conditions, the friendless intimacy into which it forces the proletariat, the contrasts, visible to hundreds of thousands, between wealth and poverty, between crime and the protection afforded by authority to the rich and privileged, are in themselves lessons in the class struggle.[7]

Many contemporary social scientists have, in fact, found that in such countries as the United States, Italy, Australia, West Germany, and France there is a general relationship between increasing size of plant and community and working-class unionization, militancy, and support for left-wing politics.[8] None of these studies were done in relatively underdeveloped countries, however, as was ours; and all, with one exception, dealt essentially with the appeals of *organized* left-wing politics such as Social Democratic or Communist parties, or with unionization, rather than with anarchism, syndicalism, or what Richard Hamilton has termed "nativist radicalism." These studies, therefore, followed

[7] *The Unfinished Revolution* (New York: Random House, 1960), p. 60.

[8] V. O. Key, *Politics, Parties, and Pressure Groups* (New York: Thomas Y. Crowell, 1952), p. 272; Juan Linz, "The Social Bases of West German Politics" (Unpublished dissertation, Columbia University, 1959), Chapter 10; Richard F. Hamilton, *Affluence and the French Worker* (Princeton: Princeton University Press, *in press*), Chapter 14; Leon Epstein, "Size of Place and the Division of the Two-Party Vote in Wisconsin," *Western Political Science Quarterly*, IX (March, 1956), 138-50; Clark Kerr and Abraham Siegel, "The Inter-Industry Propensity to Strike: An International Comparison," in *Industrial Conflict*, ed. Arthur Kornhauser *et al.* (New York: McGraw-Hill, 1954), pp. 189-212; and Seymour Martin Lipset, *Political Man* (Garden City, N.Y.: Doubleday, 1959), pp. 248ff., and the references therein.

in the tradition of the theorists who emphasized large-scale industry as the source of working-class radicalism, and attempted, rather speculatively, to locate the factors assumed to create greater amenability to revolutionary politics among the workers in the bigger plants.

In the pre-World War I period, however, there was another much less influential theoretical current which tried to explain the prevalence of revolutionary anarchosyndicalist ideology among the workers as the result of quite different factors. These theorists noted that anarchosyndicalism, in contrast to Social Democracy, apparently had its greatest strength in the small plants, and in the countries and regions where small-scale industry was characteristic. Spain, France, and Italy, for example, which were among the least industrialized countries of Europe at the time, were centers of anarchosyndicalism. France, the birthplace of syndicalism, had little industrial concentration before World War I; even in the past several decades it has remained essentially a country of small- or medium-scale industry.[9] Italian social democracy, and then communism, was strongest in the industrialized north, and "gained no foothold in the south or in Sicily, and little in central Italy." In these areas of small-scale production, "Anarchism retained its appeal."[10] In Germany, where industry was generally large-scale, social democracy never had serious syndicalist competition, and only it and communism became major working-class ideologies. The Latin American countries such as Argentina, Chile, and Cuba, that had significant working-class movements and in

[9] Andre Philip, "France," in *Organized Labour in Four Continents*, ed. H. A. Marquand (London and New York, 1939), p. 3; Warren C. Baum, *The French Economy and the State* (Princeton: Princeton University Press, 1958), p. 232; Val R. Lorwin, "France," in *Comparative Labour Movements*, ed. Walter Galenson (New York: Prentice-Hall, 1952), pp. 332-33.

[10] G. D. H. Cole, *A History of Socialist Thought*, II (London: Macmillan Co., 1954), 330; J. P. Van Aartsen, "Italy," in *Organized Labour in Four Continents*, ed. Marquand, pp. 193-94.

which anarchosyndicalism had preceded communism as the dominant working-class ideology, were also generally characterized by small-scale industry. This was true especially in the prewar period when anarchosyndicalism was at the height of its influence in the working class.[11]

In contrast to the theorists who emphasized the importance of large-scale industry in the development of working-class consciousness, the few, such as Lucien Sanial, John Spargo or Werner Sombart, who attempted to explain the ecology of anarchosyndicalism and its apparent appeal to workers in small-scale industry, emphasized the *content* of the ideologies and offered an essentially rationalistic interpretation of anarchosyndicalist appeal. They were probably compelled to do so because, rather than trying to explain the general bases of working-class radicalism, they were trying to explain the differential appeals of two ideologies which, at least superficially, appeared to be identical as ideologies of working-class protest. The particular content of each ideology, the vision they projected of the future and of the workers' role in that future, therefore, became important in the search for an explanation of these ideologies' differential appeals. They argued that anarchosyndicalism rather than Social Democracy (or communism in a later period) appealed to workers in small workshops because anarchosyndicalist doctrine taught that socialism would result in the establishment of relatively autonomous industries run by the workers themselves, rather than in state ownership of industry and central planning. Since, under capitalism, the workers were employed in small independent workshops and believed that they possessed the requisite skills and technical knowledge to run them without their bosses, the revolution would simply turn control of the factories over to the workers and eliminate the owners, that

---

[11] Robert J. Alexander, *Labour Movements in Latin America* (London: Fabian Society, 1947), p. 4; George Wythe, *Industry in Latin America* (New York: Columbia University Press, 1945).

is, the capitalist class. The ideology of anarchosyndicalism not only had greater appeal to such workers, these theorists argued, but in fact its very genesis could be explained by "the social and economic environment in which the syndicalist doctrines arose." As Werner Sombart put it:

> The fundamental conception of the future common-wealth as an organization of federated groups, [and] the theory of work . . . could have found acceptance only in a land where industries are for the most part carried on in workshops, with the master workman (*maitre-ouvrier*) at the head of each, and a few journeyman employees besides. Many of the syndicalist theories, despite the denials of the Syndicalists themselves, are based on a conception of industry which is reminiscent of the guild system.[12]

Apropos of Sombart's allusion to the affinity between the syndicalist idea and the guild system, it is interesting that in his analysis of the participation of the workers in the German revolution of 1848, Marx had observed a similar phenomenon. He wrote that in Germany at that time the mass of the working class were employed in small shops, and that as a result, the guild system still retained such a strong appeal to them that at the outbreak of the revolution, a large part of the working classes called for the immediate reestablishment of guilds and medieval privileged trades' corporations. By contrast, in the more developed manufacturing districts, "where the modern system of production predominated, . . . [and] the facilities of inter-communication" between the workers were therefore more highly developed, "a strong nucleus formed itself, whose ideas about the emancipation of their class were far more clear and more in

[12] *Socialism and the Social Movement* (London and New York: E. P. Dutton, 1909), p. 111; see also John Spargo, *Syndicalism, Industrial Unionism and Socialism* (New York: B. W. Huebsch, 1913), p. 25.

accordance with existing facts and historical necessities. . . ."[13]

In light of these early speculations concerning the relationship between anarchosyndicalist ideas and small-scale manufacturing, a recent finding by Richard Hamilton in his study of French working-class politics is particularly relevant. While he found that the "pro-Soviet" workers were more frequent in the larger plants, the "nativistic radicals" (those who expect change in the workers' condition to come through revolution), are more frequent in the *small* plants. Nativist radicalism, in contrast to the greater strength of procommunism in the large industrial towns, also is strongest in the villages. Hamilton's interpretation of this finding is that their employment in "small, non-expanding, family-dominated firms" convinces the workers, even without the presence of a political organization to transmit the "lesson" to them, that no solution for their problems is possible in this setting. Since they know the chances for promotion or pay increases are minimal, they believe "the only change for the better that could occur would be the result of a radical transformation of the social order." In larger plants, by comparison, Hamilton shows that the workers believe their chances for improvement are good. Thus, workers in this setting "can see the possibility of a direct solution" for their problems without the need for a social revolution. Hamilton suggests further that syndicalist or anarchist radicalism in Spain and Italy may have had similar origins, since these countries "are also characterized by small plants and traditionalist management."[14]

Whether Hamilton is closer to the explanation for this type of radicalism than earlier theorists or not is debatable. What is clear, however, and immediately relevant to our own study, is the fact that, like France, Cuba was also characterized by (*a*) small- (if not tiny) scale industry, and

---

[13] *Revolution and Counter-Revolution, or Germany in 1848*, ed. Eleanor Marx Aveling (Chicago: Charles H. Kerr, 1919), pp. 23-24.

[14] *Affluence and the French Worker*, Chapter 12.

(*b*) by a strong tradition in its working class, long preceding the dominance of Communists in the labor movement, of "nativistic radicalism" and revolutionary anarchosyndicalism.

(*a*) "Chinchales," so-called factories of as few as three or four workers, abounded in prerevolutionary Cuba—though they were never fully enumerated. The results of a very incomplete prerevolutionary study of the size-composition of industrial establishments in Cuba in 1952 are shown in Table 7.1, indicating that about two-thirds of the prerevo-

TABLE 7.1

Size of Cuban (Nonsugar) Plants, 1954 and 1962

SIZE	NUMBER		PERCENT OF TOTAL	
	1954	*1962*	*1954*	*1962*
5 workers or less	830	97	45.1%	8.0%
6 to 10	333	102	18.2	8.5
11 to 25	320	259	17.3	21.7
26 to 100	250	532	13.6	44.4
101 to 250	67	140	3.6	11.7
251 to 500	26	43	1.4	3.6
500 or more	14	25ª	0.8	2.4

ª 500 to 750, 18; 750 to 1,000, 4; 1,000 or more, 3.

Sources: 1954: U. S. Department of Commerce, Bureau of Foreign Commerce, *Investment in Cuba: Basic Information for United States Businessmen*, Washington, D.C., 1956, p. 73. 1962: Dirección de Trabajo y Salarios, Ministerio de Industrias, Havana, January 1962 (original memorandum prepared at the author's request and in his possession).

lutionary "factories" surveyed employed fewer than ten workers. Since the *chinchales* were out of reach of the survey to a great but unknown extent, the table undoubtedly understates their proportionate share of the population of industrial establishments. Even with the vast consolidation of industry under the Revolutionary Government, and the merging of hundreds of *chinchales* and the concentration of workers in fewer and larger industrial establishments, the craft and workshop character of Cuban industry remains dominant today.

In addition, while Cuba was relatively urbanized before the revolution, urban growth there, unlike that in much of Europe and the United States, did not come from the development of heavy industry. Rather, the high level of urbanization grew out of Spanish colonialism and the slave economy, which, to a great extent, gave the establishment of cities their impetus. Wealthy plantation owners lived in the cities, usually ports, from the income of their plantations, and these became the centers of European culture and influence, as well as dwellings of proletarianized smallholders and peasants displaced by the large plantations. The proportion of the Cuban population living in urban centers was relatively constant in this century, being about 47 percent in 1899 and 56 percent in 1953, though cities of about 25,000 population were growing faster than others in the prerevolutionary decades.[15]

Manufacturing establishments and, therefore, the homes of industrial workers, were often located far from big cities, not only in small towns but also in the countryside proper. The latter was especially true of what there was of heavy industry in prerevolutionary Cuba. The *bateyes* of the big sugar mills were, in fact, not only "factories in the field," but also urban communities in themselves which often held the homes of as many as two or three thousand mill workers. The Nicaro nickel refinery in Oriente Province, for example, not to speak of the mines at Matahambre or Moa Bay, was located in the countryside, and the majority of the workers employed there lived in small surrounding rural villages. The Ariguanabo textile plant in Havana Province, Cuba's largest factory, was located in a "company town," its inhabitants the workers and their families. Workers in the

[15] Wyatt MacGaffey and Clifford R. Barnett, *Twentieth Century Cuba* (Garden City, N.Y.: Anchor Books, 1965), pp. 47ff.

biggest plants were often actually rural dwellers, whose social existence retained a strong rural flavor. Their neighbors might be peasants. Loose goats, chickens, and pigs wandered around the workers' villages and the factory outskirts, and in their off-time many workers cultivated minuscule plots of their own. On the other hand, a multitude of small manufacturing establishments were located in the bigger towns and cities; a few provinces and a few cities within them held most of them. Something like half of the prerevolutionary manufacturing plants (the actual figure was probably even higher) were estimated to be located in Havana Province alone.[16] The large homogeneous centers of working-class population in the bigger cities, therefore, undoubtedly had a higher proportion of workers who were employed in small plants.

(b) Anarchosyndicalism preceded communism as the most significant working-class ideological influence in Cuba. The anarchosyndicalists called Cuba's first workers' congress as early as 1892; led some of her earliest and most heroic strikes, and the first, albeit unsuccessful, attempts to organize the railroad workers; dominated the strike movements preceding and continuing throughout the First World War and its aftermath, which was a particularly intensified period of social struggle in which their *comites circunstanciales* played the leading role; led the first successful organizational drives among the sugar mill workers; founded and dominated the first national working-class organization, the National Workers' Confederation; and in 1925 bore the brunt of the Machado regime's repression, which resulted in the deportation in prison ships, or murder, of their major leaders, the decimation of their organizations, and destruction of their working-class influence. In the wake of this repression, the Communists became dominant in the labor movement and the

---

[16] U.S. Department of Commerce, *Investment in Cuba* (Washington, D.C.: U.S. Government Printing Office, 1956), p. 74.

anarchosyndicalists never regained anything but the most minor working-class influence. But in those three decades of the most difficult years of working-class organization, the anarchosyndicalists undoubtedly left the workers an important political legacy. How many of their ideas remained part of the working-class's political culture and continued to exert influence on the workers even under Communist influence cannot be known definitely; but it is one which, given the influence, for instance, that the same legacy apparently retains among French workers, cannot be ignored. Further, we have to recognize that the anarchists and syndicalists also lost their early influence over the workers to the Communists in other countries of Latin America, as well as in France and Italy. Thus, as unquestionably important as the murder of their major leaders was in eliminating anarchosyndicalist influence in the Cuban working class, other factors must have been operative. One was the fact that the Cuban industry in which the anarchosyndicalists were strongest, cigar-manufacturing, was simply transferred by its owners to Florida and New Jersey in the face of the success of anarchosyndicalist organization. However, among factors common to other countries where they lost their influence, there was the attraction of Soviet power, the greater organizational coherence of the Communists, and the willingness of the Communists to formally engage in national politics.

The factor most relevant in the present context was the probable capture by the Communists of the influence of the workers in some of the largest and most important plants of these countries. That is, we know from empirical studies that their success has more or less consistently been greater among the workers in the biggest factories. Historical sources, on the other hand, indicate the relatively greater strength of the anarchosyndicalists in industries in which small-scale production predominated. Whatever the reasons (we discussed some possibilities above), the fact that the views of the anarchosyndicalists apparently are more appealing to the workers in the least strategic, least developed industries of a country, must have gone against them. One of their last pre-revolutionary strongholds in Cuba, for example, was the culinary workers. The Communists, on the other hand, succeeded in cementing their most important working-class base in the sugar industry, which was both the island's singularly most important industry and the one in which the scale of production had been developed to the optimum. Whether or not the Communists generally exerted greater influence among the workers in the bigger factories throughout Cuba is one of the central questions of this chapter.

We have pointed out so far that (a) the workers in the biggest plants often lived in the countryside proper or in small villages and towns, and that the large centers of homogeneous working-class population in the big cities had a predominance of workers employed in small shops; (b) the small factory milieu probably produced a nativist radicalism and had apparently been the historical base of the anarcho-syndicalists. Now, the question is how these facts affected the extent to which the Communists could reach or appeal to the workers.

We might surmise that the rural surroundings and consequent relative inaccessibility of workers in some of the biggest plants, and the attention any organizer would be likely to attract in such situations, might have impeded their organization by the Communists, even though they were prime organizational targets. On the other hand, since the workers in small shops predominated in the homogeneous working-class neighborhoods of the bigger cities, they should have been relatively more accessible to Communist agitation and political and electoral activity. Yet these workers were much less likely to have been organizational targets at work than the workers in the bigger plants; and even when exposed to Communist agitation, the anarchosyndicalist ideas still current among them may have resisted, or the small shop milieu itself may have impeded, organizational attempts. Thus, for the foregoing reasons, it was difficult to predict what we would find concerning the relationship between prerevolutionary procommunism and the size of the plant the workers worked in and of the community they lived in.

There was also the not insuperable but difficult "technical" problem that by the time of our survey there had been such a thorough reorganization of Cuban industry, such vast consolidation of small shops into bigger ones, and the shift of workers from one plant to another, that any relationship that politics and plant size may have had in actuality before the revolution might not be discovered by our survey. This was one reason why we designed our sample so as to increase the probability that we would interview workers in the larger plants, which were the least likely to have been touched yet by this phase of reorganization. There was also a significant influx, as we know, of ex-peasants, agricultural laborers, petite bourgeoisie, and white-collar employees into the working class since the revolution; and these workers had to be excluded from our computations so as not to further obscure any relationship between size and politics that may have actually existed. Finally, we faced the problem of small numbers. The workers in our sample actually came from only 21 plants. Thus, not only did each size-of-plant category contain a limited number of workers as a base for computations, but more important, a category might contain only one plant, or, as it turned out, no more than four.

Given these practical and theoretical reasons to be uncertain concerning the relationship we would find, it came as a surprise to discover that our data do, indeed, indicate something of a relationship between increasing plant size and prerevolutionary support for the Communists (Table 7.2). However, the relationship is clearly not entirely direct; and the workers in the very biggest plants (employing over

2,000) actually were the *least* likely to support the Communists before the revolution. These were the workers employed in the U.S. government-owned Nicaro nickel plant in Oriente and the textile plant in Bauta, in Havana Province. The first was built in 1942 by the United States Government because of the wartime emergency. It is located, as noted earlier, in the countryside, and recruited its workers, it seems likely, from the rural areas with little Communist influence. The U.S. government probably was particularly vigilant against Communist organizers, on the one hand, and, on the other, the Communists, then engaged in aiding the anti-fascist war, probably did not try to organize these workers in any case—it was left for others to do so. By the war's end the Communists were already engaged in a struggle for survival against the Cuban government's attempt to eliminate them from leadership of the labor movement and were in no position to launch an organizational drive in the Nicaro plant. As for the textile plant, it was in a company town; the company exerted strong paternalistic control, and resisted early organizational attempts until, when it was finally organized, it was by non-Communist radicals (one of whom, Jesús Soto, rose after the revolution to the position of Organizational Secretary in the labor confederation). So the finding is not unreasonable, although such post hoc interpretation is not intellectually satisfying.[17]

There is no relationship between plant size and support for the revolution (Table 7.2). In light of our earlier discussion, this finding was to be expected. That is, the revolutionary leadership was probably able to tap the latent or nativistic radicalism of the workers in the small plants, and secure them as a base for the revolution, and at the same

[17] Of course, all this interpretation may be beside the point, and our finding the result of sampling error; but since we did discover a general relationship between plant size and prerevolutionary procommunism among workers in the plants of 2,000 workers or less, this seems unlikely.

TABLE 7.2

Percent Supporting Communists or Revolution,
by Size of Plant[a]

NUMBER WORKERS IN PLANT	COMMUNISTS	REVOLUTION	(N)
26-100	24%	86%	(21)
101-250	30	90	(10)
251-500	39	66	(38)
501-750	40	80	(15)
751-1,000	28	72	(39)
1,001-2,000	46	62	(24)
2,001 or more	7	67	(15)

[a] This and the following tables in this chapter exclude those who were not workers before the revolution.

time receive the support of the pro-Communist workers in the larger plants. It is worth mentioning also that in the revolution's first years, after the conflict with the United States had become serious, many of the small workshops and factories were actually run by the workers when their owners went into exile. (This was true even in a few large plants, where managerial, administrative, and technical personnel—often American—left the country.) This may have awakened—along with the very decentralized nature of early industrial "planning" and the quasi-anarchist style of the revolutionary leaders—the dormant syndicalist sympathies of many workers. Further, the Revolutionary Government had no necessary reason to focus organizational or propagandistic efforts on the larger plants. This was not true of the Communists before the revolution, who had good reasons to make the larger plants their organizational targets.

First of all, like any other opposition, the Communists in any country have limited resources, which they have to deploy in accordance with their estimate of the strategic importance of the plants and their chances of success in organizing them. Experience has already taught labor organizers that a strike that involves large numbers of workers is more likely to succeed than one involving only a few who can easily be replaced by strike-breakers. The large enterprises are also more able to bear the cost of union organization and accede to it, even welcome it, because of the regularity and stability it usually brings to the labor force in the plant.

Secondly, the Communists aim at the larger plants and bigger cities on theoretical and ideological grounds. The more "advanced workers" are, of course, supposed to be those in the heavy industrial plants rather than in the small craft shops; the Communists have always emphasized organization on a "class" rather than craft basis; and the urban proletariat is supposed to be the "vanguard of the proletariat." Moreover, if only from their own reading of Marx and Engels, they also have reason to assume that the larger plants have the more class conscious workers in them, and to choose these as organizational targets. So, aside from any special aspects of the social relations and work contexts of the larger plants, the simple fact that the Communists probably chose them as the objects of their organizational efforts made them more likely to be the greater centers of Communist strength. The Revolutionary Government, on the other hand, has had almost unlimited access to the workers, whatever the size of the plant or community they are in, thus overriding the organizational and communication advantages of different size plants.

It is not surprising, then, that there is no systematic relationship between plant size and support for the revolution, or between community size and support for the revolution. The Communists, however, apparently had secured greater prerevolutionary support among the workers of the larger communities; though, as with plant size, the relationship is not linear (Table 7.3). The division is between the workers in the very smallest communities of under 5,000 inhabitants in which 27 percent of the workers were pro-

Communist, and all the larger ones where the proportion was 36 percent.

TABLE 7.3

Percent Supporting Communists or Revolution, by Community Size

SIZE OF COMMUNITY	COMMUNISTS	REVOLUTION	(N)
Less than 5,000 population	27%	74%	(69)
5,000-24,999	38	69	(29)
25,000-74,999	37	81	(27)
75,000 or more	33	63	(27)

Moreover, as Table 7.4 shows, plant size and community size both independently contributed to Communist support; with the exception noted earlier for the very largest ones, the workers in the larger plants were more likely than those in the small plants, whatever the size of the community in which the plant is located, to have been Communist sympathizers; and whatever the size of their plant, the workers living in the larger communities were more likely to be pro-Communist.[18]

[18] This relationship between the size of the community and pro-communism is consistent with the very fragmentary information we have on prerevolutionary voting patterns in Cuba. In the presidential elections in 1948, the last election under a relatively formal democratic (in Cuban terms) regime, the electoral returns do not reveal any striking differences between the votes received by the political parties in different provinces. However, the Communists, and an independent left-wing candidate, Eduardo Chibás, were strongest in Havana, while the moderate *Auténticos*, and the conservative Liberal-Democratic coalition were weakest there. Not only was Havana by far the most urbanized province in Cuba (over 90 percent), and Havana city by far the largest city, but it was also the center of Cuban manufacturing industry (half the known manufacturing establishments were located there). Thus, the greater combined vote of the Communists and Eduardo Chibás in Havana province probably came from the dense working-class sections of metropolitan Havana. The weakest centers

TABLE 7.4

Percent Pro-Communist before Revolution, by Plant
and Community Size[a]

NUMBER WORKERS IN PLANT	LESS THAN 5,000	5,000 OR MORE
26-250	21% (14)	29% (17)
251-1,000	26 (31)	41 (51)
1,001-2,000	39 (18)	67 (6)

[a] Simply to make exposition easier and clearer, this and the following tables in which size of plant is a variable exclude the 15 workers in plants of over 2,000 workers. *The reader should bear in mind that "2,000 or more" is a deviant case throughout.*

It should be emphasized that the size of the plant employing them apparently affected the workers similarly whether they were skilled, semiskilled or unskilled, and whether they were unemployed or regularly employed before the revolution (Tables 7.5 and 7.6). These subgroups of the working class were all more likely to support the Communists if they were located in the larger plants (again, with the exception of the very largest ones). Furthermore, the relationships between unemployment and procommunism (see Chapter 3)

of Communist electoral support were in Pinar del Río and Matanzas provinces, the provinces with the fewest known manufacturing establishments, and, therefore, probably with the smallest working-class populations. In these provinces the Center and Right did at least as well as or better than they did in the other provinces. Pinar del Río, which was the least urbanized province of Cuba, was the one in which the right Liberal-Democratic coalition received its biggest vote. Forty-two percent of Pinar del Río's votes went to the Right compared to only 28 percent in Havana. Less than two percent of the vote went to the Communists (and about 10 percent to the combined Left, if Chibás is included) in Pinar del Río, compared to almost 10 percent for the Communists (and 30 for the combined Left) in Havana Province. For the electoral figures from which I computed the percentages see William Stokes, *Latin American Politics* (New York: Thomas Y. Crowell, 1959), p. 382. On the distribution of manufacturing establishments by province, see *Investment in Cuba*, p. 74, and for urban percentages, p. 176.

and skill level and procommunism hold in both the larger and the smaller plants, so that the size of the plant, unemployment, and skill each contribute independently to the formation of a radical working-class outlook. The differences between employed and unemployed were greatest in the smaller plants and least in the larger plants. Presumably, the workers in the larger plants were more exposed to homogeneous social pressures, which diminished the political differences between them, whatever their relative economic security.

TABLE 7.5

Percent Pro-Communist before Revolution, by Plant Size and Prerevolutionary Employment

NUMBER WORKERS IN PLANT	MONTHS WORKED PER YEAR BEFORE REVOLUTION	
	9 or less	10 or more
26-250	38% (13)	17% (18)
251-1,000	44 (32)	30 (50)
1,001-2,000	50 (12)	42 (12)

TABLE 7.6

Percent Pro-Communist before Revolution, by Plant Size and Skill Level

NUMBER WORKERS IN PLANT	SKILLED	SEMI- AND UNSKILLED
26-250	33% (9)	26% (19)
251-500	43 (14)	35 (23)
501-1,000	44 (16)	36 (28)
1,001-2,000	54 (13)	36 (11)

The theoretical problem remains, nonetheless, as to what it is about the social structure of different sized plants that makes them affect their workers differently. Through what processes does the size of the plant operate to encourage political radicalism—or amenability to the appeals of radical, socialist or Communist agitators and organizers? What intervening variables are present in the different sized plants, and how do these relate to political radicalism?

We have already pointed out the possibility that radical agitators and organizers may be more likely to choose the larger plants as their targets on tactical and theoretical grounds, and that the smaller plants are less likely to have militants or political activists in them. This differential selection of different size plants as organizational objectives may also be supplemented by differential self-selection or recruitment of certain types of workers. It is possible, for example, that workers who have the ambition of becoming proprietors of small shops may prefer them to larger ones. They might believe their chances for learning a skilled trade are greater in a small shop, for instance, under the close supervision of the shopowner; and the latter may very well himself have been a worker who managed to open a shop of his own. Still possessed of the value of becoming bosses, such workers are probably less easily organized into unions or radical parties.[19] Small shops and factories, because of their comparatively less bureaucratic and less impersonal work atmospheres, might also be more attractive to workers coming from rural farm backgrounds, or petite bourgeoisie homes. In West Germany Juan Linz found that the sons of independent farmers, who were more likely than workers' sons to be conservative, were located disproportionately in the smaller shops.[20] However, our own data do not indicate any systematic relationship between social origins (*i.e.*, father's occupation) and size of plant.

Apart from possible differences in their sources of recruitment of workers, a number of other possible factors as-

[19] For a discussion of factors that operate in different sized shops to affect social interaction, see Seymour Lipset, Martin Trow and James Coleman, *Union Democracy* (Garden City, N.Y.: Anchor Books, 1962), pp. 170ff.

[20] *The Social Bases of West German Politics*, Chapter 23.

sociated with size, or assumed to be associated with size, have been suggested as possible bases of large plant radicalism. Large plants are assumed to be characterized by impersonal and arbitrary patterns of managerial authority, by less freedom for the worker to control the pace of his work, a breakdown in "sympathetic communication" between management and workers, and a lack of worker identification with the enterprise. Workers' discontent and organization to protect their interests, and their willingness to support radical political alternatives, are nurtured in such circumstances.[21] As Marx and Engels wrote in a famous passage of the Manifesto, for example, "masses of laborers [are] crowded into the factory, . . . organized like soldiers . . . of the industrial army, . . . placed under the command of a perfect hierarchy of officers and sergeants, . . . [and] daily and hourly enslaved by the machine. . . . The more openly this despotism proclaims gain to be its end and aim," they wrote, "the more petty, the more hateful, and the more embittering it is."[22] Traditionalist authority patterns tend to erode in the larger plants because the workers are more likely to be treated in accordance with standardized rules and procedures and an impersonal system of justice, which constitute a hierarchically organized system of authority and work discipline over which the workers initially have little influence. The breakdown of traditionalism, and the growth of working-class organization and class consciousness, are both cause and consequence of the workers' struggles, more likely in the larger plants, to modify and change the plant's internal system of social control.

In the larger factories, moreover, the workers tend to form an isolated class, and the consensus that develops

[21] See Robert Blauner, *Alienation and Freedom* (Chicago: University of Chicago Press, 1964), p. 178; and Lipset, *Political Man*, p. 237, on the arbitrariness of managerial authority in large plants and its relation to workers' discontent, militancy and leftism.

[22] "The Manifesto," *Marx and Engels: Basic Writings*, p. 14.

among them in the face of managerial authority, is reinforced by this relative homogeneity of their class environment. The workers have little but formal contact with nonmanual personnel, and these are usually in positions of authority over them. "A large plant," as Lipset puts it, "makes
for a higher degree of intra-class communication and less
personal contact [between workers and] . . . people on higher
economic levels."[23] Discussion of grievances, and economic or
political issues goes on almost entirely between the workers
themselves. The workers are, therefore, unlikely to be subject to political cross-pressures, to points of view or sources
of information that compete with those coming from union
and/or radical sources. They strengthen each others opinions
and definitions of their situation; and they are more likely to
reach a consensus about their common problems and interests, and a common course of action to defend those interests.
In such a situation, moreover, the union organizer or political activist is able to play a strategic role in the development
of the consensus, and help infuse it with radical political
content.

In small shops, however, there are likely to be fewer
activists to begin with, and these few may find it more difficult to dominate the informal discussions about politics, or
even issues apparently far removed from politics, since the
workers are more likely to have close personal contact with
their employers. The greater likelihood of employers being
present even during work breaks in small shops will inhibit
political discussions. The owner may himself be a "successful" former worker whom the workers knew before as a work-
mate. Close, though asymmetrical, personal relations between the workers and the shopowner may be more likely in
this setting, and workers may identify with and feel personally loyal to him. The boss's point of view concerning their
grievances may seem more persuasive to the workers since it is

---

[23] *Political Man*, p. 252.

easier for them to "understand" his problems also, and to identify with his economic difficulties. Such personal ties, in turn, tend to weaken bonds of class solidarity, class differences will seem more nebulous, and radical appeals based on the doctrine of the class struggle, of a conflict of interests between the workers and the owners, are less likely to find fertile soil.

While these speculations refer to the probable impact of plant size on in-plant social relations, and on the possibilities of interclass versus intraclass communication, communication patterns do not necessarily vary with size, or with size alone. The possibilities for inter- versus intraclass communication may vary in accordance with the relative size of the pool of managerial, administrative, and technical personnel "available" for informal social relations with the workers during working hours. Their "availability" varies, however, not only in accordance with their number proportionate to the number of production workers, but also with their physical location in the plant, the amount of freedom the work process itself allows for informal socializing during work, and the degree to which the work process makes interaction between nonmanual employees and production workers either possible or necessary.

Our own data indicate, for instance, that the ratio of managerial, administrative, and technical personnel to production workers (the so-called A/P ratio) in the plant is closely related to the workers' political attitudes. That is, we established two categories of plants, one with a "high" A/P ratio where the number of nonmanual employees is large proportionate to production workers, and one with a "low" A/P ratio where the number of nonmanual employees is proportionately small; and we found that the workers were *less* likely to have been prerevolutionary supporters of the Communists where the A/P ratio was *high*, and *more* likely to have been where it was *low* (Table 7.7). Further, it is relevant that the proportion "indifferent" rather than "hostile" to the Communists varies with the A/P ratio. This is perfectly in accord with the general hypothesis concerning the political effects of differential opportunities for inter- versus intraclass communication. The A/P ratio, though, is not necessarily a good index of interaction between manual and nonmanual employees. The latter may very well be isolated in their offices away from the production workers, and may, indeed, have nothing to do with them either during working hours, or lunch breaks, in spite of their high proportion compared to the production workers.

TABLE 7.7

Prerevolutionary Attitude toward Communists, by Plant A/P Ratio

PLANT A/P RATIO	FRIENDLY OR SUPPORTER	INDIFFERENT	HOSTILE	(N)
Low	37%	37%	26%	(98)
High	24	46	30	(54)

However, the plants in our sample with high A/P ratios are also the very ones in which the process of production more or less regularly brings production workers into contact with nonmanual personnel. Of the eight plants in our sample with high A/P ratios, four are characterized by continuous-process technology, to a great extent (two oil refineries and two breweries), and two (electric power plants) by technology which, from the point of view of our analysis, have the same social consequences. That is, their technologies require continuous consultation and checking between office staff and production workers. In these plants, as Robert Blauner points out, most workers "neither see the product nor work on it directly with their hands. Instead, they monitor automatic control dials, inspect machinery, adjust valves, and record . . . data. . . ." The workers in these plants can, to a great extent, satisfy personal needs when they feel like it, and have a great deal of freedom, compared to most industrial workers, to socialize on the job with each other "because they carry out their tasks according to their own rhythm." Blauner's observations concerning workers in continuous-process technology in the United States might just as well have been made about the workers I observed in these same types of plants in Cuba:

> The automated worker's work—light, clean, involving the use of symbols, and resulting in *regular contact with engineers, salesmen, and supervisors*—is also somewhat similar to that of the office employee. And his mentality is not far different; he identifies with his company and orients himself toward security. Like the white-collar man, this security comes from his status as an employee, from his dependence on the benevolent and prosperous company, rather than his own independence. *Generally lukewarm to unions and loyal to his employer*, the blue-collar employee in the continuous-process industries may be a worker "organization man" in the making.[24]

These plants have high A/P ratios and production processes that bring manual workers into regular contact with administrative and technical personnel; and they are also parts of industries that generally have been able to provide their workers with a regularity of employment and long-range job security that less stable industries cannot provide. It is reasonable to suggest, then, that the differences in the politics of the workers employed in them may simply be the result of their differential economic security. However, when we control for the workers' prerevolutionary employment security, we find that the structure of in-plant relations associated with the A/P ratio and the workers' experience with unemployment both independently contributed to the formation of their political attitudes. The workers who were *regularly employed* in plants with *high* A/P ratios were the *least* likely of the four subgroups to

[24] *Alienation and Freedom*, p. 181. (My italics)

support the Communists before the revolution, while those who were underemployed in low A/P ratio industries were most likely to support them (Table 7.8).

TABLE 7.8

Percent Pro-Communist before Revolution, by Prerevolutionary Employment and Plant A/P Ratio

| Plant A/P Ratio | MONTHS WORKED PER YEAR BEFORE THE REVOLUTION | |
	9 or less	10 or more
Low	43% (47)	31% (51)
High	31 (16)	21 (38)

The question now is what differences we should expect between the politics of workers in large and small plants, if the A/P ratios in these plants do not differ. That is, what are the political consequences of plant size if A/P ratio is held constant? We might reason that since the A/P ratio is constant, size ought not to affect the workers' politics, and differences between workers in large and small plants should disappear. However, our original reasoning was that the chances for interaction between workers and nonmanual personnel are greater in small plants. Thus where the A/P ratio is low in both large and small plants, the chances for such interclass interaction should still vary with size. In addition, differences in the opportunities for interclass interaction in the plant will probably be bolstered by the actual physical size and layout of the plants, and the location of the administrative and technical staff. A small shoemaking or cigar manufacturing shop is more than likely to have all the workers gathered in one large room, with the boss's "office" in the corner of the same room. He is in and out of the room throughout the workday, supervising, and likely participating himself in the work, or engaging in informal small talk with the workers, all of whom he probably knows by their first names, and whose families he is familiar with. The administrative and technical staff of a cement plant or copper mine or textile factory of over 500 employees, however, is comparatively isolated from the production workers, with whom they rarely have anything but formal businesslike contact.

Where, however, the A/P ratio is high, the work process demands regular interaction between workers and administrative and technical personnel, and the work rhythm allows for a good deal of informal socializing, the effect of plant size itself on interaction will probably be negligible. Moreover, such continuous informal interaction of workers and non-manual personnel probably prevents political militants in such plants, even if the plants are quite large, from being able to dominate the informal climate of opinion. However, in plants with low A/P ratios this would not be so, and our earlier reasoning would still apply; the target character of the larger plants would still be politically consequential. This reasoning, in any case, is consistent with our findings (Table 7.9). The proportion of prerevolutionary pro-Communist workers is essentially the same in the large and small plants with high A/P ratios. In the plants with low A/P ratios, though, the large plants have the highest proportion of prerevolutionary Communist supporters. It should be pointed out, further, that there is no difference between the politics of the workers in the small plants with low A/P ratios, and the plants, large and small, with high A/P ratios. That is, as we expected, interclass interaction is probably about the same in all these three types of plants. The large plants with high intraclass interaction (the low A/P ratio plants) stand out as the base of pro-Communist workers before the revolution.

The plant's size, its ratio of production workers to managerial, administrative, and technical personnel, and the process of production interact to create an objective structure of social relations within the plant that, in turn, determines to

TABLE 7.9

Percent Pro-Communist before Revolution, by Plant
Size and A/P Ratio

NUMBER WORKERS IN PLANT	PLANT A/P RATIO			
	low		high	
26-250	25%	(20)	27%	(11)
251-2,000	45	(69)	24	(37)

a great extent the political attitudes of the workers employed in it. Their political attitudes are also affected by how the workers perceive that structure and their place within it, and this is the subject of the next chapter.

CHAPTER 8

Alienation and Revolution

✄ "EVERY age has its key ethical concept around which it can best formulate the cluster of its basic problems"—and to many contemporary thinkers that concept is alienation.[1] The frequent use in social science today of some variant of the concept testifies to what Robert Nisbet calls "the central place occupied by the hypothesis of alienation."[2] Much of the concept's value in sociological analysis, however, is diminished because in the very process of trying to "remove the critical, polemic element in the idea of alienation,"[3] the concept itself has become alienated from its classical meaning as a radical attack on the existing social structure. In fact, in most sociological writing it is "no longer clear what alienated men are alienated from."[4]

The concept, in one of its most important classical meanings, was an attack on the exploitation of the worker in industrial capitalist society. Thinkers as diverse as John Stuart Mill, Tocqueville, Marx, and Engels independently arrived at a similar critique of the worker's alienation from his work through observations of developing capitalism. Mill, for example, thought the workers' alienation from their work would lead them to become discontent with the existing social order:

[1] Lewis Feuer, "What is Alienation? The Career of a Concept," in *Sociology on Trial*, ed. Maurice Stein and Arthur Vidich (Englewood Cliffs, N.J.: Prentice Hall, 1963), p. 127.

[2] *The Quest for Community* (New York: Oxford University Press, 1953), p. 15.

[3] Melvin Seeman, "On the Meaning of Alienation," *American Sociological Review*, XXIV, 6 (December 1959), 784.

[4] John Horton, "The Dehumanization of Anomie and Alienation," *British Journal of Sociology*, XV (December 1964), 284. A major study appeared recently, however, which is an excellent exception to this criticism, namely, Robert Blauner, *Alienation and Freedom* (Chicago: University of Chicago Press, 1964) which attempts to locate

I cannot think it probable that they will be permanently contented with the condition of laboring for wages as their ultimate state. To work *at the bidding* and for the *profit of another, without any interest in the work* . . . is, *not even when wages are high*, a satisfactory state to human beings of educated intelligence who have ceased to think themselves naturally inferior to those whom they serve.[5]

Mill therefore proposed a reorganization of industry which would allow the workers to share in both the management and profit of industry, as means of "healing the widening and embittering feud between the class of laborers and the class of capitalists. . . ." He could not be persuaded "that the majority of the community will forever, or even for much longer, consent to hew wood and draw water all their lives in the service and *for the benefit of others*; or . . . that they will [not] be less and less willing to cooperate as subordinate agents in any work, when *they have no interest in the result*. . . ."[6]

To Marx, it was in "the relation of the worker to work, to the product of his labour and to the non-worker, and the relation of the non-worker to the worker and to the product of his labour," that the essence of any social structure—its form of social domination and exploitation— was located.[7] "The whole of human servitude," he argued "is involved in the relation of the worker to production, and every relation of servitude is but a modification and consequence of this relation."[8]

---

the differential conditions of work under which industrial workers are likely to feel estranged from their work.

[5] *Principles of Political Economy*, 2 vols. (Boston: Charles C. Little and James Brown, 1848), II, 327. (My italics)

[6] *Ibid.*, p. 338. (My italics)

[7] Karl Marx, *Economic and Philosophic Manuscripts of 1844*, ed. and trans. Martin Milligan (Moscow: Foreign Languages Publishing House, n.d.), p. 83.

[8] *Ibid.*, p. 82.

In common with Mill and Tocqueville, Marx and Engels emphasized what they believed were the generally destructive psychological consequences of the worker's position in industrial production. In Marx's and Engels' famous formulation:

> Owing to the extensive use of machinery and the division of labour, the work of the proletarians has lost all individual character and, consequently, all charm for the workman. He becomes an appendage of the machine, and it is only the simplest most monotonous and most easily acquired knack that is required of him.[9]

In particular, however, Marx focused on two levels of the organization of capitalist production in which alienation is inherent:

(1) The locus of control over the organization of production within the plant itself. Marx argued that the worker is deprived of his individual rationality to the extent to which the process of production is made rational from the standpoint of the organizer of production, namely, the capitalist. Because control, planning, and organization of production are the prerogative of the capitalist, the worker is degraded to the level of a mere productive force, separated or alienated from his own knowledge, judgment, and will, which are now required only for the plant as a whole.[10]

[9] "The Manifesto of the Communist Party," in *Karl Marx and Friedrich Engels: Basic Writings on Politics and Philosophy*, ed. Lewis Feuer (Garden City, N.Y.: Anchor Books, 1959), p. 14. For Tocqueville's views see *Democracy in America*, 2 vols. (New York: Vintage Books, 1945), II, 168-71. Also see the ideas of the young, "pre-Marxian" Engels in *The Condition of the Working Class in England* (New York: Macmillan, 1958), pp. 133-34.

[10] *Capital* (New York: Modern Library, 1906), pp. 396-97, 708-709. It might be worth noting the evident kinship between Marx's concept of individual rationality and rational organization, and Karl Mannheim's concept of "substantial rationality" as opposed to "functional rationality." Cf. *Man and Society in an Age of Reconstruction* (New York: Harcourt Brace, 1954), pp. 52-60, 216.

(2) The locus of control over the means of production and the products of production within the capitalist system as a whole. Neither the tools that the worker works with nor the products he produces are his property. Therefore, in the very process of production, the worker becomes alienated from his work because it is not in his own interest but in that of the capitalist. The more the worker produces, and the more he expends himself in his work, the more *the owner of his labor power* benefits. Thus, at work, the worker himself is the property of the capitalist, and is alienated not only from his work and the products of his work, but from himself.[11]

As a result of the process of alienation of both the worker's rationality and his product, "every remnant of charm in his work" is destroyed and it becomes transformed into "hated toil."[12] Usurped of their individual rationality and their collective product, the workers, Marx believed, would not only find their work degrading and suffer psychological deprivation, but also would become discontent with the capitalist system as a whole. This discontent, in turn, would be a major revolutionary motivating force. Marx assumed, in other words, that the *objective* relationship of the alienation (*i.e.*, separation) of the workers from the control of the social organization of production and the products of their work would result in their *subjective* estrangement from the capitalist system. This process of estrangement, along with the problematic development of class consciousness, would lead eventually to the proletarian revolution and the "emancipation of the working class." As Marx put it,

[11] *Economic and Philosophic Manuscripts*, pp. 71-73, 78-80. This aspect of alienation, the objective separation of the worker from the products of his work, was the conceptual germ of Marx's later concept of exploitation in which the value created by the worker over and above the value he is repaid in wages is appropriated by the capitalist.
[12] *Capital*, p. 708.

The proletarian class . . . feels itself crushed by this self-alienation, sees in it its own impotence and the reality of an inhuman situation. It is . . . a revolt to which [the class] is forced by the contradiction between its humanity and its situation, which is an open, clear and absolute negation of its humanity.[13]

Since Marx there has been a tradition in political analysis of relating work and its discontents to the development of radical working-class politics. In the sociological literature on working-class politics, the connection between worker dissatisfaction, social resentment, and political radicalism has often been noted.[14]

There is also a literature on the working class that has been aptly termed the "sociology of cynicism," in which more often implicitly but occasionally explicitly, attitudes of general hostility toward and resentment of society are linked to alienation from work.[15]

[13] *Die Heilige Familie, Marx-Engels Gesamtausgabe*, Vol. III, Part 1, 205-206, quoted in *Karl Marx: Selected Writings in Sociology and Social Philosophy*, ed. T. B. Bottomore and M. Rubel (London: Watts and Co., 1956), pp. 231-33.

[14] Seymour Lipset, Paul F. Lazarsfeld, Allen Barton, and Juan Linz, "The Psychology of Voting: An Analysis of Political Behavior," in *Handbook of Social Psychology*, Vol. II, ed. Gardner Lindzey (Cambridge, Mass.: Addison-Wesley, 1954), 1,124-70. See also Lipset, *Political Man*, p. 237.

[15] Donald Clark Hodges, "Cynicism in the Labor Movement," *American Journal of Economics and Sociology*, XXI, 1 (January 1962), 29-36; Ely Chinoy, *Automobile Workers and the American Dream* (Garden City, N.Y.: Doubleday, 1955); Paul Goodman, *Growing Up Absurd* (New York: Random House, 1960); George Friedmann, *Anatomy of Work* (New York: The Free Press of Glencoe, 1961); C. Wright Mills, *The New Men of Power* (New York: Oxford University Press, 1948); Hadley Cantril, *The Politics of Despair* (New York: Basic Books, 1958); Karl Bednarik, *The Young Worker of Today: A New Type*, ed. J. P. Mayer, trans. R. Tupholme (Glencoe, Ill.: The Free Press, 1955).

Ironically, Ely Chinoy's interviews with auto workers in Detroit convinced him that the workers' alienation explained the widespread interest among them in small business and, to an extent, in farming, "and their responsiveness to the values of the small-business tradition." He concluded, therefore, that

> Paradoxically, the very process of alienation which Marx thought would transform workers into class conscious proletarians has instead stimulated their interest in small business and in small-scale private farming, institutions which Marx asserted were doomed to extinction.[16]

Chinoy did not try to measure the political attitudes of the workers he interviewed, however, nor examine the extent to which their longing to get out of the factory represented hostility toward a society that exploited them and their work. The fact is that despite the theoretical orientations and the numerous suggestions for research on the subject, there have been few studies of the relationship between work attitudes and political attitudes,[17] or of the political meaning of alienation from work.

Alienation and Revolution

The Cuban revolution gave new public esteem and respect to manual labor, nationalized industry, and abolished the private appropriation of the workers' products.[18] Social relations in the plant were also altered radically in an egalitarian direction by the revolution. Here, then, was an exceptional opportunity to study the political meaning to the workers of fundamental changes in their work situation—

[16] Chinoy, p. 86.

[17] See Richard Centers, *The Psychology of Social Classes* (Princeton: Princeton University Press, 1949), pp. 160, 170-72, 203; Richard F. Hamilton, *Affluence and the French Worker*, Chapter 12; and Juan Linz, "The Social Bases of West German Politics," unpublished dissertation, Columbia University, 1959, pp. 215ff.

[18] Cf. *Twentieth Century Cuba*, p. 168.

in their role in the organization and control of production and of the products of their work.

Of the twenty-one plant administrators we met and spoke to, eight were workers before the revolution: in the Uruguay sugar central, the brewery in Manacas, the cigarette factory in Vedado, the leather factory in Managua, and the agricultural equipment plant in Vibora, the administrators were civilians, while the worker-administrators of the textile plant in Ariguanabo (whose assistant had been a union delegate before the revolution), and of the Matahambre copper mine and chemicals plant in the port of Santa Lucia were members of the Rebel Army. The salaries of most administrators were no higher than skilled workers in their plants, the modal salary of the administrators we interviewed being $350 monthly, with some earning as low as $250 monthly. Salaries of the administrators were still relatively low at the time of our interviews not only because the Minister of Industries, "Ché" Guevara, asserted this as a socialist principle, but also because wages were then frozen, and administrators therefore received the same wages they were receiving in their previous jobs. Of course, many administrators had such "fringe benefits" as cars, if their work required it, but, in general, the status gap between administrator and worker, as we observed them, seemed barely existent.

Yet it seemed clear that the workers who were supposed to participate in directing production did not do so. Participation was to take place through the Technical Advisory Councils, theoretically composed of the most dedicated and conscientious workers. Many workers, however, seemed to be almost unaware of the councils' existence.

In contrast, the Grievance Commissions (*Comisiones de Reclamaciones*) apparently had succeeded to a great extent in gaining the workers' approval. The commissions were three-man bodies composed of representatives of (1) the factory administration, (2) the Ministry of Labor (elected by the workers), and (3) the factory work force (also elected by the workers). The commissions were empowered to decide questions involving workers' individual grievances, such as sick leaves, work transfers, dismissals, and wages. Once a decision was taken, the worker concerned could appeal to an Appeals Commission, and even directly to the Minister. When I asked Jesús Soto and Carlos Fernández R., two high-ranking CTC officers, what a worker could do if after going through the whole process of appeal he was still unsatisfied, they apparently did not understand the implications of the question. "Ché," however, said that a worker could appeal to his union to intervene in his behalf, and involve it in the defense of what he considered his infringed rights.

Even when they thought the commissions "bureaucratic," however, most workers compared them favorably with the burdensome, lengthy, and often corrupt process to which even the simplest grievance was subjected in prerevolution days.[19]

Whatever the nature of the actual changes in the workers' role in the organization of production, however (changes about which we could not be certain from our limited observations), we could analyze how the workers themselves perceived these changes and their new existential situation, and how these attitudes related to their view of the revolution.

We asked the workers, for instance, how well they thought the administrators of their plant were doing their jobs; 23 percent thought their plant administration was doing either a poor (seven percent) or merely acceptable (16 percent) job. In some instances, the workers indicated they had little to do with the administration of the plant, as, for example, the electrical worker in Santiago who told us: "I really don't know the administrative part of the plant, and I have no

[19] See my article, "Labor in Cuba," *The Nation* (October 20, 1962), pp. 238-41, for a detailed discussion of my observations of the workers during the period of my research in Cuba.

information about the way the administrators are working."
A sugar worker at the Enidio Díaz central saw. no significant
change: "This mill," he said, "goes as it always did." Another sugar worker, at the Venezuela central, voiced a
familiar working-class gripe: "As far as I'm concerned [the
administrator] is doing all right. I don't worry about it.
You've always had to watch the boss, or you get fired. It's
always been the same." Most workers, though (56 percent),
thought their administrator was doing his job well despite
the fact, as a worker at the Uruguay central put it, that "he
was a worker in another central before the nationalization.
He's doing well, but he's not as well prepared or trained as he
should be." Other workers, like an old anarchist in the Manacas brewery, were proud that the administrator was a former
worker: "I think everyone agrees," he said, "that our administrator is one of us, nothing more. He attends to everything
well. He gives us his ideas and takes ours. He is one of the
workers here. He worked as a mechanic before the revolution,
and the government selected him from there." "They must do
their jobs well, now," a worker at the Argelia Libre central
said, "because they are receiving the government's guidance
and, besides, we now can protest if they do something wrong,
call a general assembly of the workers here, and—if we
must—remove them from their positions." A minority of
workers (20 percent) were even enthusiastic about the new
administrators. "Oh, he's a fine *compañero*. He was a worker
and he understands the workers' lives," said a worker at the
nationalized Shell and Esso refineries in Regla (which were
now under unified management), "and this is the reason we
selected him for the administration." A nickel worker
emphasized that the new administrator "shares with the
workers. He does not have privileges like they had before,
and like the office workers had." An electrical worker in
the Matanzas plant said the administrator was distinguished
from the workers only by "his technical knowledge, but he
works for the same interests as the workers," while to an old

West Indian worker in Vibora's agricultural equipment plant the change was simple and fundamental. As he told me in his special brand of English: "In everythin' we work pretty contented. Work is not like in time gone past by when you got to run and kill yourself. With this government who rule now, I work more contented. The other government abused the workin' people. This one try to help 'em."

These different perspectives on the way their plants were now run are reflected, of course, in the position the workers take on the revolution. As Table 8.1 indicates, there is a direct relationship between their judgment of the caliber of their plant administrators, and their attitudes toward the revolution.

TABLE 8.1

Workers' Opinions of Plant Administration and Their Attitudes toward Revolution

PLANT ADMINISTRATORS ARE DOING THEIR JOBS[a]	FAVORABLE	INDECISIVE	HOSTILE	(N)
Poorly or acceptably	51%	11%	38%	(47)
Well	70	17	13	(114)
Very well	90	0	10	(21)
Excellently	90	0	10	(20)

[a] The question was: "Do you think the administrators of your plant are doing their jobs poorly, acceptably, well, very well or excellently?"

If the structure of formal and informal relations between administrative personnel and production workers, as the worker perceives them, has an important impact on his general perspective toward his society, so, too, has his conception of opportunity in the plant. A worker who sees a huge gap between himself and his peers, on the one hand, and the management on the other, is not likely to believe he has much of a chance of advancing in the plant (even if it is no longer under capitalist ownership and management).[20]

[20] Cf. Blauner, *Alienation and Freedom*, p. 178.

When we asked the workers what they thought the chances for promotion or for wage raises were in their plant, two-thirds of them thought the chances good, another 13 percent fair, and the remaining fifth or so, poor. Their remarks emphasized the structural changes wrought by the revolution and their new collective—rather than individual and individualistic—opportunities. Many workers pointed out that they themselves knew workers who were now plant administrators or technicians. Others, as did this brewery worker, for example, emphasized the expectations they had for the economic development of the country, and the expanding educational opportunities: "Well, the industries are growing. Almost all of us are studying and many will become administrators and engineers. Before, we could not have done such a thing." An electrical worker in Santiago said: "Our opportunities for promotion are excellent because the capacity of our plant is being raised, as is its production. Besides, there is a project afoot for an electric turbine plant of seventy thousand kilowatt hours, and another one in Gibara nearby, that will raise our generating capacity—as well as our need for workers." Elimination of the need to have "pull" or to bribe someone to get ahead, and the application of universal standards of judgment now, were among the more frequent reasons the workers gave for believing their chances for improvement were now good. A Havana brewery worker said: "You get ahead now according to your capacity, and by strict examination, as well as in accordance with the years you have been working in the plant, and if the one in line can't do it, then the next one gets the chance. The costs of production are all posted and the wage costs are made public and we know exactly what everyone earns, and this is much different. Today one doesn't come in off the street, and pay off someone, no. Now he has to stand in line with the rest and earn it in accordance with his ability." Others, of course, were not quite so sanguine about their opportunities: An oil worker at the former

Texaco plant in Santiago said: "Before, at least the unions tried to raise wages. Now you work, and you work, and you work once again, and still the wages are frozen." A cement worker (unintentionally emphasizing the new egalitarianism), said: "There aren't any [opportunities], not for now anyway. You work at the same wage you got before, no matter what place you are working, so what's the point? For example, the chief of personnel here gets the same he got when he worked here as an electrician." Thus, these different perceptions of the opportunity structure are also related to the workers' views of the revolution, as Table 8.2 indicates. The better he thinks his chances for promotion or higher

TABLE 8.2

Perception of Opportunity for Promotion or Higher Wages, Compared with Attitude toward Revolution

THE CHANCES FOR PROMOTION OR HIGHER WAGES IN THIS PLANT ARE[a]	FAVORABLE	INDECISIVE	HOSTILE	(N)
Good	81%	12%	7%	(131)
Fair	65	11	23	(26)
Poor or "don't know"	42	11	47	(45)

[a] The question was: "What do you think the chances are for promotion or higher wages for a worker in this plant?"

wages are the more likely the worker is to support the revolution.

I think the excerpts from our interviews with the workers indicate that many of the workers believe the revolution *and the nationalization of industries,* has had a profound impact on their work attitudes. Many made spontaneous allusions to the effects of nationalization on their attitudes. But our questions asked about their *present* attitudes, without reference to the past. The important point, however, is what *changes* have actually occurred in how they view their work since the nationalization of industries. What did they think of their work before, and what do they think since? To answer this question, as posed, is impossible, since we have no prerevolutionary survey data on the workers' attitudes toward their work. It *is* possible, though, for us to see *how the workers themselves think the nationalization of industries affected their view of their work.* What do they say when asked a simple open-ended question as to why they hold their present attitudes toward work? We asked the workers the following questions: What do you think of your particular work? Would you say you like it a lot, more or less, or a little? What are your reasons for thinking this way about your work? Did you think differently before the industries were nationalized? If so, how?[21]

These questions made it possible for us to (*a*) separate the workers who said they had changed their attitudes toward work since nationalization from those who reported no change; and (*b*) construct a typology of the four possible types of attitude-change that could have occurred since nationalization among the workers who were workers before the revolution.[22]

[21] Admittedly, this is a rather crude way to measure the workers' attitudes toward their work, but our major concern here is their relationship to attitudes toward the revolution, rather than the absolute magnitude of work satisfaction among the Cuban workers. For a discussion of the difficulties in measuring work attitudes, see Arthur Kornhauser, "Psychological Studies of Employee Attitudes," in *Human Factors in Management*, ed. S. S. Hoslett (Parkville, Mo., 1946); and for an excellent synthetic discussion of the literature on work satisfaction, see Robert Blauner, "Attitudes Toward Work," in *Readings in the Economics and Sociology of Trade Unions*, ed. Walter Galenson and Seymour Martin Lipset (New York: Wiley, 1960).

[22] Unfortunately, I did not think of asking the workers a forced-choice question about their prenationalization attitudes toward their work paralleling the question about their present attitudes. Had I done so, constructing the typology would have been a simple task, and the typology would have been more precise. As it is, we were compelled to infer, by analyzing the workers' replies to the open-ended question about the changes in their work attitudes since nationalization, what their prenationalization attitudes were—that is, infer at least to

Taking the present work attitudes of the workers who said they like their work "a lot," and defining them as "positive," and the remaining workers' attitudes as "negative," and classifying their prenationalization attitudes by inference, also as positive or negative, we get the four types in Table 8.3.

The typology is meant, quite simply, to indicate how the workers themselves see the relationship between their present work attitudes and those they held before nationalization. Does the worker think his attitude has changed, and if so how?—in what direction? It is then quite valid to compare the differing support for the revolution among these differ-

---

the extent of classifying those prenationalization attitudes as "positive" or "negative." In practice, fortunately, this was not particularly difficult to do, and there was little or no guesswork involved, since the question obviously tapped feelings the workers wanted to discuss at length. The answers of some workers did pose classification difficulties, though, not only because they were insufficiently specific about the past, but also because not all changes were qualitative changes. Some were simply changes of degree. Some workers, in other words, liked their work less, but still liked it sufficiently well to say they liked it a lot; others liked their work more, but were still generally negative about their work. As a result of these two kinds of difficulties, we found it best to exclude five workers from our typology of work attitude changes, because the change that had occurred in their attitudes since nationalization was not clear.

Another and more subtle methodological problem is that we interviewed the workers, after all, some two years after the nationalization of industries. By then, of course, the connection between the causes and consequences of their work situation and work attitudes may have become transparent. Some workers (we have no way of knowing how many) may have now realized that they had been discontent with their work before the industries were nationalized, although they had not known this consciously before. The workers' retrospective reports of their work attitudes are, therefore, not necessarily the same as the actual attitudes they had toward their work before nationalization. It was the very transformation of their work situation which made them aware of their past discontent—a discontent which they may have felt only vaguely or not at all in the past. What this means, quite simply, is that had we really interviewed the workers before the industries were nationalized, their work attitudes might have been quite different from the ones they recall having at the time of the interviews.

TABLE 8.3

Change in Work Attitudes, and Nationalization of Industries[a]

ATTITUDE TOWARD WORK			
BEFORE NATIONALIZATION	SINCE NATIONALIZATION	(N)	PERCENT
Negative	Positive	(64)	43%
Negative	Negative	(25)	17
Positive	Positive	(53)	36
Positive	Negative	(5)	3
	Total	(147)[b]	99

[a] Those who were not workers before the revolution are excluded from this and the following tables in this chapter.

[b] The type of change in the work attitudes of five workers was not clear, and they are not included here or in the following tables.

ent types of workers, as long as we remain clear about the nature of our data.

What is striking about the way the workers report that their attitudes have changed (Table 8.3), is that nearly three-fourths of those dissatisfied with their work in one way or another before the nationalization of industries say nationalization positively transformed their attitudes toward their work. For them, apparently, socialization of the means of production was not a romantic myth or an empty political slogan; for with it came a fundamental change in their work and their commitment to it. Socialism provided them with a desire to work which they had not experienced before. This transformation in their work commitment, in turn, has been basic to their support of the revolution.

Clearly, as Table 8.4 indicates, the workers who think that their work attitudes have been transformed positively since nationalization are more likely than others to support the revolution. Moreover, the contrast is sharper when only the workers who are very favorable to the revolution in each type are compared. Then we find that 70 percent of the workers whose work attitudes became positive since nationalization are very favorable to the revolution, compared to 44 percent, 32 percent, and none, respectively, of the other three types shown in Table 8.4.

TABLE 8.4

Attitude toward Revolution, by Change in Work Attitude since Nationalization of Industries

CHANGE IN WORK ATTITUDE	FAVORABLE	INDECISIVE	HOSTILE	(N)
Negative-positive	84%	9%	7%	(64)
Negative-negative	72	8	20	(25)
Positive-positive	62	15	23	(53)
Positive-negative	20	0	80	(5)

In accordance with most prior theory, we have assumed, to this point, that the work attitude is the intervening variable in the psychological process leading to the development of the worker's political outlook. That is, the objective structure of work relations creates an attitude toward work that may be a starting point for the worker's developing attitude toward the existing social structure in general. It is probable, of course, that in the complex world outlook each worker develops, the attitudes he has toward his work and toward society as a whole are inseparable, and reciprocally interact with and affect each other. The process might even be that the worker's *political outlook* is the *source* of his attitude toward his work. Radical workers who believe that whatever the specific conditions of their work, they are necessarily exploited in a capitalist system, may be more likely to consider their work degrading. George Friedmann has made a similar point:

> There is no doubt that a job takes on a sense of greater value in the worker's mind when he feels himself in sympathy with the aims of the community as a whole. . . . Therefore, when a considerable proportion of the work-

ing population of a capitalist country contract out of it because of their conviction that they are being exploited, any
attempt to overcome the harmful effects of specialization
is rendered vain in advance.[23]

We might want, then, to look at the relationship in Table
8.4 differently, namely, at how the work attitudes of workers
who view the revolution differently have changed since
nationalization. As Table 8.5 indicates clearly, the relationship, when looked at in this way, is also strongly in the predicted direction: the revolutionary workers are far more
likely to report positively transformed work attitudes since
nationalization than the indecisive or hostile workers.
Being "in sympathy with the aims of the community as a
whole," their work has taken on "a sense of greater value."

TABLE 8.5

Attitude toward Revolution Compared to Change in Work Attitude
since Nationalization of Industries

ATTITUDE TOWARD REVOLUTION	NEGATIVE-POSITIVE	NEGATIVE-NEGATIVE	POSITIVE-POSITIVE	POSITIVE-NEGATIVE	(N)
Favorable	51%	17%	31%	1%	(106)
Indecisive	37	13	50	0	(16)
Hostile	16	20	48	16	(25)

My own view, however, on both theoretical and historical
grounds, is that the order of attitude development was from
work to revolution. My basic assumption, supported by
my own research as well as the research of other political
sociologists, is that the pressures arising from the work
situation are among the major ones impinging on the
worker, and are decisive in the development of his political
attitudes. Prior theory and research tells us this, but we

[23] The Anatomy of Work, p. 90.

know it also on simple logical grounds of time order. The nationalization of industries took place in the late summer of 1960 and was a decisive event in the revolution's radicalization—in fact, in defining the nature of the revolution itself. It was this event, perhaps more than any other, which politically divided the Cuban population, essentially along class lines, and which was certainly *the* event of most significance in the working lives of the workers. Thus, it seems more than likely that the changes at work and in the situation of their fellow workers and themselves in the society that resulted from the nationalization of industries, and, consequently, the change in their work attitudes, was a major variable in the development of their attitudes toward the revolution, rather than the reverse. Of course, once set in motion, it is obvious that the two attitudes (toward work and the revolution) probably have interacted with and reinforced each other.

How important their changed work attitudes are in the workers' conception of the revolution can be seen from the fact that even when we control for their prerevolutionary economic insecurity the workers whose work attitudes have been transformed positively since nationalization are still more likely than others to support the revolution (Table 8.6). Moreover, work attitudes more clearly differentiate the political attitudes of the economically secure workers than of the insecure ones, among whom the common experience of unemployment and underemployment has already served as a spur to radicalism. Finally, as expected, the prerevolutionary unemployed are more likely than the employed to support the revolution, whatever the change in their work attitudes since nationalization.

Estrangement

In our discussion so far we have equated "estrangement" and work dissatisfaction. To a great extent that is a valid equation, since the general theoretical question posed is the

TABLE 8.6

Percent Pro-Revolution Compared to Change in Work
Attitude since Nationalization of Industries and Prerevolutionary
Employment

| CHANGE IN WORK ATTITUDE | MONTHS WORKED PER YEAR BEFORE REVOLUTION | |
	9 or less	10 or more
Negative-positive	92% (36)	75% (28)
Negative-negative	82 (11)	64 (14)
Positive-positive	80 (15)	55 (38)
Positive-negative	— (0)	20 (5)

interconnection between work discontent and general social discontent. Marx, however, was not attempting to analyze the general sources of work dissatisfaction—although he gave many insights in that direction. In his analysis, he focused on the historically specific form of work dissatisfaction which he thought to be inherent in the structure of capitalist production relations. That is, estrangement (*entfremdung*) was specifically the result of the workers' alienation (*entaüsserung*) from ownership of the means of production, and control of the organization and products of production. It was this objective structure that would lead, Marx believed, to the workers' estrangement, first from their work, and then from capitalism as a whole. Work and politics—estrangement and class consciousness—would meet: the workers would become aware that in order to abolish the conditions which led to their estrangement from work, they would have to destroy the conditions of their class's existence and, thereby, the capitalist system.

Thus, presumably implicit in Marx's theory of alienation would be the following hypothesis: The workers whose source of work discontent, as they see it, is their objective alienation from control over the organization and products of production, would be more likely to become politically radical not only than other workers but than *other workers who are also discontent with their work.* To test this hypothesis it would be necessary, then, to distinguish subtypes of work discontent among which would be "estrangement" in Marx's sense, and relate workers having these subtypes to those having given types of political attitudes and behavior. In practice, however, it would be difficult to distinguish such types for analysis.

In Chinoy's study of automobile workers' attitudes, there is a clue to one analytically important way of operationally distinguishing such subtypes. Thus, a machine operator told Chinoy:

> *The main thing is to be independent and give your own orders and not have to take them from anybody else.* That's the reason the fellows in the shop all want to start their own business. Then the profits are all for yourself. When you're in a shop there's nothing in it for yourself. When you put a screw or a head on a motor, *there's nothing for yourself in it.* So you just do what you have to do in order to get along. *A fellow would rather do it for himself. If you expend the energy, it's for your own benefit then.*[24]

This machine operator was emphasizing, I believe, exactly what Marx called the alienation of the workers from the products of their work, and also was indirectly alluding to the workers' loss of control over the organization of production. For this machine operator, alienation apparently was the reason for his discontent with his job and his desire to get out of the plant and run his own small business if possible.

This suggests that it might be of value to distinguish (*a*) the workers whose discontent with their work derives (*as they themselves perceive it*) from their lack of control over the organization and/or the products of their work, from (*b*) the workers whose source of work discontent lies elsewhere.

---

[24] *Automobile Workers and the American Dream,* p. 86. (My italics)

The former workers would presumably fit the specific Marxian category of estrangement. In short, on the basis of their spontaneous answers to open-ended interview questions, we could categorize workers as "estranged" or not, and then ask: are the estranged workers more likely to be politically radical than other workers—in particular, than other workers who are also discontent with their work?

This question, certainly, is not directly relevant here, since the revolution has "turned things 'round." Cuba is a society in which the relationship we might expect in a capitalist system between the two attitudes has been stood on its head. Whereas estrangement and revolutionary socialist politics should, according to the Marxian hypothesis, be directly related among workers under capitalism, it is now those who are *not* estranged who should be the revolutionaries, because theirs is now a society in revolution.

The relevant question, then, is: Do the workers who believe the abolition of alienation was the reason for the positive change in their work attitudes differ from other workers in their view of the revolution? In particular, are these workers who believe they were estranged from their work before nationalization more likely to support the revolution than the other workers whose work attitudes have also become positive only since nationalization?

In our interviews, as we noted already, we asked the workers what their reasons were for their present work attitudes, and whether or not and in what way they thought differently about their work before the nationalization of industry. We can, therefore, categorize the workers in accordance with the themes of their answers to this question. I have categorized as estranged before nationalization those workers whose answers expressed the conviction that the positive change in their work attitudes occurred because, in contrast to their situation before nationalization (*a*) the workers and the administration of the plant or factory in which they worked were now one and the same, (*b*) the

products of their work were now their own, and/or
they were now working in the interest and for the benefit of
themselves and their fellow workers.

There was, for example, the brewery worker who said:

> The boss paid us a miserable salary. The revolution put
> the workers to work, and paid more. The profits of the
> industries are now used for schools and for highways that
> we build ourselves. . . . We don't have a boss now. We
> ourselves run the brewery. There are no overseers, but
> rather *responsables* [persons encharged with responsibility
> for a particular task]—because we need technical advisers.
> . . . Before I didn't want to work. Now, I work of my own
> will, at whatever is necessary.

A sugar refinery worker also emphasized the common effort
of the workers for their common benefit:

> Everything is now done as is necessary for the workers.
> Now we have decent human beings who work with us, as
> we work with them. Before, we didn't know whom we
> were working for or whom we were working with. When I
> work now, I work of my own free will [*mi propia fuerza*],
> not like before when I worked only out of need. Now, the
> chief helps us resolve any problems. Say something breaks,
> he doesn't say: "Fix it!" but "C'mon, let's see what *we*
> can do"—and we do it. It's a job we do because we want
> to.

A copper miner was brief and to the point:

> Before, a raise in production benefited *the bosses*. Not
> now.

The same was true for a nickel furnace-tender:

> We worked for the boss before. We work for ourselves
> now.

Other workers spoke with greater eloquence, but expressed
the same essential idea:

"I sacrificed a part of my youth to learn my trade, and it is only now that I am working for myself—since the foreign enterprises passed into the hands of the revolution."

"I work freely now. It is as if I am my own boss. I did not work with the same emotion before, or feel the same importance. . . . The administrators, the workers, they are the same thing, so that if something is functioning well— or badly—now, it is our doing."

"There is more for the workers now. I have security and can now provide for my family. If I want, I can now have guests without shame or fear. Before, I would say, 'I have nothing.' Now I welcome my friends to my house with pride. From now on, if there are cars produced, then workers will have cars, too; if there is medicine, *we* shall have medicine— and doctors!"

"The difference is the following: Before, I worked for another individual or for a company. Now I work for the people, that is, to provide hospitals, houses, et cetera, and whatever else the country needs most."

In contrast to these workers, the majority of workers whose attitudes toward their work had become positive since nationalization focused in their replies essentially on the overall improvement in their personal well-being, dignity, and economic security, rather than on the abolition of alienation. Typical of these workers was the maintenance man at a sugar central who said: "I never knew when I was going to [have] work before; how could I like that?" In different words, workers in the paper mill, tobacco factories, oil refineries, nickel processing plant, and so on, emphasized the elimination of maltreatment at work and of the fear of layoffs and unemployment:

"The bosses pushed us around before. Now they don't expect enough of us!"

"Now, if I want to talk to a fellow, I don't have to look over my shoulder."

"Now I have secure work. I don't worry about getting sacked or laid off."

"Before, I always worked—sixty-one years old and I worked since I was a kid. There was no other way to live. But I couldn't even work most of the year. I left for home at the end of the *zafra*. Now I work the whole year."

To others, the factory was now more than a place to work, it was a place to learn:

"I am trying to improve myself now. I attend classes in *Mínimo Técnico* [elementary technical training]. Before, I didn't even have work."

"A worker can stay right here after work and study if he wants. Before, he left this place as quickly as he could!"

Others were poetically obscure: "Because of the light shed on us now, and the road we are traveling."

To what extent, then, do these latter workers differ in their support of the revolution from those workers who were "estranged" from their work before the industries were nationalized? The difference is clear. Every one of the 25 workers to whom the abolition of alienation was the crucial reason why their work attitudes became positive, favors the revolution (Table 8.7). Further, 84 percent of those estranged are very favorable to the revolution, compared to 61 percent of the other workers whose work attitudes have become positive since nationalization. Thus (*a*) the workers whose attitudes toward work were transformed positively by the nationalization of industry are more likely than other workers to support the revolution, and (*b*) especially distinct, given their unanimous support of the revolution, are the workers who attribute their changed work attitudes to the abolition of alienation.

This, it might be argued, should have been "obvious." For, looked at differently, those workers whom we have termed "estranged" before nationalization quite clearly were expressing the conviction that they had been exploited in the

TABLE 8.7

Prenationalization Work Discontent and Attitude toward
Revolution among Workers Whose Work Attitudes
Have Become Positive since Nationalization

TYPE OF PRENATIONALIZATION WORK DISCONTENT	FAVORABLE	INDECISIVE	HOSTILE	(N)
Estrangement	100%	0%	0%	(25)
Other discontent	74	15	10	(39)

past under capitalism. Here, perhaps, is the conceptual and actual connection between *alienation* and *exploitation,* wherein *estrangement* is a *sense of exploitation.* It is, therefore, inherently a *political* attitude. For once the worker develops the conviction that he is not working in his own interest, but in the interest of the owners and managers, he has, in fact, developed the conviction that he is being exploited; he has developed something akin to a radical political outlook.

In contrast, the argument might continue, the workers whose primary concern was their general economic security and working conditions, were on a level of consciousness that is not necessarily political in its implications. Their outlook is akin to "bread and butter unionism." Their demands, moreover, conceivably could be solved under capitalism. However, for the workers to whom their alienation from control of their work and the products of their work is crucial, only a social revolution could suffice to eliminate their estrangement.

I think there is much of substance in this argument. It is, in essence, the hypothesis suggested earlier, except that it is phrased as an assertion that estrangement and radical politics *must* go together, that, indeed, they are one and the same. That, however, is precisely the question, since whether or not the sense that one is being used for the profit of others necessarily leads to hostility to the system as a whole that translates itself into a leftist political outlook is an *empirical question*. Whether—and how—they respond *politically* probably depends on the alternatives the workers have the opportunity to see. As we have seen, for instance, Chinoy's research on American auto workers suggested to him that estrangement may express itself in the urge to establish an independent small business—perhaps, even to move into the position of exploiting others—rather than in the political demand for the abolition of capitalism.

Our data have suggested, in contrast, that estrangement is more likely than other types of work dissatisfaction to lead to a revolutionary political outlook. The reminder must be added, of course, that we dealt here with the workers' retrospective views of their situation under Cuban capitalism rather than with their actual views, which may have differed considerably. The big question, then, is whether or not the same relationship between estrangement and revolutionary politics exists among workers in capitalist countries. If this is so, then the implication is clear that no matter how high their wages might become, nor how comfortable their nonworking lives might seem, a core of workers will continue to exist under capitalism who will be estranged from the system itself, and who cannot and will not be at one with themselves until that system is abolished.

CHAPTER 9

Political Generations

✍ THIS chapter is concerned with the formation of political generations in the working class, and the relevance of these generations to the revolution. Its thesis is that (a) different political generations were formed among the Cuban workers as a result of the impact on them of distinct historical experiences, and (b) that the differential response of these generations to the revolution is understandable in terms of these experiences.[1]

[1] The concept of political generation focuses on the intersection of biography, history, and social structure. It compels us to pay attention to crucial variables of explanatory value that we might otherwise overlook. However, despite the wide interpretive use to which some variant of the concept of generation has been put (whether in creative literature, literary criticism or qualitative political analysis), its use has been infrequent in the sociological analysis of politics, and especially so in the analysis of data gathered through survey research methods. Seymour Lipset, for instance, recently noted again that "unfortunately, there has been no attempt to study systematically the effect of generation experiences with modern survey research techniques." (*Political Man* [Garden City, N.Y.: Doubleday, 1960], p. 265.) The statement also appeared much earlier in Lipset, Paul F. Lazarsfeld, Allen Barton, and Juan Linz, "The Psychology of Voting," in *Handbook of Social Psychology*, ed. G. Lindzey (Cambridge, Mass.: Addison-Wesley, 1954), II, 1,124-70. The most significant lack in the study of political generations is that there have been no studies of the formation of political generations elsewhere than in the advanced industrial societies of the West. (Although there are some very cogent words on the subject in S. N. Eisenstadt, *From Generation to Generation* [Glencoe, Ill.: The Free Press, 1956]; and Alex Inkeles and Raymond Bauer, *The Soviet Citizen* [Cambridge, Mass.: Harvard University Press, 1961]).

On generations in literature see Malcolm Cowley, *The Exile's Return*, rev. ed. (New York: The Viking Press, 1956), especially the prologue. Cf. also Julius Petersen, *Die Literarischen Generationen* (Berlin: Junker und Dunn-Haupt, 1930); Henri Peyre, *Les Generations Literaires* (Paris: Bowin, 1948); Yves Renourard, "La notion de generation en histoire," *Revue Historique*, CCIX (January-March 1953), 1-23; John Clellan Holmes, "This is the Beat Generation," *New York Times Magazine*, November 16, 1952.

My approach to the problem of generations in Cuba is based essentially on Karl Mannheim's general formulation. He suggested that common experiences during their youth might create a common world view or frame of reference through which individuals of the same age group would tend to view their subsequent political experiences. Sharing the same year of birth, they "are endowed to that extent, with a common location in the historical dimension of the social process." Much like the effect of class on its members, the generation also limits its members "to a specific range of potential experience, predisposing them for a certain characteristic mode of thought and experience, and a *characteristic type of historically relevant action*."[2] Thus a generation in this view consists of individuals for whom their common experiences at the same age were differentially relevant not only at that point but in their subsequent behavior. Historical events may, as Bennet Berger has put it, "create sudden discontinuities between the age groups upon which they have

---

On generations in politics see Marvin Rintala, "A Generation in Politics: A Definition," *The Review of Politics*, xxv, 4 (October 1963), 509-22; Herbert H. Hyman, *Political Socialization* (Glencoe, Ill.: The Free Press, 1959); Sigmund Neumann, "The Conflict of Generations in Contemporary Europe," *Vital Speeches*, v (August 1, 1939), 623-28; Helmut R. Wagner, "A New Generation of German Labor," *Social Research*, xxiii (Spring 1956), 151-70; Lewis Feuer, "Rebellion at Berkeley," *New Leader*, xlvii (December 21, 1964), 3-12; Reinhard Behrendt, "Die Offentliche Meinung und das Generationsproblem," *Kölner Vierteljahrshefte für Soziologie*, xi (1932), 290-309; William Evan, "Cohort Analysis of Survey Data: A Procedure for Studying Long-term Opinion Change," *POQ*, xxiii, 1 (1959), 63-72; Hans Gerth, "The Nazi Party: Its Leadership and Composition," *American Journal of Sociology*, xlv (January 1940), 517-41, esp. 529-30; Joseph R. Gusfield, "The Problem of Generations in an Organizational Structure," *Social Forces*, xxxv (May 1957), 323-30; Rudolf Herberle, *Social Movements* (New York: Appleton-Century-Crofts, 1951), pp. 118-27 and the references therein.

[2] "The Problem of Generations," in Mannheim's *Essays on the Sociology of Knowledge*, ed. Paul Keckskemeti (New York: Oxford University Press, 1952), pp. 290-91. (My italics)

had a sharp impact and the age groups to which they are only history."[3]

From the standpoint of our analysis, it is particularly significant that the Cubans themselves see their history to a great extent in generational terms, a fact which is not at all surprising, given the dramatic and profoundly traumatic nature of the events that formed several Cuban generations. Cuban literature—political, historical, fictional—is replete with references to the "generation of '68" or the "generation of '95" or the "generation of the thirties," generations formed during singularly significant historical epochs in Cuba (respectively, the Ten Years' War against Spain [1868-78], the War of Independence [1895-98], and the abortive revolution of the thirties [1933-35]). Of the generation of the thirties, Teresa Casuso (who at 20 was the leader of the "Ala Isquierda," the left wing of the students' movement in the revolution of the thirties) has written: in "the twenty years that passed between the collapse of the general strike of March 1935 and my meeting Fidel Castro, I lived . . . like a ghostly survivor" of the generation of the thirties, "a generation that came to an untimely end, as a unified force, in the March strike."[4]

Especially significant is the fact that the movement led by Fidel Castro, in common with other revolutionary nation-

[3] "How Long is a Generation?", *British Journal of Sociology*, XI (March 1960), 10-23. Cf. "A whole 'political generation' may [develop] . . . for whom the socio-economic events of their youth served as bases for permanent political norms. . . . Presumably an age generation can be transformed by political events and social conditions into a political generation based on class considerations—a generation that retains its allegiances and norms while succeeding generations are moving in another direction." Bernard Berelson, Paul F. Lazarsfeld, and William McPhee, *Voting* (Chicago: University of Chicago Press, 1954), p. 61.

[4] *Cuba and Castro* (New York: Random House, 1961), p. 77. Miss Casuso, who was Ambassador Plenipotentiary of the Cuban Revolutionary Government to the UN, resigned her position in 1960 and sought asylum in the U.S.

alist and anticolonial movements, placed special emphasis on its being a new generation, shorn of the cynicism and the betrayal of revolutionary ideals typical of their elders. Its cadre were predominantly young people in their late teens and early twenties and, to this extent, shared with revolutionary youth movements an identification of the general social movement with their particular generation.

Writing of the distinctive "youth ideology" often developed in anticolonial movements, S. N. Eisenstadt has pointed out: "The essence of these ideologies (from the point of view of our analysis) is that the changes which they advocate and struggle for are more or less synonymous with rebellion against the 'old' order and generation—a rebellion of youth, a manifestation of the rejuvenation of national and social spirit. In them the usual modern emphasis on youth as bearers of the common values—in these cases of the *new* types of values—is accentuated and geared to realization of the movement's political and social goals. In some cases . . . the whole movement identifies itself with such a romantic ideology and values."[5]

The very first lines of the manifesto of the 26th of July movement, which stated the movement's general aims in the anti-Batista struggle, were: "The 26th of July Movement is resolved to take up the unfulfilled ideals of the Cuban nation and to realize them. To accomplish these ends, the movement counts on the contribution and the presence of *the reserves of youth* who are anxious for new horizons in the chronic frustration of the Republic. *That is its credential and its distinctive feature.*" (My italics.) The manifesto condemned "the colonial mentality, foreign economic domination, [and] political corruption" of the republic, and the regime of exploitation and oppression installed by Batista, and implicitly repudiated the older generation:

[5] *From Generation to Generation*, p. 311.

Against this storm of horror and shame only the reserves of youth of the country have resisted without bowing. This is highly significant and demonstrates the urgent necessity for renovation which the nation feels. With the fall of its natural civic defenses—the parties and their leaders, the organs of publicity and the tribunals of justice—the youth literally has had to come forward to take combat positions. With that authority, sealed with blood and the lives of comrades fallen in the struggle or killed by the dictatorship's executioners, we declare that nothing and nobody will make us surrender the responsibility that rests upon us, and that we will be faithful to the ethics and program of the Revolution.

Tracing its roots directly to the "generation of the thirties" which had also fought against "the intact chains of the past," the manifesto declared:

Workers and students marched in the vanguard of the movement, thus demonstrating the rebellion of the second republican generation violently divorcing itself from the traces of the colonial reality which the regime of Gerardo Machado embodied at that time.

Of that "generation of the thirties," despite its romantic immaturity, it is necessary to note a favorable credit balance in the account of the republic. In the "100 days" that the revolutionary forces held power, they did more in the defense of the interests of the nation and of the people than all the governments of the preceding thirty years. . . . It was this that permitted the group to come to power [in 1944, when Batista relinquished power] which appeared to be most identified with the movement: the Cuban Revolutionary Party, "*autentico*." . . . The two "*auténtico*" governments of Grau San Martin and Prio Socarras were tremendous frauds. . . . Not only did they leave unresolved the basic problems of the country, the economic, industrial, agrarian, educational, judicial, military, etc., but also they opened an immense floodgate of frivolity and scandal through which the anti-revolutionary forces sneaked back into power, significantly led again by Fulgencio Batista.

If one ember of the revolutionary fire of the thirties remained alive, the reactionary coup of March 10th extinguished it completely.

Thus, on the one hand, the young rebels of the 26th of July movement identified with the generation of the thirties, its accomplishments and aspirations; on the other, the movement condemned that generation for its failure to fulfill the ideals of its youth, and its capitulation to reaction—a capitulation which led to the need for the revolutionary movement of the new generation:

> The gang of anti-national elements that took power thanks to the March 10th coup cancelled ipso facto all hope of Cuba for its economic independence. . . . Only the decisive and active eruption, in the first place, of its youth, formed and indoctrinated in a firm national and patriotic conviction, can save the Cuban nation. They have the urgent task of completing the unconcluded revolution, and of repairing the harm done to the country by the 10th of March and by the conformity, cowardice, and submission shown by those who had the unavoidable debt of repelling it. . . . Together with its epic realism, the action of the Sierra Maestra is highly symbolic. It represents *the battle of the new and pure sap of the nation* against the poisonous vapors that are undermining and destroying it. . . . Either the Revolution will triumph, thanks almost solely to the strength of the youth, inaugurating a new order of dignity, liberty, and national reconstruction, or the governing gangsters of Batista will prevail. . . .[6]

---

[6] "Manifiesto-programa del Movimiento 26 de Julio," Appendix to Enrique González Pedrero, *La revolución cubana* (Mexico: Universi-

Not only did this generational animus characterize a good deal of the rebel movement before the conquest of power, but apparently it has also continued as one significant source of self-identification since the revolution. In one of his first public speeches (January 8, 1959) after the fall of Batista's regime, Fidel Castro again identified the youth of his generation as one of the decisive social bases of the revolution: "When the 26th of July movement organized itself and initiated the war, it realized that the sacrifices would be great and the struggle long. . . . It was evident that the 26th of July movement had the sympathy of the people, and it was evident that it had *the nearly unanimous support of the youth of Cuba.*"[7]

The generation of '53, the generation of Fidel Castro and his fellow rebels, is held up as a model of sacrifice and heroism on the nation's behalf. The special quality of his generation has been reiterated in many speeches by Fidel Castro. "This generation," he has said,

> had nothing to learn from the society in which it grew up.
> . . . It had to find the source of its valor in itself. If it took
> an example from anyone it was from men like Guiteras,
> Mella, Martí, Maceo, Agramonte.[8] This generation drew

---

dad Nacional Autonoma de Mexico, 1959), pp. 89-91, 97-99, 103-105, 125. (My italics)

[7] *Guia del pensamiento politico económico de Fidel* (Havana: Diario Libre, 1959), p. 92. (My italics)

[8] Antonio Guiteras, Secretary of Government, Army, and Navy in Grau San Martín's Cabinet, leader of Young Cuba, the left wing of the anti-Machado opposition, and the young martyred hero of the repression of the revolution of the thirties; Julio Antonio Mella, student leader, founder of the Communist Party at age 22, assassinated by Machado's agents in 1929; José Martí, foremost leader and ideologist of the independence movement against Spain, died in battle in the War of Independence in 1895; Antonio Maceo, a Negro, leading general of the War of Independence, who lost his life in that war; Ignacio Agramonte, legendary young martyred hero of the Ten Years' War against Spain, whose body was burned by the Spaniards attempt-

upon itself for dignity, civic responsibility, pride, patriotism, and for the strength to win the battle that we have just won and all the battles that we will have to wage in the future. This generation has been heroic; but the next will be better. It will be better because we did not have many examples to follow, but it will have the example of the present generation.[9]

"Ours is the generation," Castro said on another occasion, "to which no one gave a good example. . . . It drew upon itself for the idealism, virtue, and courage necessary to save the Fatherland. . . . *It is the best generation that the Fatherland has had.* It grew in the midst of negation and bad examples. But the coming generation will be better than ours. It will be inspired not only by the generations of '68 and '95 but also *by the generation of 1953*."[10]

Thus, given what appears to be the relatively developed self-consciousness of the generations themselves, formed in a historical context characterized by relatively abrupt political and social transitions and clearly demarcated political intervals, it is probable that distinct political generations were formed in Cuba whose consciousness prepared them for significantly different responses to the revolution. In particular, it may be stated as a hypothesis that *the historical period* (and/or phase of development of the economic and political organization of the working class) *during which succeeding generations of workers first became involved in the labor movement had significant consequences for the formation of their political outlooks.* Shaped by the early experiences of their youth in the labor movement—that movement's struggles, organizations, tactics, strategy, ideology, and

---

ing to prevent his grave becoming a shrine of the colonial struggle for independence.

[9] *Guia del pensamiento politico economico de Fidel*, p. 44. (My italics)

[10] *Ibid.* (My italics)

leadership—political generations emerged in the Cuban working class which have measurably different attitudes toward the Castro revolution.

For our purposes, the concept of political generation will be defined as Rudolf Heberle has put it: "those individuals of approximately the same age who have shared, at the same age, certain politically relevant experiences."[11] Formulated in this way, the concept leaves open to empirical investigation the decision as to (a) which age groups to isolate for analysis and (b) which experiences to delineate as having decisive political relevance for that age group.[12]

Thus, in our analysis of political generations in the Cuban working class and their contemporary relevance in the context of the revolution, two strategic methodological decisions were necessary: (1) which *age category or categories* to locate in time and (2) in *which historical periods*, depending on which experiences were hypothesized to be politically relevant.

(1) Normative expectations of political involvement in Cuba were established and perpetuated by the political activities of students, whose agitation and action since the foundation of the Republic were often decisively bound up with the politics of the working class—whether in the anti-Spanish colonial struggle for independence or in the abortive revolution of the thirties. The late teens and early twenties have been viewed in Cuba as a period demanding political commitment and involvement—the period of coming to manhood politically. Towns and villages throughout Cuba display plaques bearing the names of patriotic martyrs in by-

[11] *Social Movements*, pp. 119-20.

[12] This concept is therefore also essentially identical with the concept of "cohort" usually employed in demographic analysis: Cf. "A cohort may be defined as the aggregate of individuals (within some population definition) who experienced the same event within the same time interval." Norman B. Ryder, "The Cohort as a Concept in the Study of Social Change," *American Sociological Review*, XXX (December 1965), 845.

gone social struggles, a majority of whom were youth "whose obsession seems to have been not so much to live gloriously as to die gloriously."[13] In two of Cuba's most significant political periods, moreover, the political cadre who predominated in the movement were young men and women; the short-lived government of Ramón Grau San Martín during the revolution of the thirties rested to a considerable extent on the support of the youth. Raúl Roa, a student leader at that time, and presently Foreign Minister of Cuba, dubbed that regime "the ephebocracy," or teenage government.[14] And in the guerrilla struggle and urban *resistencia* against Batista, men and women in their late teens and early twenties likely formed the majority of the movement's leaders and cadre, whatever their class of origin.[15] On these grounds, therefore, of the normative expectations relevant to political ac-

[13] Robert Taber, *M-26: Biography of a Revolution* (New York: Lyle Stuart, 1961), p. 14.

[14] Teresa Casuso, *Cuba and Castro*, p. 64.

[15] Exact information is difficult if not impossible to obtain even about the ages of top revolutionary leaders, let alone of typical rebel cadre. Fidel Castro's biographies, for example, are not consistent; Spanish sources usually place his birthdate at August 13, 1927, English as August 13, 1926. Cf. Gerardo Rodríguez Morejón, *Fidel Castro: Biografía* (Havana: P. Fernández, 1959), and such American sources as Jules DuBois, *Fidel Castro: Rebel Liberator or Dictator?* (Chicago: Bobbs-Merrill, 1959); Taber, *M-26: Biography of a Revolution*. Nonetheless, from talking to individuals who "should know" in a variety of positions in Cuba, including *commandantes*, administrative personnel, and union officials, aside from the workers interviewed in our study who had fought in the hills, a consensus emerged that the typical age of the rebel youth was 18-25 years in 1952, when Batista came to power. Reasonably reliable ages of some of the more important leaders in 1962 when we did our research in Cuba, are: Fidel Castro, 35; "Ché" Guevara, 34; Raul Castro, 30; Armando Hart, 31; Osmany Cienfuegos, 32; Augusto Martínez Sánchez, 36; Camilo Cienfuegos, one of Fidel's top *commandantes* during the guerrilla war, who died in a plane crash in 1959, was about 30 when he died; Enrique Oltuski, a leader of the urban *resistencia*, was 31 in 1962; Faustino Pérez (coordinator of the abortive 1958 general strike and head of the urban *resistencia*), 31; Vilma Espin (Raul's wife and an active leader of the *resistencia*, known romantically as "Deborah" during the war), 28; Haydeé Santamaría (another rebel heroine), 32.

tivity in Cuba, the age category of 18-25 years is employed here to locate the generations temporally.

In addition, I chose this age category on more general sociological grounds. First, that the meaning of age varies in accordance with social norms governing specific activities and their relationship to age, and that it is precisely at the age at which coming to manhood is normatively defined that the individual becomes more responsive to the impact of social change, since he is relatively less subject to parental influence in his new role. That is, it is likely that the individual who has come of age is more "responsive to the impact of social change" than the child who is still "insulated from it by his home environment."[16] It is therefore reasonable to assume that the experiences of workers in the period after they enter the labor force and assume their own support, and are no longer under parental supervision, would be particularly significant to them, especially if this occurs in a period of social upheaval.

Second, it is a central assumption of this book that the social pressures arising out of the work situation are fundamental to the worker's political outlook. A recent study found, for instance, that French workers were more likely than other Frenchmen to discuss politics at work.[17] Much of the most significant political socialization of the worker—insofar as that involves assimilation of the political orientations current in his class—occurs after the inception of his *work* career. It follows, therefore, that some time must elapse between the worker's entrance into the labor market (and labor movement) and his assimilation of the political standpoint of his coworkers. This being so, crucial events impinging on the working class are more likely to affect his personal politics if he has been working a few years than if he has only begun to work. Hamilton reports a study of French

[16] *Ibid.*, p. 131.
[17] Richard F. Hamilton, *Affluence and the French Worker*, Chapter 4.

workers by Maupeau-Leplatre which found that young
workers did not have class-conscious attitudes at age 14
when they first began to work, but had a "marked change in
outlook by age 18. If workers' 'education' occurred at home,
it seems unlikely," Hamilton points out, "that young workers
would have the outlooks described."[18] For these additional
reasons, I chose to focus on the historical events surrounding
the workers when they were in their late teens and early
twenties rather than when they were younger.

(2) From the standpoint of our analysis of political generations, five critical periods in Cuban political history of the
past several decades can be distinguished. Their general
social conditions, political issues, and "concrete internal
political and social struggles"[19] constitute the decisive politically relevant experiences of succeeding Cuban generations—that is, of those who were 18-25 years of age when
each of these critical periods began. In Table 9.1 I have
briefly indicated the decisive events of each political generation analyzed in this chapter, and the predicted political
consequences of those events. The latter deserve fuller descriptions, nonetheless, so that the reader may himself judge
their significance.

Sugar speculation in the aftermath of the First World
War ended abruptly with Cuba's economic collapse in the
early 1930s (partly as a consequence of the Great Depression
in the United States), and the country entered a period of
profound social upheaval. Mass working-class and student
political strikes throughout the country resulted in the violent overthrow of the repressive and authoritarian Machado
regime. There were also increasingly more militant political
initiatives. The students took control of the University of
Havana and demanded its "autonomy" from government
interference; and the workers seized and occupied several
railroad terminals, public utilities, ports, and 36 sugar cen-

[18] *Ibid.*   [19] Heberle, *Social Movements*, pp. 122-23.

TABLE 9.1

Temporal Location, Decisive Political Events of Political Generations, and Predicted Political Consequences

AGE CATEGORY AT TIME OF STUDY (1962)	PERIOD WHICH BEGAN WHEN WORKERS WERE IN 18-25 AGE CATEGORY	DECISIVE POLITICALLY RELEVANT EVENT(S)	PREDICTED RANK OF GENERATION'S SUPPORT FOR	
			Communists	*Revolution*
21–27	1959 on	The establishment of the Revolutionary Government and ensuing revolutionary changes, including nationalization of industry and declaration of "socialist" regime.	[a]	4
28–35	1952-53–1958	Batista's *coup*, guerrilla war and urban resistance led by Castro, agitation and organization in working class, rebirth of working-class economic struggle, abortive national general strike, fall of Batista.	3	1
36–43	1944–1951	Relative political democracy and economic stability, alliance of government and anti-Communist labor officials, purge of Communists from CTC leadership.	4	5
44–51	1936-37–1943	Suppression of insurrection, reemergence of Communist leadership of labor movement, collaboration with Batista, achievement of tangible socio-economic benefits for organized workers.	2	2
52–59	1928–1935	Mass working-class and student insurrection, "dual power" of "Soviets" under Communist leadership, establishment of radical nationalist regime.	1	2

[a] The youngest generation's response to the Communists before the revolution is excluded here and in the following tables, since the question about their prerevolutionary attitudes toward the Communists refers to an attitude held before they were adults.

trals, along with a number of adjoining towns. In many centrals they established "soviets" of workers, peasants, and soldiers. Students, young intellectuals, and workers, aside from taking independent political action, were in liaison with each other, and the students acted in many instances as workers' delegates to the short-lived radical nationalist Grau regime, and as a transmission belt for the workers' demands. The young Communist Party was dominant in the leadership of the working class and, despite the equivocal role of the Communists in the final overthrow of the Machado regime, they maintained and increased their influence among the workers throughout the revolutionary period. Repression of the revolutionary movement by Batista, a sergeant who had led a revolt of the enlisted men and noncommissioned officers and gained leadership of the army, led to his consolidation of power in late 1936 and early 1937.

The suppression of the revolution, forceful dissolution of working-class organizations, and the advent on the international Communist scene of the Popular Front period, resulted in the transformation of the radical and independent workers' movement. It became a reformist movement under Communist leadership, that inaugurated an era of government-labor collaboration. The relative stability and economic security in Cuba during the Second World War accentuated even further the workers' movement's reformism, as well as growing bureaucratization. Under Communist leadership, the organized workers were able to gain many tangible economic and social benefits.

Batista relinquished power in 1944, and a period of relative political democracy began—a period, however, that also included an alliance of the government and anti-Communist labor officials which increasingly harassed the Communist leadership of the labor movement by extra-legal and violent methods. The Communists were thus finally ousted by force in 1947 from official leadership of the *Confederación de Trabajadores de Cuba* (CTC), the central labor organization unifying workers throughout the country, which the Communists themselves had formed in 1938 under Batista's aegis. The growing bureaucratization of the unions, their loss of contact with the mass of the workers, and collaboration with the government was heightened during this period of comparative internal economic stability and "prosperity."

CTC officials, under the leadership of Eusebio Mujal (whence comes the derogatory term "mujalista"), did not resist Batista's coup d'état of March 1952, in which he regained power. In the years following, and throughout the guerrilla war and *resistencia*, the CTC was largely an appendage of the regime, and often a weapon against the workers themselves; and the already significant union corruption of recent years became increasingly supplemented by gangsterism and intimidation of the workers. The Communists, having lost the government's tutelage, and been outlawed by Batista, regained a measure of grassroots influence among the workers, and led some important victorious strikes, especially in the sugar industry. But the regime fell, not as the result of a working-class insurrection, which never materialized on a mass level, but in conflict with the guerrilla forces and urban *resistencia* under the leadership of Fidel Castro's 26th of July movement, whose cadre were predominantly young men and women. As a result, their age peers, whether active in the anti-Batista movement or not, and whatever their class, were both more suspect to the police and the military and more likely than Cubans of other ages to suffer arbitrarily at the hands of the regime.[20]

[20] "Every sunrise [throughout the anti-Batista struggle] revealed dozens of corpses hanging from lampposts or lying crumpled on the pavement. Two girls, innocent of any political activity, the Giralt sisters, were ferociously murdered in their home in Havana, their screams sounding through the neighborhood as they were battered to death. The most barbaric methods of torture, not excluding castration, were daily incidents in the police stations, where *the groans of a whole generation of youths* were heard as they were tortured for information, or for having aided the revolutionary movement." (Teresa Casuso,

The role of the workers in the anti-Batista struggle contrasts strikingly with their decisive insurrectionary role against the Machado regime. Nonetheless, the years of the Batista regime saw a reinvigoration of the Cuban tradition of independent working-class economic struggle—under the leadership of Communists and non-Communists alike. The apparent political quiescence of the workers should not be exaggerated lest our understanding of this period and its impact on the workers of this generation be diminished. For instance, in the 1955 strike in the sugar industry, there were several highly militant actions, and the sugar workers were joined by other workers in cities such as Santa Clara and some sugar towns of Camaguey and Havana provinces, and their economic demands became coupled with such political slogans as "Down with the criminal government!"

In eastern Cuba and in Santiago, the country's second largest city, there were especially significant instances of mass working-class political support of the anti-Batista movement. A spontaneous political strike set off by the funeral of two young 26th of July leaders (Frank País and Raúl Pujol) on August 1, 1957 spread from Santiago to other cities in Oriente Province, including several other towns outside the province. The strike was complete in Santiago; the Nicaro nickel plant and city shops were shut down for five days. In subsequent months "Strike Committees" were organized in the plants by 26th of July organizers, collaborating with other opposition elements in preparation for a general strike in 1958. The general strike, which the 26th of July leaders called for April 9, 1958, collapsed in several hours in Havana, with little mass support. But just as in the previous August, the strike completely paralyzed industry and com-

Cuba and Castro, p. 134. [My italics]) Similar descriptions of the Batista regime's arbitrary violence against young people during the guerrilla war appear in all the accounts of this period, such as Jules DuBois, *Fidel Castro*; Robert Taber, *M-26*; and Ray Brennan, *Castro, Cuba, and Justice*.

merce in Santiago; workers stayed out despite the regime's threats of arrest and its offers of immunity from prosecution to anyone killing an advocate of the strike. The events mentioned here, then, were certainly significant in the movement against Batista's regime and must have had an impact on the workers' political outlook.[21]

Now, if it is correct that the struggle against Batista and the events flowing from it were of decisive significance in shaping the political outlook of the workers of this generation of '53, then clearly they should be far more likely than the members of other generations to support the revolution.

Comparison of the workers in the different generations confirms this expectation (Table 9.2). United by the common political frame of reference its members developed

TABLE 9.2

Attitude toward Revolution, by Political Generation

AGE CATEGORY AT TIME OF STUDY (1962)[a]	FAVORABLE	INDECISIVE	HOSTILE	(N)
21-27	55%	19%	25%	(36)
28-35	90	2	8	(51)
36-43	61	17	21	(51)
44-51	69	15	15	(26)
52-59	70	9	22	(23)

[a] This and the following tables exclude eight workers who were under 21 and seven who were over 59 in 1962.

during the anti-Batista struggle, it is the rebel generation of Fidel Castro, the generation of '53, which stands out as the decisive generational base of the revolution. Further, the

[21] For a more detailed account of these events, and a general political history of the Cuban working class, see the author's unpublished dissertation, "Working Class Politics in Cuba: A Study in Political Sociology" (University of California at Berkeley, 1964).

two other generations that stand out are precisely those whose members themselves experienced the revolutionary events of the thirties as young men. It is, of course, possible to argue that the fact that they experienced an abortive rather than a successful revolution should make them cynical and pessimistic rather than optimistic about the Castro revolution—an argument which does make a good deal of sense. Yet it is not to be forgotten that while the *social* revolution was crushed, the Machado regime *was* overthrown and thus the political revolution in the narrow sense was a success. Moreover, seen in retrospect, the revolution also yielded significant gains for the workers in subsequent years—especially the legitimation of their right to political and economic organization, a right which allowed them to win substantial economic benefits. It is also relevant that the repression of the revolution of the thirties, which, in any case, had significant "anti-imperialist" overtones, was widely believed in Cuba to have been the result of United States political intervention.[22] The anti-imperialism of the Revolutionary Government may, therefore, be another source of their support. Thus, it is understandable (even if not quite so predictable as the response of the generation of '53) that these generations may view the present revolution as the renascence and continuation of the struggles of their own youth, and be more disposed to support it than, for example, the generation of workers who came to manhood during the republican interregnum of relative stability and political democracy, or even

[22] "The principal revolutionary groups," as Dana Gardner Munro put it, "not only sought to destroy the evils of the traditional political system, but also to do away with United States 'economic imperialism.'" (*The Latin American Republics: A History*, 2nd ed. [New York: Appleton-Century-Crofts, 1950], p. 501.) See also Charles A. Thompson, "The Cuban Revolution: Reform and Reaction," *Foreign Policy Reports*, XI (January 1, 1936), 261-71; Teresa Casuso, *Cuba and Castro*, pp. 68ff.; Robert F. Smith, *The United States and Cuba: Business and Diplomacy, 1917-1960* (New York: Bookman Associates, 1959), pp. 148-56; and the author's dissertation, pp. 30-46.

than the present generation of workers for whom prerevolutionary struggles are mere "history."[23]

The low proportion, and relative rank, of the latter generation in support of the revolution is unexpected. My own prediction was (see Table 9.1) that this generation would be outranked by the generations of '53 and the thirties, but would itself outrank the republican generation. It might be suggested that an explanation lies in the fact that the workers of this generation knew little if anything through personal experience about the prerevolutionary situation of the working class. Many of them (55 percent) were not even workers before the revolution, and were essentially entering the working class at the time of the establishment of the Revolutionary Government. Thus, it was unlikely that they would or could appreciate the positive changes in the situation of the working class wrought by the revolution. As we shall see below (Table 9.5), if the proportion favorable to the revolution among the few prerevolutionary unemployed of this generation is compared to the proportion favorable among the unemployed of the other generations, the intergenerational differences are significantly reduced.

The impact of the anti-Batista struggle on the workers of the generation of '53 has made it the generational base of the revolution. Peculiar to the decisive experiences which shaped it, moreover, is the fact that in a significant sense it was, indeed, their generation which brought the Revolutionary Government to power. The very leaders of the revolution it-

[23] The historical events I have postulated as being of decisive political significance in the formation of different political generations were probably significant for the Cuban population as a whole. In particular, however, it is the impact of these events on different *working-class generations* which most concerns us theoretically. Therefore, we should expect the generational relationships to be even clearer if we look only at those workers in our sample who *were workers before the revolution*, while excluding those who have come into the working class since the revolution. Our findings confirm this hypothesis and it is true throughout our analysis.

self, it will be remembered, those who led the *resistencia* and were the rebel cadre in the hills and cities, are members of the generation of '53. Thus, members of this generation were subject not only to the general influences of this period, but also to the specific impact on them of the fact that their peers formed the leadership and cadre of the 26th of July movement. Put differently, in accordance with the hypothesis of political generations, the fact that the members of this generation acquired their political frame of reference in the course of the anti-Batista struggle should have made them more likely than members of other generations to support the revolution now, *regardless of the generation to which the rebel leaders themselves belonged*. That, indeed, the rebels *were* predominantly of their own generation may, therefore, have been an additional source of their support for and identification with the rebels and their cause. It may be surmised that the rebels became, in a significant sense, collectively the reference group of that entire generation, and the chief rebel leaders its foremost culture heroes.[24] That the rebel leaders also couched much of their program in generational terms may also have considerably increased the likelihood that the members of the generation of '53 would identify with them. In turn, this act of identification may itself have reinforced the attitudes which this generation was developing in response to the set of stimuli created by the historical situation.[25]

[24] Technically, "reference individuals." As Robert Merton conceptualizes it, "Emulation of a peer, a parent, or a public figure may be restricted to limited segments of their behavior and values and this can be usefully described as adoption of a role model. Or, emulation may be extended to a wider array of behavior and values of these persons who can then be described as reference individuals." *Social Theory and Social Structure* (Glencoe, Ill.: The Free Press, 1959), p. 303.

[25] The process of identification may be likened—although it is by no means entirely parallel—to the act of identification which may occur in racial, ethnic, or religious minorities when certain of their members become outstanding public figures either because of indi-

If our assumption is correct that identification with the members of their generation who were actively participating in and leading the rebel movement, was one more element in the complex of elements comprising the distinct politically relevant experiences of the generation of '53, then, at the very least, we should expect a similar identification in the present. Therefore, the question is, are members of the generation of '53 more likely than the members of the other political generations to identify with the leaders of the revo-

vidual "success" or as leaders of a social movement based on that group. As Norman Ryder has pointed out, the cohort, or generation, "conceptually . . . resembles most closely the ethnic group: membership is determined at birth, and often has considerable capacity to explain variance, but need not imply that the category is an organized group." ("The Cohort as a Concept in the Study of Social Change," p. 847.) Yet there is this fundamental difference, especially in the present analytical context, and that is that "members" of a cohort, or generation, do not have the "visibility" of an ethnic group that makes them distinctly recognizable as "one of your own kind." This raises the question, therefore, as to whether or not, and if so, why, individuals are more likely to choose "public figures" as reference individuals who are in their own age cohort than public figures who are not and, conversely, whether or not individuals who are not in the same age cohort as a given "public figure" are less likely to identify with him than individuals who are in the same cohort. Our assumption here is that there is a tendency for reference individuals to be chosen from one's own age cohort. This is warranted as a working assumption on (1) the general sociological grounds that "identification with groups and with individuals occupying," as Merton puts it, "designated statuses does not occur at random but tends to be patterned by the environing structure of social relationships and by prevailing cultural definitions." (*Social Theory and Social Structure*, p. 302.) Peer emulation, of course, is also held in sociological theory to be one of the more significant socialization agencies; (2) this assumption is warranted also on the general psychological grounds that "other things being equal, it seems that we identify ourselves most readily with those perceived to be like ourselves (or like our self-ideal). The bases of the perceived similarity may be many kinds—sex, *age*, group membership, skin color, etc." (David Krech and Richard S. Crutchfield, *Elements of Psychology* [New York: Alfred Knopf, 1958], p. 214. [My italics]) In any case, relevant evidence concerning this question, so far as this study is concerned, is presented below.

lution—at least so far as to perceive them as reference individuals?

Using the question "Aside from personal friends or relatives—of all the people you hear or read about—could you name three individuals whom you admire very much?" as a rough, empirical indicator (sufficiently precise to differentiate sub-groups from each other), we found that the generation of '53 *is* distinct in this regard.[26] Its members were more likely than those of other generations to name a revolutionary leader (Fidel Castro, Raul Castro, "Ché" Guevara, Juan Almeida, etc.) as at least one of the three individuals whom they admire greatly (Table 9.3).

That the political generations vary in their response to the revolution in accordance with their historical location in prerevolutionary Cuba suggests also that they should have varied in their prerevolutionary political orientations as well. The political strength of the Communists in the working class, for instance, was significantly different in the critical periods which formed the political generations. We might, therefore, predict that the workers varied in their attitudes toward the Communists before the revolution in accordance with the role of the Communists during the workers' common youthful experience in the labor movement. If the Communists were then a significant independent political force, then the workers of that generation should have been more likely to support the Communists before the revolution than workers in political generations whose youthful experience in the labor movement came during a period of Communist weakness or irrelevance.

Comparison of their prerevolutionary attitudes toward the Communists indicates that the political generations did view the Communists in expectedly different ways (Table 9.4). That is, the two generations with the highest proportion of

[26] This question was borrowed from the study then in progress by Gabriel Almond and Sidney Verba, *Civic Culture* (Princeton: Princeton University Press, 1963), and I gratefully acknowledge my use of it.

TABLE 9.3

Political Generation and Reference Individuals[a]

AGE CATEGORY AT TIME OF STUDY (1962)	PROPORTION NAMING AT LEAST ONE REFERENCE INDIVIDUAL WHO IS A						
	Cuban revolutionary leader[b]	*Communist political figure*[c]	*Cuban hero or martyr*[d]	*Popular celebrity*[e]	*High culture figure*[f]	*Anti-Castro political figure*[g]	*(N)*
21-27	55	11	11	17	25	8	(36)
28-35	78	18	12	14	18	2	(51)
36-43	55	14	13	9	22	2	(51)
44-51	54	19	4	23	13	4	(26)
52-59	57	4	9	4	22	13	(23)

[a] Percentages do not total 100 because three responses were required. Categories in which no more than 10 percent of any generation named a reference individual are excluded from this table.

[b] "Fidelistas" or "new Communists."

[c] Cuban PSP leaders ("old Communists") or international Communist figures; *e.g.*, Mao, Khrushchev, Lenin, Ho Chi Minh.

[d] Historic heroes or martyrs such as José Martí, Máximo Gómez, Antonio Maceo, Antonio Guiteras, or martyrs of the anti-Batista struggle such as Frank País, José Antonio Echevarría.

[e] Athletes, movie stars, radio and TV entertainers, etc.

[f] Scientists, novelists, artists, philosophers, poets, etc.

[g] Counterrevolutionary leaders such as Carlos Prío Socarras, José Miro Cardona, Manuel Urrutia, or political figures such as Presidents Kennedy and Eisenhower, or Allen Dulles.

workers who were sympathetic to the Communists before the revolution are those that were formed, respectively, during the anti-Machado struggles and the abortive revolution of the thirties in which the Communists played a leading political role, and when the Communists were dominant in the leadership of the CTC. Moreover, despite the fact that the workers of the generation of '53 might be expected, since their generation is disproportionately favorable to the revolution, to retrospectively "recall" favorable attitudes toward the Communists in the prerevolutionary period, their generation scarcely differs in this respect from the generation

TABLE 9.4

Prerevolutionary Attitude toward Communists, by
Political Generation

AGE CATEGORY AT TIME OF STUDY (1962)[a]	FRIENDLY OR SUPPORTER	INDIFFERENT	HOSTILE	(N)
28-35	29%	43%	27%	(51)
36-43	29	35	35	(51)
44-51	38	38	23	(26)
52-59	39	39	22	(23)

[a] The youngest generation of workers (21-27 in 1962) is excluded from this table since the question about their prerevolutionary attitudes toward the Communists refers to an attitude held before they were adults.

of republican stability. The latter, however, has a higher proportion of workers who were hostile to the Communists, in fact, the highest proportion of all generations. It was during the republican interregnum that the Communists were at their weakest level in the working class (especially among the economically secure workers, as we shall see below). During this period, they were purged from official leadership of the CTC, and the workers who entered the labor movement at this time were therefore less likely than other workers to develop pro-Communist political orientations. As for the attitudes of the members of the '53 generation toward the Communists before the revolution, there are good historical reasons why they should have been, at best, ambivalent about the Communists. Fidel's leadership of the assault on Moncada was denounced by the Communists as a bourgeois romantic and "putschist" adventure,[27] and throughout the guerrilla war against Batista—until it entered its last months —the Communists' official attitude was equivocal. As late as May 1958 the Communists were still referring to the 26th of July movement as "those who count on terroristic acts and

[27] The *Daily Worker*, August 10, 1953, p. 2.

conspiratorial coups as the chief means of ousting Batista," although they described the movement as the "most militant and progressive sector of the non-Communist opposition."[28] In the unsuccessful April 9, 1958 attempt at a general strike the Communist leadership—though not opposing it—declared that the movement did not have enough support to succeed; this statement, circulated by Batista, was construed by the 26th of July movement as detrimental to the strike effort. As late as June 28, 1958, when the guerrilla war had reached a high point, the Communists had not reconciled themselves fully to the necessity for armed struggle, and a declaration of the party's National Committee called for "clean, democratic elections" to eliminate Batista.[29] The fact is, the Communists, despite the influence they still retained among the workers, were the tail end of the anti-Batista struggle, with the unquestioned leadership of the struggle residing with the 26th of July movement. Thus it is understandable that members of this generation of '53 were no more likely than the generation of the republic to view the Communists favorably. (This interpretation gains further credence from other findings to be presented below.)

So far, our analysis of the political generations has treated them in terms of their members' common location in the historical dimension of the social process. From this standpoint, the common politically relevant experiences of their members have, taken as a whole, differentiated the political generations from each other and produced intergenerational differences in political attitudes consistent with our understanding of their historical location. It is clear, however, that the generations are themselves internally differentiated by structural factors, and that individuals of the same generation sharing different locations in the social structure will have

[28] Quoted in the *Daily Worker*, May 4, 1958, p. 6.
[29] See the author's dissertation, "Working Class Politics in Cuba," pp. 92ff.

experienced the politically relevant events of their youth differently.

As Bennet Berger has put it: "The temporal location of a [generational] group must first be kept analytically distinct from its structural location; second, when considering them together, we should be aware that the impact of structural (e.g., occupational) factors on the nature of the temporal location may, under some conditions, be such as to fragment the cultural 'unity' of a generation beyond recognition. . . ."[30]

Now one of the most significant structural determinants of the Cuban workers' differential response to the revolution, it will be remembered, was their prerevolutionary employment status. It is, therefore, important to consider the impact of their prerevolutionary employment status on the workers of different political generations. Our findings in this regard are quite interesting (Table 9.5). As we might expect, within every political generation the workers who were unemployed and underemployed are more likely to support the revolution than those who were regularly employed before the revolution.

Moreover, both among the unemployed workers and the regularly employed, the generation of '53 exceeds the other generations in the proportion of revolutionary workers; among the employed workers it is the generation of the thirties which is second to the generation of '53, as we should expect. Among the unemployed workers, however, the generation of the republican interregnum has as great a proportion of revolutionary workers as does the generation of the thirties. Here is a particularly instructive instance of how the

[30] "How Long is a Generation," p. 16. Cf. also, "In the comparison of different age groups in the *aggregate*, or the same age groups at different historical periods in the *aggregate*, any differences that appear to be generational may simply be *artifacts* of the different social composition of the groups. . . . In principle, this can be solved by the introduction of certain controls or matchings, but it may often be neglected in practice." Hyman, *Political Socialization*, p. 130.

TABLE 9.5

Political Attitudes, by Political Generation and Prerevolutionary
Employment[a]

AGE CATEGORY AT TIME OF STUDY (1962)	UNDER- AND UNEMPLOYED[d] PERCENTAGE			REGULARLY EMPLOYED SUPPORTING		
	Revolu- tion	Commu- nists	(N)	Revolu- tion	Commu- nists	(N)
21-27[b]	75%	—%	(8)	42%	—%	(12)
28-35	100	31	(22)	85	35	(20)
36-43	81	41	(21)	43	17	(23)
44 plus[c]	82	64	(11)	68	39	(31)

[a] Those who were not workers before the revolution are excluded from this table, so that the relationship between political generation and the structural factor of unemployment is not "contaminated."

[b] See note a, Table 9.4 of this chapter.

[c] This category combines the generations of the second Machado regime and the first Batista regime, and is referred to in this chapter as the "generation of the thirties."

[d] "Under- and unemployed" refers to workers who worked, on the average, nine months or less per year before the revolution, while "regularly employed" refers to those who worked 10 months or more.

same generational members, located differently in the social structure, are differently affected by historical events. The relative stability, prosperity, and political democracy of the republican interregnum left the problem of unemployment and underemployment untouched. These proved, from the perspective of the unemployed workers, to be irrelevant to their situation and may indeed (as our evidence seems to indicate) have inclined them toward radical solutions to their problems (even more than their unemployment may otherwise have done). This interpretation is supported further by our findings concerning the differential effects of unemployment on the prerevolutionary attitudes of the workers toward the Communists in the different generations.

As Table 9.5 indicates, among unemployed workers, those in the generation of the republican interregnum were second only to the generation of the thirties in their prerevolutionary support of the Communists. Also consistent with our findings on aggregate generational differences in prerevolutionary attitudes toward the Communists, it is the generation of the thirties, both among the employed and unemployed, which had the greatest proportion of prerevolutionary Communist sympathizers.

Looking at the relationships differently, it might be expected that since the unemployed were generally more likely to support the Communists before the revolution, this would also be true in each political generation. In fact, this is true in every political generation *but one*. In the generation of '53, unemployed workers were *not* more likely than their employed peers to sympathize with the Communists. In view of the experiences of the different political generations with the Communists, however, as we pointed out earlier, this finding makes more sense than had the unemployed of this generation, indeed, been more likely to support the Communists than the employed. The most significant radical movement on the contemporary scene for the generation of '53, the movement possessing the political initiative and clearly leading the anti-Batista struggle of that period, was not the Communist but the 26th of July. There is little reason, then, why the unemployed *of this generation* should have been more responsive to the Communists than were their employed peers. Not only were the *Fidelistas* leading the anti-Batista struggle, but the content of their agitation among the workers was also radical in social content, and perhaps even more radical than the agitation of the Communists who continued to counsel moderation for so long.

Indeed, we already know that the unemployed of this generation of '53 are more likely to support the revolution than the employed workers, though they were not more likely to support the Communists before the revolution.

Finally, it is important to note that it is among the regularly employed workers that the relationships between generations most closely approximate those found when the generations are viewed as a whole. This is especially worthy of emphasis, since it is where unemployment (which tended to override the effects of their historical experiences) is absent that the generational relationships we predicted from knowledge of Cuban history are strongest and clearest. Thus, for instance, among the employed workers of the generation of the republican interregnum, whose historical experiences were not "contaminated" by unemployment (thus providing another basis for radicalism), the ideology developed under the impact of the republican experience became operative. Our findings are therefore consistent with the view that ideology will have its greatest importance precisely among the workers who "objectively" have the least to gain from revolutionary politics.

Conclusions

Not only does comparison of the political generations in the aggregate reveal significant political differences between them in accord with hypotheses based on the concept of political generations, but comparisons of intrageneration subgroups are also in accord with those hypotheses.

The general theoretical significance of our findings lies, first, in their demonstration of the analytic utility of formulating specific hypotheses in terms of the concept of political generations. It may, indeed, be correct, as Herbert Hyman has argued, that the "generic process of learning of politics" does not include generational influence, and that "susceptibility to this influence may not be universal or may be constrained in many cases by other factors."[31] However, this hardly merits relegation of the concept to the conceptual dustbin, as is implied in Hyman's otherwise incisive and valuable discussion.[32] In fact, of course, it is precisely one task of

[31] *Political Socialization*, p. 124.

[32] *Ibid*. Hyman repeatedly refers to the concept of generation as "doctrine," saying, for example, "the doctrine must be regarded in a

sociological inquiry to discover under what conditions a particular type of social determinant may or may not be operative, and to modify theory appropriately. The fact that some
simple nonliterate societies do not have social classes, for instance, and that therefore "susceptibility to this influence
may not be universal," hardly merits discarding the concept
of social class. On the contrary, such empirical findings lead
to further conceptual and theoretical development. Failure
to use the generation concept because its empirical demonstration is difficult is detrimental to the analysis of political
behavior. It is especially important from a theoretical standpoint to analyze the effects of generations in societies characterized by comparatively greater social instability and internal
conflict than the advanced industrial societies of the West.
Until now, it is only in the latter societies that the few
empirical studies utilizing the concept (whether implicitly
or explicitly) have been done. This is important not only
because of the necessary comparative perspective on generational politics such studies could provide, but also because
generational politics seem to be most associated with differences in social stability during the period in which the
different generations came of age.[33] Thus our findings, based
as they are on interviews with workers now living through a
social revolution in a country whose history has been marked
by social and political instability, are of particular theoretical
interest.

Second, our findings and the demonstration of the utility
of the concept of political generation impinge indirectly on
the issue of the relevance of "history" to sociological analysis
and theory. The very concept itself is a statement of the

---

modest light"; the evidence "patently argues against the general significance of the doctrine"; and "the empirical demonstration of the doctrine is attended by great difficulty."

[33] Lipset, *Political Man*, p. 267; Richard Centers, *The Psychology
of Social Classes* (Princeton, N.J.: Princeton University Press, 1949),
p. 168; Hamilton, *Affluence and the French Worker*, Chapter VI.

hypothesis that social processes, relationships, norms, and values are often inexplicable without reference to the events of the past, and that analyses limited to consideration only of contemporary relationships may be deficient in significant ways.

Third, to the extent to which the concept attempts to link up behavior and character with *non*institutionalized but historically significant forms of social interaction, our findings impinge also on social psychological theory. That is, such decisively relevant experiences as may be included under the rubric of "historically significant events" (*e.g.*, major political issues, concrete internal struggles, general social conditions) may or may not themselves have significant consequences for the social structure and, therefore, for the character, norms, and values of the men selected and formed within it. But these very events may have independent psychological effects on their participants, aside from their institutional consequences.

"The historical and structural features of modern society," as Hans Gerth and C. Wright Mills have said, "must be connected with the most intimate features of man's self. That is what social psychology is all about. And that, we think, cannot be done by dealing only in microscopic observations."[34] That the historical and structural features of the society in which they came to manhood played a significant role in the formation of the political identities of succeeding generations of Cuban workers (their political allegiances and norms and their response to the revolution) is, of course, precisely the point of this chapter.

[34] *Character and Social Structure* (New York: Harcourt, Brace, 1953), p. xix. See also Anselm Strauss, *Mirrors and Masks: The Search for Identity* (Glencoe, Ill.: The Free Press, 1959), p. 164.

CHAPTER 10

Revolutionary Workers and Individual Liberties

✍ RADICALS and socialists typically have emphasized the democratic potential of the working class, its anti-elitism and egalitarian values, and its solidarity with other exploited and oppressed classes elsewhere. They have looked forward to the "conquest of power" by the workers as the first phase in the realization of "that democratic programme for which the bourgeoisie once stood. . . . As the lowest of all classes, [the working class] is also *the most democratic* of all classes." Once in power, the workers "would extend universal suffrage to every individual and establish complete freedom of press and assemblage."[1] To Friedrich Engels, the Paris Commune, born in working-class revolution and based on the armed might of the workers, was a genuine political democracy characterized as it was by universal suffrage, the right of recall of all public officials, the limitation of the salaries of officials to the amount earned in wages by the workers, and binding mandates on all delegates in the governing representative bodies of the Commune—all procedures instituted by the workers themselves. "Do you want to know," he asked, "what [the dictatorship of the proletariat] looks like? Look at the Paris Commune. That was the Dictatorship of the Proletariat."[2]

In contrast, a recurrent theme in the essentially conservative and antidemocratic ideology of the upper and middle classes and their spokesmen, has been the characterization of the workers as barbaric, impulsive, anticulture, childlike, lacking in the capacity for reason and judgment, and requiring the discipline and guidance of their "betters" in matters of

[1] Karl Kautsky, *The Social Revolution* (Charles H. Kerr and Co., 1903), pp. 107-108. (My italics)

[2] Introduction by Engels to Karl Marx, *The Civil War in France* (Moscow: Foreign Languages Publishing House, 1952), pp. 27-29.

government. In different periods this view has taken different forms and been expressed in different ideological guises.[3] Characterizations of the workers in these terms had become so frequent and vocal in intellectual circles half a century ago, that Karl Kautsky was moved to exclaim that "the proletariat which will . . . make its own laws [once coming to power] has a much stronger instinct for freedom than any of the servile and pedantic professors who are crying about the prisonlike character of the future state."[4]

In recent years, this negative image of the working class has again gained advocates and adherents—this time among "intellectuals of the democratic left who *once* believed the proletariat necessarily to be a force for liberty, racial equality, and social progress."[5] Lewis Feuer, a prominent academic philosopher, has argued that "the masses" have been *the most consistently anti-intellectual force in society. . . .* It was the American lower classes, not the upper, who gave their overwhelming support to the attacks in recent years on civil liberties. It is among the working people that one finds dominant those sects and churches most hostile to the free spirit."[6] In the writings on "mass culture" occasionally explicit and often implicit identification of "masses" and "working class" is made, and the impoverished commercial culture is explained by its alleged audience base in the lower

[3] In Reinhard Bendix's excellent study of changing ideological justifications for class rule, or what he calls "ideologies of management which seek to justify the subordination of large masses of men to the discipline of factory work and to the authority of employers," *Work and Authority in Industry* (New York: John Wiley and Sons, 1956), sufficient evidence to support this statement appears throughout.

[4] *The Social Revolution*, pp. 124-25.

[5] The words are Seymour Martin Lipset's in his *Political Man* (Garden City, N.Y.: 1960), p. 97. (My italics)

[6] Introduction to *Marx and Engels: Basic Writings on Politics and Philosophy* (Garden City, N.Y.: Anchor Books, 1959), pp. xv-xvi. (My italics)

classes.[7] Samuel Stouffer and Seymour Martin Lipset have adduced quantitative evidence allegedly demonstrating the "authoritarian" propensities of the working class.[8] Among the qualities of working-class life and culture which "are part of the complex psychological basis of authoritarianism," says Lipset, are

> greater suggestibility, absence of a sense of past and future (lack of a prolonged time perspective), inability to take a complex view, greater difficulty in abstracting from concrete experience, and lack of imagination (inner "reworking" of experience). . . .[9]

[7] See the various articles collected in *Mass Culture*, ed. Bernard Rosenberg and David M. White (Glencoe, Ill.: The Free Press, 1957); and especially the article by Ernest van den Haag, "Of Happiness and Despair We Have No Measure."

[8] Samuel A. Stouffer, *Communism, Conformity, and Civil Liberties* (Garden City, N.Y.: Doubleday and Co., 1955); Lipset, *Political Man*, chapter entitled "Working-Class Authoritarianism." This chapter (which appeared originally as an article in the *American Sociological Review*, xxiv [1959], 482-502) has provoked a great deal of discussion and controversy and stimulated new research; it is probably the single most important contemporary statement and attempted documentation of the thesis that the working class is politically authoritarian. It is for this reason that I focus on it here.

[9] *Political Man*, p. 115. If, with the exception perhaps of his charging the workers with "lack of imagination," this *sounds* like a description of *children* rather than of workers, Lipset is quite willing to make this comparison of children and the working class *explicit*. A few pages later (p. 121) in a note to a similar description of the workers, as he sees them, Lipset says: "Most of these characteristics have been mentioned by child psychologists as typical of adolescent attitudes and perspectives." Thus the view Lipset has put forth in sociological language has long roots, reaching into the late seventeenth century view that "the poor were children, they must be disciplined, they must be guided, and on occasion they might be indulged," as Bendix describes it in *Work and Authority*, p. 61. Lipset's elitist view of the workers as childlike and unable to "take a complex view" of politics also leads him to believe that the workers need not be a threat to democracy, if they receive the *proper guidance* from his fellow "intellectuals of the democratic Left." As he says: "The Western labor and socialist movement has incorporated [democratic] values

Given these qualities, says Lipset, it is evident why "extremist and intolerant movements in modern society are more likely to be based on the lower classes than on the middle classes."[10] "No other party," he states, "has been as thoroughly and completely the party of the working class and the poor," as has the Communist Party; and yet, "the threat to freedom posed by the Communist movement is as great as that once posed by Fascism and Nazism."[11] What, then, would happen to "freedom" if a revolution should come to power based upon the working classes?—indeed, a revolution not only based upon the support of the workers but also led by men who, in the very thick of internal class conflict and nationalist confrontation with the power formerly dominant in their country, proclaimed themselves to be "Marxist-Leninists," and called for unity with the existing Communist Party, as happened in Cuba?

This article is about the attitudes of Cuban revolutionary workers toward civil liberties for opponents of the revolution. It contributes, therefore, both to the recent discussions among social scientists of so-called working-class authoritarianism and to the long historic debate to which this question is heir, namely, the consequences of working-class emancipation and political power.

---

into its general ideology. But the fact that the movement's ideology is democratic *does not mean that its [working-class] supporters actually understand its implications.* The evidence seems to indicate that understanding of and adherence to these norms are highest among leaders and lowest among followers. *The general opinions or predispositions of the rank and file are relatively unimportant in predicting behavior as long as the organization to which they are loyal continues to act democratically.* In spite of the workers' greater authoritarian propensity, their organizations which are anti-Communist still function as better defenders and carriers of democratic values than parties based on the middle class." (My italics) As long, in other words, as the workers are loyal to and willing to be guided by their betters, rather than following their own opinions or predispositions, democracy will not be in danger!

[10] *Ibid.*, p. 97. [11] *Ibid.*, p. 99.

A test of the thesis of working-class authoritarianism based on interviews with revolutionary workers in a country where there is a socialist revolution underway led by self-proclaimed "Marxist-Leninists" is of unique theoretical importance because proponents of the thesis assert or implicitly assume that: (a) working-class existence under capitalism tends to create a "complex psychological basis" for authoritarianism; (b) workers, therefore, tend to be "hostile to the free spirit," intolerant of social or political dissenters, and opposed to allowing them individual liberties; (c) workers tend to support "extremist" or revolutionary or Communist movements because such movements' immoderation, rigidity, and "lack of democracy" are especially appealing to them; and (d) revolutionary or Communist workers, therefore, are a special "threat to freedom."

Cuba provides us with a unique opportunity to test these assumptions and assertions, and to demonstrate how little they are founded on valid evidence. Here is Cuba in the summer of 1962 when we interviewed the workers for this study —a Cuba in the midst of revolution, a Cuba but one year away from repelling a major counterrevolutionary invasion attempt, a Cuba mobilized, propagandized, and ready for another invasion, a Cuba under arms, and in which hundreds of thousands of citizens (and 55 percent of the workers in our sample) were in the militia, a Cuba in which there was a widespread anticipation and fear of another invasion, a Cuba, in other words, in which one would hardly expect revolutionary workers to accept dissent, free speech, and public criticism of the Revolutionary Government—especially if workers are, as if by nature, supposed to be "authoritarian."

We shall see that it is an individual's relative political involvement and level of education that determines the likelihood of his being politically "authoritarian," not the fact that he is a worker or has grown up in the working class, or even that he is a Communist or revolutionary worker.

Revolutionary Workers and Individual Liberties

We asked each of the workers in our sample, about mid-way through the interview, "What do you think should be done to an individual who publicly criticizes the government or the revolution?" What, in other words, did he think of free speech for dissenters and critics of the revolution? Would the workers tolerate it, or would the "deep-rooted hostilities" (Lipset's phrase) that the workers might have been expected to develop as members of an oppressed and exploited class in prerevolutionary Cuba be expressed in "political authoritarianism?"

There were, indeed, only a minority of revolutionary workers (27 percent) who said that criticism of the revolution ought not to be tolerated by the government. Many saw the revolution's critics as class enemies: "This person who criticizes [the revolution] would have to be someone who was in the privileged class before," a sugar worker asserted, "and the government must take measures against his kind." A chemicals worker who had worked in the sugar fields before the revolution said: "Such an individual should ask the pardon of 'Nuestro Señor' [the Lord] and be sent to work sowing *malanga*, because there is no reason to criticize. I have always lived by my hands, so I cannot criticize. Only those who have never worked can [criticize]." "Well, simply," a skilled electrical worker said, "any revolutionary could discuss with this individual the reasons for his discontent with the revolution, and if he persists and expresses himself publicly in the extreme, in terms even more aggravated and disrespectful, he should be interrogated by the revolutionary police. Indeed, as is known, such persons who regularly express themselves in forms so depreciative of the revolution must have been exploiters of the people—and for that reason cannot be allowed to return to exploit us again. Nothing unjust should be done to anyone of course, as they did under the tyranny, when revolutionaries were tortured and assassinated." A leather worker saw the question of free speech and criticism directly in terms of class justice. "If he's a *worker*," he said, "then you must try to convince him and bring him over to our side. He is simply confused. If he's a *capitalist*, send him out of our country. We are in the process of liberation. We, the workers, are responsible for pushing the work of the government forward, and are struggling for our rights."

Some workers thought it was a simple question of right or wrong, having nothing to do with personal judgment or differences of opinion: "If what he says is correct," as one told us, "fine, it would have to be taken care of. But if he's wrong, he must be punished." A worker in a chemicals plant thought that an attempt should be made "to give him counsel and advice, first, and a chance to correct himself. People should try to convince him of his errors, but then, if necessary, he may have to be put in prison for a while."

"It is a question for the tribunals to handle and the judges to decide," said a sugar worker, "they will know what to do with him." A few workers (exactly four of the 142 revolutionary workers) demanded the death penalty. One, a Nicaro nickel worker, volunteered to be the executioner: "I myself would kill whoever spoke against the revolution." A worker in the Uruguay sugar central was somewhat more generous, saying that "first, you try to convince him. But if you can't convince him, you shoot him, no?"

The vast majority (73 percent) of the revolutionary workers, however, clearly and without hesitation told us, as did a miner, that the "revolution must be generous to our enemies. This is a free revolution, and he should be counseled, but no more." "Only if he actually acts against the revolution," a cigar worker declared emphatically, "should something be done to him. *Never for merely expressing his opinions.* All speech is free—but," and here his tone changed "if he tries to do something more, to *act* against the revolution, he must be taken before the tribunals, and be judged, and have a penalty imposed on him as the case requires. Those that try something *militarily* against the government,

I think, should be shot." A cement worker said essentially the same thing in different words, echoing what most of the revolutionary workers thought: "Nothing [should be done to him]. After all, he has his criteria, I have mine. Nothing should be done to them for talking: if they bomb or sabotage or kill, of course, we must act against them. But as to speech itself, I speak with people who are against the revolution all the time and they are free to do so." Some workers expressed the same idea, but with a bit of a wry humorous twist, as the sugar worker who told us that "this fellow who criticizes the revolution is probably illiterate, and has no consciousness of what the revolution has done for him and for all of us. I would suggest to him that he watch television so that he can learn about what is really happening." "We would think," said another worker," that this guy must be missing something in his head, and just leave him alone." The tolerance of others came from their confidence in the strength of the revolution: "Nothing should be done to stop criticism," said a paper mill worker, "because for everyone who speaks against the revolution, there are ninety-nine who will defend it. *Teach* him, he is not functioning too well intellectually. Otherwise, let him alone." An electrical worker said it differently: "The majority of the people, of course, are with the revolution, and nobody would even bother to listen to his lies, so why bother with him? Someone might try to clarify his problems for him. Nothing more." " 'Look, *chico*,' I'd say," said a brewery worker, " 'this revolution is correct. Its laws are for the working class.' That's what I usually tell them. I discuss things with many *compañeros* who don't agree with the revolution, who don't sympathize with it, and try to convince them. But nothing more than that. They don't convince me either." Another worker summed up the general view of the revolutionary workers in these quiet words: "Nothing happens, and nothing should happen to those who do no more than *speak out* freely against the revolution—for we now live in a time that is completely different from the past."

What kind of revolutionary workers, then, were more likely, what kind less likely, to oppose free speech for the revolution's critics?

We simply separated the revolutionary workers into two groups: those who clearly affirmed the right of free speech for opponents of the revolution, and those who either clearly wanted this right *denied* opponents of the revolution or who seemed to have some doubts about it, and called the first group of workers "Libertarian," and the second "Authoritarian." A worker who *opposed* the revolution, of course, would want free speech for himself and the revolution's other opponents, but this would in no way indicate whether or not he was, indeed, committed to free speech *as* free speech. A revolutionary worker, in contrast, who is both committed to the revolution, and also affirms the Cuban citizen's right to freely speak out *against* the revolution without any government interference or punishment, seems to be worthy of the name "Libertarian."

Education

An outstanding political sociologist has assured us that "the findings of public opinion surveys in thirteen different countries [indicate] that the lower strata are less committed to democratic norms than the middle classes"; but these are essentially *unanalyzed* "findings," without an attempt to control for variables which might be *associated* with but *not integral* to the working-class situation, such as, for example, differential formal education. We know that where education is controlled, differences between workers and others tend to disappear, and "the increases in tolerance associated with higher educational level are higher than those related to higher occupational level." Moreover, although he assures us that "the evidence from various American studies is also clear and consistent—the lower strata are the least tolerant,"[12] recent reanalyses of opinion surveys in the

12 *Ibid.*, pp. 109 and 103.

United States in the 1950s seriously contradict his claim. Lewis Lipsitz found, for example, that (*a*) different indices of so-called authoritarianism give quite different results, and most important that (*b*) the relatively greater authoritarianism of the workers

> as opposed to the middle class, appears to be largely a product of lower education. *With education controlled,* middle-class individuals who were surveyed in the 1950s are *not* consistently less authoritarian than working-class individuals. A comparison of those in both strata with high school education or less reveals that *workers tend to be less authoritarian on questions more closely related to politics.*[13]

The direct relationship between formal education and people's attitudes toward dissent and free speech has been documented by a number of studies. These have been done, however, in relatively stable political contexts and in countries in which the right of dissent has been more or less institutionalized and/or protected by law or custom. Cuba before the revolution certainly was not such a society, though some dissent was tolerated by the regime, as long as it remained unorganized and ineffective, and was not voiced either too consistently or too daringly. Censorship of newspapers, intimidation and bribery of publishers and editors, arrest and imprisonment, even torture and murder, of political opponents was common under prerevolutionary regimes; and even the interval of somewhat democratic government from 1944 to 1952 was not free of such practices. Violence was the stuff of prerevolutionary political life. The right of dissent allegedly protected by the 1940 Constitution

[13] "Working-Class Authoritarianism: A Re-evaluation," *American Sociological Review*, xxx (February 1965), 109. (My italics) See also Richard F. Hamilton, "Working Class Authoritarianism," *Papers of the XVIII World Congress of Psychology* (Moscow, 1966).

had little meaning in real life. The very word "democracy" was itself sullied by the lip service paid it by dictators and corrupt politicians, and democracy was often denounced from all sides "as a system giving power to the rich and riches to the powerful," but nothing but misery to the people. One common premise of the political beliefs of right and left, therefore, reportedly was "the need for government-imposed order [which] justified a disregard of constitutional procedures and the use of violence in the struggle for power. . . ."[14] Under these circumstances, there is reason to doubt that democratic norms were deeply imbedded in the political culture of the working class (or of any other class) in prerevolutionary Cuba. As to the role of the educational system in the inculcation of politically relevant values, the private school curricula were heavily laden with the anti-rationalist values of revealed truth, and the free public education received by the workers was in general of very poor quality, whatever the formal grade they achieved. Thus the extent to which formal education served to broaden the individual's perspective and increase his respect for other's views and his tolerance of ideological diversity is questionable.

If the prerevolutionary heritage of the workers makes difficult any prediction of what effect differential education might have on the holding of libertarian attitudes, so too does the very situation which the revolutionary workers were living through—one in which nationalist sentiment, class consciousness, political passion and ideology might be expected to cut across educational lines and, so to speak, collapse any attitude differences that might otherwise have resulted from differences in education. Some of the most sophisticated and educated workers might very well also be the most

[14] Wyatt MacGaffey and Clifford Barnett, *Twentieth Century Cuba* (Garden City, N.Y., 1965), pp. 147-48.

passionate ideologues, ready to defend the suppression of free speech and dissent as necessary concomitants of the making of a revolution. It was, after all, not uneducated workers but often university-educated intellectuals who gave the world the extensive rationalizations and justifications for authoritarian rule that we have become familiar with under the governments of some newly independent countries and revolutionary regimes.

Education, moreover, can encourage individuals not only to recognize the need for diversity but also to understand (or to make themselves think they understand) the complex needs of a country in revolution. Many such individuals, therefore, whose formal education might otherwise dispose them to libertarian values, might be precisely the ones whose political "education" has also convinced them that economic development is not possible while allowing the full play of dissent—which, they believe, might dissipate national energies and impede the purpose of social reconstruction. Dictatorship may very well be seen as an indispensable phase of development during which institutions are created that will then make possible the establishment of a viable political democracy. By no means is this simply an ideological conception emanating from the so-called totalitarian Left. In their recent study, *The Civic Culture*, for example, Gabriel Almond and Sidney Verba have written,

> The resources available to the elites of the new nations are scarce, and there are limits on the capacities of these societies to assimilate these resources rapidly and effectively. Other goals compete for the same resources. *We cannot properly sit in judgment of those leaders who concentrate their resources on the development of social overhead capital, industrialization, and agricultural improvement, and who suppress disruptive movements or fail to cultivate democratic tendencies.* . . . Few Western states-

men have ever been called upon to cope with such a range of issues and choices all at once.[15]

There is ample reason to believe, then, that in the midst of a social revolution in an underdeveloped country that has never had an established democratic tradition, the "typical" or "normal" relationship between formal education and political tolerance found in comparatively stable political democracies might be upset.

The fact is, however, that whatever may have been the effect of the various factors discussed, the formal education of the workers is quite clearly related to the likelihood of their denying the right of free speech to critics of the revolution (Table 10.1). The revolutionary workers with the least education are the least likely to be "libertarian." This seems to be a rather striking confirmation of the importance of education in fostering civil libertarian attitudes—since even "when the chips were down" in a revolutionary situation the revolutionary workers most willing to grant their opponents the right to express themselves about the revolution without hindrance were the most educated ones.

TABLE 10.1

Formal Education and Libertarianism among
Revolutionary Workers[a]

GRADE COMPLETED IN SCHOOL	LIBERTARIAN	(N)
None	30%	(10)
1-3	62	(34)
4-6	81	(68)
7 or more	82	(28)

[a] Two workers who "didn't remember" what grade they had completed are excluded from this and Tables 10.3 and 10.4.

[15] (Princeton: Princeton University Press, 1963), p. 504. (My italics)

Political Interest

One assumption often made in the interpretation of the education-political tolerance relationship is that the less educated are less exposed to and less involved in the cross-currents of debate and clash of viewpoints that is more typical of the more educated and are, therefore, not as likely as the latter to value the right to dissent from the views of others. Those, therefore, who take no interest in the world around them, who find "politics" boring or irrelevant to their lives, who rarely, if ever, participate in political activity of any kind, even so much as to cast their votes in national elections, are not likely to value the rights of others to speak and act in the political arena. The Nazis, for example, apparently drew important support from "the ranks of the antipolitical apathetics," once Hitler became Chancellor. A number of contemporary studies also have found that the nonvoters and politically apathetic are more likely to be intolerant than those who vote and take an interest in political affairs.[16] The revolution in Cuba overcame the political apathy of many people, made them familiar with political problems and gave them the confidence to speak and to act politically for the first time in their lives. Yet even while their country was undergoing the most profound and rapid social change and was deeply involved in internal and external political conflict, even at a time when hundreds of thousands of persons participated in demonstrations denouncing "imperialism," when the mass media were saturated with political "news" and comment, and hundreds of political slogans decorated the walls of buildings, bulletin boards at work, billboards on city streets and country roads, and even shown in neon lights, some people remained indifferent to "politics."

This was true even among revolutionary workers, despite the fact that as a group they were far more likely to take an

[16] Lipset, *Political Man*, pp. 32 and 111, and the references therein.

interest in political affairs than workers who were indecisive about or hostile toward the revolution. When we asked the workers whether they took an interest in the political affairs of their country regularly, occasionally, or never, 12 percent of the revolutionary workers could still say they took only an occasional interest, and 16 percent of them that they never took any interest in politics.[17] And these politically apathetic but revolutionary workers were, in fact, more likely than the politically interested revolutionary workers to be "authoritarian" (Table 10.2). Strongly committed to the revolution but unwilling to take the effort necessary to follow political affairs and inform themselves, they were more likely than their fellow revolutionary workers who did take a regular interest in political affairs, to demand penalties against those who publicly criticized the revolution.[18]

Of course, this relationship between political interest and libertarianism may be spurious. Both political interest and

TABLE 10.2

Political Interest and Libertarianism among
Revolutionary Workers

POLITICAL INTEREST[a]	LIBERTARIAN	(N)
Regular	75%	(102)
Occasional	65	(17)
None	65	(23)

[a] The question: "Would you say that you take an interest in the political affairs of your country, regularly, occasionally, or never?"

[17] Among workers "indecisive" about the revolution, 25 percent said they took regular interest, 33 percent occasional, and 42 percent that they never took an interest in politics. Among the "hostile" workers, the figures, respectively, were 28, 11, and 61 percent.

[18] There is a similarity here to the "indignant style" of politics of those individuals who are high in political commitment but low in competence in the typology described in the article by David Riesman and Nathan Glazar, "Criteria for Political Apathy," in *Studies in Leadership*, ed. Alvin Gouldner (New York: Harper and Bros., 1950).

libertarianism may simply be attitudes which vary according to formal education, and any inference as to the importance of political interest as an intervening variable in the development of libertarianism may be incorrect.

Our findings do not support this objection. First, it *is* correct that political interest is a function of formal education; there is a direct relationship between the two, so that the proportion of workers who say they take a regular interest in political affairs is highest among the most educated and lowest among the least educated. Further, *lack* of interest is *inversely* related to the amount of formal education (Table 10.3). On the other hand, when we control for education, the relationship between political interest and libertarianism tends to hold, as does the relationship between education and libertarianism (Table 10.4). Whatever their education, those who take a regular interest in politics are most likely to be libertarian; and the *least* educated, whatever interest they take in politics, are also the least likely to be libertarian. Thus political interest (even interest in *revolutionary* politics!) itself apparently acts as an important intervening variable in the development of libertarian attitudes.

Family Patterns

The lower education and comparative political apathy of the workers, which contribute to their "authoritarian predis-

TABLE 10.3

Formal Education and Political Interest among Revolutionary Workers

GRADE COMPLETED IN SCHOOL	NONE	OCCASIONAL	REGULAR	(N)
None	30%	10%	60%	(10)
1-3	23	18	59	(34)
4-6	16	10	74	(68)
7 or more	4	11	86	(28)

TABLE 10.4

Political Interest and Percent Libertarian,
by Formal Education

GRADE COMPLETED IN SCHOOL	REGULAR	OCCASIONAL OR NONE
Third or less	58% (26)	50% (18)
Fourth to Sixth	84 (50)	72 (18)
Seventh or more	79 (24)	— (4)

positions," it has been suggested, are reinforced by their "authoritarian family patterns." "The lower class individual," it is asserted, "is likely to have been exposed to punishment, lack of love, and a general atmosphere of tension and aggression since early childhood. . . ." These experiences "tend to produce deep-rooted hostilities expressed by ethnic prejudice, political authoritarianism, and chiliastic transvaluational religion." In contrast, socialization in middle-class families, in which reasoning, systematic rewards and punishments, and "love-oriented" techniques of disciplining children are supposed to be typical, produces, so we are told, sophistication and ego-security that, in turn, are necessary for the "acceptance of the norms of democracy."[19]

[19] *Political Man*, pp. 115-21. This view is based on several undemonstrated and perhaps unwarranted assumptions about the nature of the "evidence" used to illustrate the alleged authoritarian patterns of working-class families. A great deal of consistency and reliability in the studies of working-class life is assumed; yet the findings of these studies have been far from consistent. The reader should refer to Urie Bronfenbrenner's comprehensive review of studies on child-rearing patterns in the U.S., for example, on which Lipset leans so heavily. ("Socialization and Social Class Through Time and Space," in E. E. Maccoby, T. M. Newcomb, and E. L. Hartley, eds., *Readings in Social Psychology* [New York: Henry Holt, 1958].) There, one of the central and unexplained questions raised by the review was why, until about twenty-five years ago, the vast majority of studies on class family patterns suggested that the *middle-class family* was comparatively authoritarian and rigid compared to the working class's freer and less compulsive concern with discipline, toilet

Our findings, however, indicate no relationship between differential class socialization and libertarianism. The working class recruits individuals from other strata and classes as well as through internal reproduction. These individuals, as we have seen in Chapter 6, tend to vary in their prerevolutionary views of the Communists and their attitudes toward the revolution in accordance with the class in which they grew up and internalized politically relevant attitudes. Now, if the alleged authoritarian family patterns of the workers were a source of political authoritarianism, we should expect to find that workers who were *not* socialized in the working class would recognizably differ from the sons of workers in their attitudes toward civil liberties. Further, the workers coming from middle-class families ought to be the least authoritarian of all workers. However, no such systematic relationship between class origin and libertarianism is revealed by our findings (Table 10.5). The likelihood of their having libertarian attitudes is about the same whatever the workers' class origins. This finding is especially worth emphasizing, I

---

training, neatness, etc. See also Arnold Green, "The Middle Class Male Child Neurosis," in Bendix and Lipset, eds., *Class, Status, and Power* (Glencoe, Ill., The Free Press, 1953), pp. 292-300; Eric Fromm, *Escape from Freedom* (New York: Reinhart, 1941); Henry V. Dicks, "Some Psychological Studies of the German Character," in T. H. Pear, ed., *Psychological Factors of Peace and War* (London: Hutchinson, 1950), pp. 193-218; Theodore W. Adorno *et al., The Authoritarian Personality* (New York: Harper, 1950). Eclectic selection of such "evidence" could certainly make a good case for "middle class authoritarianism." Certainly Lipset's own writings on the middle-class social base of fascism would serve such a middle-class authoritarianism thesis well. (*Political Man*, pp. 170ff.) See also Martin Trow, "Small Businessmen, Tolerance, and Support for McCarthy," *American Journal of Sociology*, Vol. 64 (November 1958), 270-81.

Other very significant criticisms and relevant evidence on the general thesis are contained in S. M. Miller and Frank Riessman, " 'Working-Class Authoritarianism': A Critique of Lipset," *British Journal of Sociology*, XII (September 1961), 263-76; Lipsitz, "Working-Class Authoritarianism: A Re-evaluation."

think, since implicitly at least, the alleged fact of authoritarian patterns of working-class socialization constitutes a major plank in a much-discussed "theory" concerning the origins of working-class political authoritarianism. While the worker may be able to overcome his initial low education and political apathy in the course of his life, implicit, for instance, in Lipset's argument is the thesis that the worker cannot overcome his authoritarian upbringing, and that his political consciousness is indelibly stamped with an authoritarian imprint. There is nothing, however, in sociological or psychological theory, in the findings and arguments on the question presented by others or in the findings I have presented here to support this view.

TABLE 10.5

Percent Libertarian by Father's
Occupational Status,[a] among Revolutionary Workers

	LIBERTARIAN	(N)
Agricultural laborer or peasant	73%	(33)
Worker	75	(69)
sugar central	78	(18)
urban	75	(51)
Petite bourgeoisie	73	(22)
Salaried (nonmanual) employee	78	(9)

[a] Nine workers who didn't know fathers' occupations are excluded.

Communism, Revolution, and Authoritarianism

In current political writing "extremism," "communism," and "authoritarianism" are often used interchangeably. In fact, the leading contemporary exponent of the thesis of working-class authoritarianism has gone so far as to assert that the workers support the Communist parties because the workers prefer authoritarian to democratic political leadership:

Some socialists and liberals have suggested that [work-ing-class support for Communist parties] proves nothing about the authoritarian tendencies in the working class, since the Communist Party often masquerades as a party seeking to fulfill the classic Western-democratic ideals of liberty, equality, and fraternity. They argue that most Communist supporters, particularly the less educated, are deceived into thinking that the Communists are simply more militant and efficient socialists. I would suggest, however, the alternate hypothesis that *rather than being a source of strain*, the intransigent and *intolerant* aspects of Communist ideology *attract* members from . . . the working class.[20]

Thus, the democratic and egalitarian slogans of the Communist parties, the militancy of the Communist unionists and political leaders, their comparative personal incorruptibility, their organizing skills and dedication, the actual gains won by the workers under Communist leadership are, as it were, largely irrelevant, we are supposed to believe, to the support the Communists get from the working class. If, for example, in the Cuban Constitutional Convention which promulgated the democratic Constitution of 1940, "the Communist delegates fought strongly for the inclusion"[21] of provisions on behalf of the workers, this was irrelevant to the workers' views of the Communists. If the *Confederación de Trabajadores de Cuba* "was able through its skillful Communist leadership, to obtain many of labor's demands by government decree,"[22] this too was irrelevant. Irrelevant also, perhaps, are judgments by democrats and anti-Communists that "the enormous gains achieved by the workers" under

[20] *Political Man*, pp. 99-100. (My italics)

[21] Republica de Cuba, *Censo de 1943* (Havana: Dirección General del Censo, 1945), p. 475.

[22] Barbara Ann Walker, "The Labor Policy of the Cuban Government Since 1925," unpublished thesis (University of California, Berkeley, 1947), p. 95.

Communist leadership and "the discipline and integrity of the
Communist leaders, an integrity to which Cuban labor was
little accustomed, won the respect of the rank and file . . .
[and] the support of the masses of the workers. . . ."[23] If
the Communists' "bitterest enemies" could say, in 1953
after the Communists had been purged from official control of the labor movement, that "indisputably, all the
improvements that we have achieved for the worker have
been achieved by Communism, [sic]"[24] perhaps these also
were irrelevant to the workers. Rather, we are asked to believe
that the workers are attracted by the "intolerant aspects of
Communist ideology," and are ready "to follow leaders who
offer a demonological interpretation of the evil forces (either
religious or political) which are conspiring against them."[25]

If the Marxists hypothesize that the workers will be compelled by their social situation to recognize the realities of
long-term social and economic trends in the capitalist system,
and will come to realize that their objective interests
would best be served by revolutionary socialist leadership,
some political sociologists would stand this Marxian hypothesis on its head: Lipset, for one, argues that "working-class
life seems to *prevent* the realities of long-term social and
economic trends from entering working-class consciousness."
It is for this reason that the workers support the Communists.
The workers support the Communists, in short, not on the
rational grounds that they believe the Communists are defending their interests, but because of an irrational preference for "extremist movements which suggest quick and easy
solutions to social problems and have a rigid outlook."[26]

Thus, the one great undemonstrated hypothesis running

[23] Charles A. Page, "The Development of Organized Labor in
Cuba," unpublished dissertation (University of California at Berkeley,
1952), pp. 112-13.

[24] A statement by a well-known Cuban anti-Communist journalist,
María García, in a discussion with Calixto Masó, author of "Labo-
rismo y Comunismo," *Cuadernos de la Universidad del Aire del Cir-
cuito CMQ*, XLI (Havana: CMQ, April 1953), p. 313.

[25] *Political Man*, p. 121   [26] *Ibid.*, p. 100.

like a red thread throughout the argument in favor of working-class authoritarianism is "that (. . . other things being equal) they will be *more attracted* to an extremist [and undemocratic?] movement than to a moderate and democratic one, and that, once recruited, they will not be alienated by its lack of democracy."[27] It is, therefore, remarkable, that the leading exponent of this thesis—namely, Professor Lipset—offers *no direct* (as contrasted with inferential) evidence to support it. At the least, we might have expected him to show that the same workers who vote Communist and who support them in the labor movement are the ones who disproportionately give "authoritarian" responses to the various questions he deems indicative of political tolerance or intolerance. Comparison of the attitudes of pro-Communist and non-Communist workers toward civil liberties would give us some indication whether or not it is "the intolerant aspects of Communist ideology" that attract the workers to the Communists. Such a reanalysis of Lipset's data on working-class comparative politics, as well as the analysis of other data on workers' politics, is essential for the testing of this hypothesis.

In our sample, it will be remembered that 29 percent of the workers said they were supporters of the Communists in the prerevolutionary days. If it were correct that the "intolerant aspects" of Communist ideology and political action form a major attraction for the working class, then those workers in our sample who supported the Communists before the revolution certainly ought to differ substantially—especially in the midst of a socialist revolution—from those who were indifferent or hostile to the Communists; that is, they ought to be more likely than non-Communist workers to demand penalties against critics of the revolution, and to refuse them the right to speak freely. In short, they would more likely be "authoritarian" and less likely "libertarian" than workers who were not Communists. The fact is, how-

[27] *Ibid.*, p. 101. (My italics)

ever, that we find no such relationship between "authoritarianism" and pro-Communism among the workers in our sample. As Table 10.6 indicates, the proportion of "libertarians" is essentially the same among the workers who were pro-Communist as among those who were anti-Communist before the revolution; thus Lipset's major hypothesis and an outstanding implicit assumption in much current political discourse is *contradicted* by our findings.

TABLE 10.6

Percent Libertarian among Revolutionary
Workers, Compared with Prerevolutionary Attitude
toward Communists

	LIBERTARIAN	(N)
Friendly or supporter	72%	(54)
Indifferent	76	(55)
Hostile	70	(33)

Testing the same hypothesis differently also yields results not at all in accord with what should be found if the equation of authoritarian and revolutionary views were correct. If the intolerant aspects of "extremist" movements and their "chiliastic view of the world" have special appeal to the workers, if such movements secure the support of the working class, as Lipset claims, "often by stressing equality and economic security *at the expense of liberty*,"[28] then we should certainly expect to find that revolutionary workers—supporting a self-proclaimed Marxist-Leninist "dictatorship of the proletariat"—advocate the suppression of free speech. The intensity of their commitment to the revolution ought to be reflected in a greater propensity for "authoritarianism." If Lipset were correct, the more committed the workers are to the revolution, the greater should be the likelihood that they are "authoritarian." Yet if we compare the workers whom

[28] *Ibid.*, p. 131. (My italics)

we classified as "very favorable" to the revolution with those who are "moderately favorable" to it, we find no meaningful difference in the proportions among them who would deny critics of the revolution the right to speak freely (Table 10.7).

TABLE 10.7

Percent Libertarian among Revolutionary
Workers, Compared with Attitude toward Revolution

	LIBERTARIAN	(N)
Very favorable	73%	(100)
Moderately favorable	71	(42)

Conclusions

Our findings confirm the importance of formal education in the development of political tolerance since even in this difficult and dangerous period of the revolution formal education proved to be directly related to advocacy of free speech for critics of the revolution. Our findings also confirm the importance of political interest in sensitizing individuals to the necessity and desirability of competing views, since the revolutionary workers who evinced the least interest in politics were most likely to be "authoritarian," even with education controlled for. Apparently the very act of taking an interest in political affairs itself makes individuals aware of the fact that a variety of perceptions, interpretations, and value-responses to the same events are possible. These individuals probably have often been involved in political discussions where they found themselves in the minority; respect for the other man's viewpoint may therefore have been the result. These findings concerning the relationship of education and political interest to "libertarian" political views are quite consistent with the findings of other studies done in entirely different contexts. However, we found that two major hypotheses concerning working-class "authoritarianism" suggested by Lipset were not confirmed by our findings. Contrary to his view that the roots of authoritarianism are deep in working-class family-patterns, we found that the workers who were socialized in the middle class were no more likely than those socialized in the working class to be "libertarian." This finding seems all the more important since differences in class origins *were* reflected in attitudes both toward the revolution and the Communists before the revolution. Finally, we found that the contention that support for the Communists indicates the authoritarianism of the working class, and that Communist chiliasm, rigidity, and intolerance are especially appealing to the workers, is baseless. If this view were correct, the prerevolutionary Communist workers should have been the most likely to be "authoritarian," as should the more committed of the revolutionary workers. In reality, however, we found no such relationship between support for the Communists or greater commitment to the revolution and "authoritarianism." Thus our findings indicate that precisely the hypotheses which are most critical to the thesis of working-class authoritarianism prove to be without foundation. And these findings are especially important theoretically; for it is hard to imagine a better test of the thesis of working-class authoritarianism than that provided by a study of the willingness of revolutionary and pro-Communist workers to deny civil liberties to critics of their revolution.

One of the major findings of this chapter is that the vast majority of revolutionary workers, though living through a socialist revolution and a period especially likely to arouse passions against the "internal enemy," believe in freedom of speech for opponents of the revolution. Why should this be so? Does it mean, perhaps, that under certain circumstances a revolutionary movement in our day (to the extent that its course is determined by those who constitute its base) may be the carrier of humanist traditions and a way of realizing them in the life of the masses? Are socialist revolutions that preserve many individual liberties, even in their most critical moments, realistic possibilities for other quasi-colonial countries in which capitalist political democratic forms have never existed? Or has the Cuban revolution taken place under such special conditions that it represents a historical fluke never to be repeated?

None of these questions is simple, and any attempt to answer them here would take us well beyond the purview of this book. There are two questions, nonetheless, that are quite relevant and that deserve at least a few comments:

1. Why have the vast majority of revolutionary workers been willing to tolerate open criticism of the revolution by its opponents? 2. What aspects of the prerevolutionary social structure and of the revolutionary process have made the preservation of many individual liberties possible under the Cuban revolution?

1. First, the role of the revolutionary leaders, chiefly Fidel Castro and Ché Guevara, has been important, for they have tried to inculcate by example and precept respect for the ideas of others, and for free inquiry.[29] On many occasions, they have declared their commitment to a revolution in liberty. The workers, of course, have heard these speeches, either in person or via others, or seen them in print, and know that their leaders have claimed, in Castro's words, to want "a revolution that may meet [Cubans'] material needs without sacrificing their liberties. . . . Should we accomplish

[29] The fact that Guevara, in his capacity as Minister of Industries, made it possible for an American sociologist to do a study of workers' *political* attitudes, without hindrance, and to interview them whenever and wherever the sociologist felt necessary, indicates two things of importance: first, that the revolutionary leaders had no fear of what an objective sociological study might find; second, that—at the very least—they were not opposed to free inquiry about the revolution, even by a citizen of a country that they conceive to be their mortal enemy.

our revolution in this way," he said, "the Cuban revolution will become a classic revolution in the history of the world."[30] This was but the first of many occasions on which Castro stated his commitment to the preservation of individual liberties within the revolution.[31] Only several weeks before we started to interview the workers for this book, Castro delivered a number of lengthy speeches attacking

[30] A long extract from this important speech on May 21, 1959, concerning the "olive green revolution," appears in Maurice Zeitlin and Robert Scheer, *Cuba: Tragedy in our Hemisphere* (New York: Grove Press, 1963), p. 109. The even longer extract in Spanish that this is translated from appears in *Guía del Pensamiento Politico-económico de Fidel* (Havana: Diario Libre, 1959), p. 48.

[31] One of the most startling examples of Fidel Castro's personal willingness to subject his views to public examination came in his television debates with captured counterrevolutionaries after the abortive invasion of Cuba in April 1961. It was what Castro called "the unique spectacle of a government head conducting a public discussion with prisoners who came to overthrow him. . . ." As Richard Eder described the debate in *The New York Times* (April 28, 1961), there were moments in which Castro was surrounded by prisoners who "shouted indignant denials that they were mercenaries. One told him: " 'Sir, I came to combat communism; to have elections; to uphold the Constitution of 1940, free enterprise, and the rights of citizens. We accept the consequences. The most we can pay is with our lives— our ideals will remain.' "

According to Eder, "As the Premier talked on, outlining the benefits he said the Cuban regime was bringing to the people, many of the prisoners appeared to respond to his words. Even before his advocacy of clemency, he was interrupted several times by applause."

Several months after the invasion, on December 2, 1961, in a lengthy television speech to the nation (*the same one in which he declared that he was now a "Marxist-Leninist"*), Castro stated the view that "with all its power, socialism does not abuse it. It is calm. It is conscientious. It struggles to overcome all its defects. It struggles to overcome extremism, sectarianism, abuses, injustices, simply because it is socialism, simply because it is what Marx and Engels conceived of, what Lenin and all the revolutionaries fought for—a better life for man, a happier life for the people, a freer life for the people, that replaces the regime of class oppression, the regime of an exploiting class over the workers, with a workers' democracy. In Marxist terms this is known as the 'dictatorship of the proletariat.' " The text of this speech appears in *El Mundo*, Havana, December 3, 1961, special supplement, section B.

what he called that "myopic, sectarian, stupid and warped conception of history and of Marxism" held by some of his "old Communist" comrades that tried to impose their views by force. "What must the revolution be?" he asked. "The revolution must be a school of courageous men. The revolution must be a school in which there is liberty of thought!"[32] Such speeches as these by the revolutionary leaders may have modified many workers' views and increased their political tolerance.

Second, we know that *formal* education has a profound effect on attitudes toward individual liberties. Since the revolution has raised the general level of education in the working class significantly,[33] one effect may have been to enhance the workers' willingness to listen to a variety of ideas, even those they find repugnant. This is to speak of classroom education alone. Much of the workers' education since the revolution, however, has been received in informal discussions, and as the result of taking on tasks that have forced them to face large problems and develop new skills and knowledge.

Third, we know that political interest, awareness, and participation tend to increase the willingness to let others speak their political minds. The workers in Cuba have entered massively and decisively into the political process since the revolution. They have become more familiar with political issues and the complexities involved in solving them. Many have gained political skills—organizational ability, confidence, poise, oratorical talents, and education. Castro's speeches themselves, as the London *Observer* (April 23, 1961) correctly observed, "give his mostly illiterate com-

[32] "Contra el sectarismo y el mecanicismo," *Cuba Socialista*, II, 8 (April 1962), 6.

[33] Forty-one percent of the workers we interviewed were attending one type of class or another started by the Revolutionary Government's Ministry of Education. These included beginning and intermediate instruction in the "three r's," as well as courses designed to teach the workers technical skills.

patriots a sort of lecture-course on the theory and practice of socialism." An ideology which insists on the workers' participation in the direction of their society has become a national creed. The workers have become involved in countless formal and informal ways in the running of agriculture and industry. Immediate necessity, political expediency, and revolutionary socialist ideology coincided to propel workers into activities and roles demanding skills in leadership and organization, as well as technical knowledge. With the emigration of many professionals, technicians, former political officials, government bureaucrats, managers and other administrative personnel in the plants, the mines, the sugar centrals, and so on, the workers were encouraged by the Revolutionary Government to take over these responsibilities. Participation in public affairs has become a reality for masses of workers—in work assemblies, neighborhood associations, political rallies, militia exercises, union activities, and political party work.

In the process, the workers have increased their awareness of the world and grown in political competence.[34] They have developed new leaders and acquired a sense of their own collective strength and ability to affect the destiny of their country. Their armed militias have been a pillar of the revolution. A strong sense of identification between themselves and the government has been forged. For this reason, they do not think of criticism of the revolution as a "clear and present danger." With this self-confidence and sense of their power, the workers may view criticism of the revolution

[34] In this connection, it is interesting to note that Robert K. Merton, Patricia S. West and Marie Jahoda have shown that a New Jersey shipyard workers' housing project that incorporated as a town inhabited only by workers, which compelled them to assume the town's government, resulted in a major change in the workers' political interest and participation. See their *Patterns of Social Life: Explorations in the Sociology and Social Psychology of Housing* (New York: Bureau of Applied Social Research, mimeographed, n.d.). Also see Lipset, *Political Man*, pp. 193-94.

much as politically tolerant middle-class citizens of a capitalist political democracy view "extremists." The workers can afford to be magnanimous. The "outs" are now in, and the "ins" out, and what the latter have to say is not of much consequence and is easily tolerated.

2. The Revolutionary Government was able, for reasons to be noted, to rapidly and easily consolidate its power and transform the old society. This made it possible for the humanistic commitment of its leaders to sustain itself.

(a) There was no prolonged civil war between different sectors or strata of the population to leave the masses exhausted, Cuba's economy in ruins, and the society in relative chaos. The spirit and energies of the people were waiting to be tapped. Rather than have to confront an armed, powerful counterrevolutionary army with a mass base in order to consolidate its power, the revolutionary movement fought against an army and a regime that was increasingly isolated from almost all strata of the population except those directly implicated in the regime. The army disintegrated under the blows of the guerrillas and urban resistance, and because of the lack of either concrete interests or ideological commitment to the old regime on the part of the great majority of the soldiers and lower echelon officers. The military apparatus was therefore easily dissolved when the revolutionaries assumed the reins of the government. By the time a military threat to the Revolutionary Government presented itself, a new army had been recruited from the revolutionary masses and the workers and peasants had been armed.

(b) The Cuban revolution took place in a capitalist country. Capitalism permeated and penetrated, defined and limited the entire range of socio-economic relations in the cities and countryside. Inherited quasi-feudal or traditional values and social relations existed in something of a complex mix with capitalist ones, but the latter dominated the society and were clearly ascendant when the revolution occurred. "Precapitalist forms of economic organization—traditional, feudal, or mercantile—were in no way important features of the old society."[35] Some consequences of profound importance to the revolution were the following: (1) The former ruling strata had only nominal roots in their own society and whatever legitimacy they may once have possessed had long since been dissipated or eroded. The prerevolutionary agrarian structure was relatively modernized, rationalized, detraditionalized and secularized. The peasantry—predominantly a rural proletariat, plus a sector of independent proprietors selling cash crops on the market—had little particularistic loyalties to the old privileged classes. Therefore they were not available for organization as a mass base for the counterrevolution. Nor was the Church a significant social force that could mobilize the masses against the revolution; its base was limited to the old upper and upper middle strata.

Moreover, the quasi-colonial nature of Cuban capitalism meant that these strata were discredited, given the nationalist, anti-imperialist nature of the revolution. The upper strata were in sometimes open, sometimes covert, alliance with and dependence upon a foreign government and foreign-owned industries. They had no real base in the country from which to rally opposition to the revolution and to genuinely threaten its continued development. The counterrevolution was exported, or exported itself. Rather than choosing to stay and fight, the great majority of counterrevolutionaries, therefore, chose to emigrate—and were encouraged to do so by the Revolutionary Government.

The split in the population over the revolution generally fell along class lines, with the former propertyless wage laborers of city and country becoming the revolution's decisive social base. Cuban capitalism had created a national working class—urban and rural—that was the biggest and most cohesive class, well organized and highly politicized.

[35] James O'Connor, "On Cuban Political Economy," *Political Science Quarterly*, LXXIX, 2 (June 1964), 233.

Revolutionary socialist ideology had long been fundamental to its political culture.[36] For these reasons, despite the fact that the United States has opposed the revolution in Cuba, it has, paradoxically, had a relatively secure base on which to develop. Thus, the revolutionaries have *not felt compelled* to take such extreme measures as would almost inevitably degenerate into the repression of individual liberties.[37] (2) Cuba's peculiar form of capitalist misdevelopment meant that when the revolutionaries came to power they had a reservoir of potential productive facilities that were waiting to be employed rationally. The establishment of control over them and their *reorganization* was sufficient to make possible

[36] This is not to deny that a real disparity may exist—and did exist in Cuba—between the essentially reformist line and "business unionism" of the Communist Party and the socialist ideas, models, and theories learned by the workers under the party's leadership, as well as the socialist lessons that the workers drew from their own experience.

[37] The material and moral aid of the Soviet Union, a country opposed to capitalism and to the international interests of the United States, was also of fundamental importance in objectively buttressing the security of the revolution, as well as providing the leaders with what may have been even more significant, namely, a strong *sense* of security. This in turn meant the revolutionaries would be unlikely to feel the need to repress personal liberties. On the other hand, the role of Soviet "aid" has been ambiguous. Among other things, it has provided the revolutionary leaders with a model of economic and political development in which repression of dissent and severe restrictions on personal liberties was crucial. Perhaps of greater importance, the Soviet leaders have probably strengthened the hand of the elements in the revolutionary leadership to whom individual liberties are nothing more than a "bourgeois legacy" having no place under socialism. Much of the authority enjoyed by many old Communists derives essentially from their long adherence to Soviet communism. More recently, the reported pressures exerted on Fidel Castro by the Soviets to tow the line on the Sino-Soviet dispute have led to Castro's decreasing willingness, in public at least, to engage in rational debate. A tendency to try to defame even supporters of the Cuban revolution with whom he has political differences has begun to appear in his speeches. (See especially his speech at the Tricontinental Conference, Havana, January 15, 1966.) The long-range consequences of Soviet aid are therefore yet to be weighed.

a "redistribution of income from the propertied classes to the working classes of probably fifteen percent or more of National Income" within the revolution's first three months alone.[38] This undoubtedly helped to secure the revolution's base in the working classes. Of greater importance, capitalism not only had all but eradicated the traditionalist mentality of the peasantry and created a rural proletariat, but it had also made it possible for the agrarian reform to be put through rapidly, and without the incomparably greater dislocations in agricultural production faced by the Soviet, Mexican or Bolivian revolutions. The revolutionaries were not compelled to parcel out the land—either as an act of "social justice" or to secure the peasants' allegiance. By the middle of the revolu-

---

[38] Felipe Pázos, "Comentarios a dos artículos sobre la Revolución Cubana," in *El Trimestre Económico*, XXIX, 113 (January-March 1962), 9. Pázos, former director of the Banco Nacional de Cuba, in exile in the United States, also writes: "In its first months, the revolution realized a redistribution of great magnitude of the national income in favor of the workers and employees, in the countryside and the city, whose real incomes rose about 25 percent to 30 percent." *Ibid.*, p. 7.

The Bureau of Foreign Commerce Publication, *Investment in Cuba* (Washington, D.C.: U.S. Government Printing Office, 1956), pp. 5-6, states: "Cuba is not an underdeveloped country in the sense usually associated with that term. The industrial segment of the sugar industry is a highly mechanized and efficient operation, national networks of railways and highways blanket the country, and numerous well-equipped ports provide easy access and egress for a flourishing foreign trade. On the other hand, *few countries carry a heavier overhead of underutilized productive facilities*. Cuba's sugar mills work for only a few months a year, its railways, highways, and ports handle less than their capacity of traffic." The publication also states, p. 5: "Nowhere else in Latin America, except perhaps on the Argentine pampas and the great plains of western Brazil, do greater potential opportunities appear for raising the productivity of agricultural labor." Allowing for some exaggeration, these remarks give us an indication of the immense developmental possibilities inherited by the Revolutionary Government. Cuba's "bootstrap operation" is not comparable in magnitude to that faced by Soviet or Chinese leaders; and, at least on this count, similar restrictions on personal freedom are less likely to be viewed as necessary for economic development by the Cuban leaders. But see note 40.

tion's second year, 41 percent of the land under cultivation in Cuba was already in socialized large-scale units of agricultural production—the so-called *granjas del pueblo* (peoples' farms) and the short-lived agricultural cooperatives.[39] The Cuban leaders were thus not compelled to fight the peasantry, as the Soviet leaders found necessary, in order to modernize agriculture and create efficient and large-scale forms of agricultural production. The socialist forms of property that replaced the sugar centrals in Cuba, on the contrary, helped to cement the already existing political and social bonds between the specifically agricultural proletariat and the industrial workers in the sugar centrals. Thus many revolutionary measures simultaneously increased economic rationality and strengthened the base of the socialist revolution. This in turn meant that the humanistic features of the revolution would be more likely to survive and be institutionalized as the contours of the new system emerged.[40]

[39] Mexico and Bolivia, on the other hand, had agrarian reform programs which required parcelization of the land and thereby imposed severe obstacles to these countries' attempts to develop modern agriculture. Moreover, actual distribution of the land was slow and has yet to provide economic security to the Mexican and Bolivian peasants. Either through land speculation, as in Mexico, or excessive legalism in Bolivia, with several possible stages of juridical appeal allowed the *hacendados* whose land was to be expropriated, these countries' agrarian reforms were severely impeded. Several years ago it was estimated, for example, that were Bolivia to continue to implement its agrarian reform at the rate it had been doing for the previous decade, it would take another quarter of a century before Bolivia would complete redistribution of the land subject to expropriation— an estimate which recent political events in Bolivia may yet make over-optimistic. See Robert J. Alexander, *The Bolivian National Revolution* (New Brunswick, N.J.: Rutgers University Press, 1958), p. 79.

[40] The hostility of the United States toward the revolution, its continued attempts to isolate Cuba from either government-to-government relations or economic trade in Latin America, its imposition of major economic sanctions—present cumulative problems to the Cuban Revolutionary Government. Their effect on the Revolutionary Government's policies is not easily measured. Under such pressures and tensions as these economic difficulties present, the attitudes of the

leadership may change. Dissent may become increasingly less tolerable in a situation in which the workers' sense of security, and their sense of well-being, deteriorates. These pressures may be even of greater importance than any military threat from the United States. Thus there are a number of imponderables in the situation. Any analysis that attempts—especially as briefly as this one—to weigh the aspects of social structure and of the revolutionary process that affect the relative strength of repressive tendencies within a revolution, must be incomplete.

CHAPTER 11

Revolutionary Politics and the Cuban Working Class

◆ THE revolution in Cuba is a working-class revolution; the workers in the cities, in the sugar centrals, and in the countryside are its social base. Before the revolution they formed by far the biggest and perhaps most cohesive class in the country. Split more or less evenly between urban and rural wage workers, the working class—not counting servants—constituted some 56 percent of the labor force, compared to an urban middle class only two-fifths as large and essentially lacking in class consciousness. The workers in the island's major industry—sugar—were probably Cuba's most politically conscious and militant workers before the revolution and are the outstanding base of the revolution itself. These very workers, moreover, have been in constant contact with and drawn to a great extent from rural wage laborers, who were themselves politicized and well organized before the revolution despite the seasonal nature of their employment. Thus in spite of the sparsity of manufacturing industry outside greater Havana, the working class formed a *national* class whose local struggles tended to take on the character of a national class struggle; the centrals tended to link up industrial with rural workers; and their employment in the same industry, subject to the same seasonal cycle allowed them, nay, compelled them, to coordinate local strikes into an industrywide, therefore nationwide, effort.

The workers' active and armed support of the Revolutionary Government has been decisive in the consolidation and defense of its power. Without their support the revolutionary leadership could not successfully have transformed the old order and created Cuban socialism. The revolution was not a workers' revolution in the classical Marxian sense, however. The workers did not initiate the struggle for power, as they had done three decades earlier in the insurrection against Machado. Then it had led rapidly to the formation of "Soviets" of workers, peasants, and soldiers throughout the country. In the Castro revolution, however, it is through their mass, organized support for and defense of revolutionary measures put through by the Revolutionary Government that the workers' role has been strategic. The role of the workers in the anti-Batista struggle—though not as an organized class—was also important. There were a number of violent conflicts with the old regime involving masses of workers. This was especially true in eastern Cuba, where general strikes paralyzed Santiago and outlying plants twice in eight months. Both strikes, the most recent in April 1958, were specifically political and revolutionary in origin.

The fact is that the struggle against the Batista regime profoundly affected the political consciousness of the workers. In general, the specific historical period in which succeeding generations of Cuban workers first became involved in the labor movement had significant consequences for the formation of their political outlooks. In particular, the workers about 18-25 years old who were entering the labor movement during the conflict with Batista were shaped by the experiences of the struggle and the events flowing from it. The members of this generation, the "generation of '53," are far more likely than members of other generations to support the revolution and to identify with the revolutionary leaders. Further, the two other generations that stand out in support of the revolution are precisely those whose members experienced the revolutionary events of the thirties—in which the Communists had played a leading role—as young men. These latter two generations of the thirties were also the ones with the highest proportion of workers sympathetic to the Communists before the revolution. The profound impact of the anti-Batista struggle on the political consciousness of the workers of this generation is especially evident among those who were employed regularly before the revolution. Conventional theory would have it that such workers would not be likely to support the revolution since they were economically secure under the old regime. Yet not only do the prerevolutionary employed workers of the generation of '53 support the revolution far more than do other employed workers, but they also are as likely as the prerevolutionary *unemployed* workers of other generations to support the revolution. One could never have predicted the revolutionary potential of workers in this generation from a mere knowledge of their relative economic security in prerevolutionary Cuba—despite the vast importance economic insecurity had in generating revolutionary consciousness.

Nor could the revolutionary potential of the high income, economically secure workers have been predicted from any theory in which material deprivation alone or even primarily is assumed to account for anticapitalism and support of revolutionary change. The majority of these workers, well paid and working regularly, and thus supposedly conservative in their politics, not only support the revolution but nearly a third of them were pro-Communist *before* the revolution. This proportion was *higher* than among the *low income* regularly employed workers. The same is true of the skilled workers who in the aggregate were living better on all counts than other workers. Higher wages, more prerevolutionary economic security, better working conditions, greater work satisfaction, more formal education—and still the skilled are just as likely as the less skilled workers to support the revolution. What is more, despite their far better material conditions of existence, the skilled workers, in every subgroup but the so-called privileged sector, were much *more* likely to support the Communists than the semiskilled and unskilled workers. From their peculiar vantage point, the irrationalities of the capitalist wage structure in Cuba were apparently more easily perceived and more strongly felt. Often earning the same or even lower wages than less skilled workers they likely thought of themselves as especially burdened by these irrationalities—and, paradoxically, as being the most exploited stratum of the working class.

Unemployment and underemployment in the working class served as a constant source of radicalism, not because of the deprivation involved but rather because of the "transparency" of the connection between the workers' unemployment and the economic structure as a whole. The irrationality of a system that could give them full employment scarcely more than a part of the year, and the recurrence from year to year of this "boom and bust" experience of employment and *dis*employment, was visibly rooted in the peculiar nature of Cuban capitalism, and, too, in its ultimate dependence on and control by foreign capital. It was in reality a system in chronic and repeated economic crisis, unable to stabilize itself or to grow. It was a system which, apart from the nakedness of its structural irrationalities and the specific economic deprivations it imposed on the workers, was interlocked with a corrupt and oppressive dictatorship. It was a system whose "insides" were recurrently exposed to view, a system, therefore, which itself created the belief in its dissolution, and provided the objective basis for a revolutionary movement dedicated to that end.

Yet, Negro workers, despite the fact they bore the brunt of the old system's irrationalities, were *not* more likely than white workers to give their support to the Communists before the revolution, and were even more likely to be anti-Communist. The Negro unemployed were less likely than white unemployed to support the Communists before the revolution; and, what is more important, they were even less likely than regularly employed Negroes to do so. On the other hand, Negro workers are more likely than whites to support the revolution, whether or not they had secure pre-revolutionary employment. To the Negro unemployed before the revolution, who very likely saw their racial membership as the prime cause of their situation, a class conscious or pro-Communist political orientation probably seemed meaningless. The revolution apparently made the connection between their fate and the fate of white workers, and the prerevolutionary economic order, distinctly recognizable —where once it had been obscure. Thus their racial membership and prerevolutionary unemployment now reinforced each other, making them even more likely than the white prerevolutionary unemployed to support the revolution. The revolution, therefore, simultaneously increased the Negro workers' revolutionary consciousness and cemented the links between them and white workers, thus providing itself an even more secure social base in the working class.

The revolution also was able to secure, as had the Communists before the revolution, significant support in strata that bordered on, but were not in, the working class. The *"clase popular"* included small traders, independent artisans, and even the lowest rungs of clerical and sales employees. Social interaction between their families and the families of industrial workers was probably regular and frequent; they also suffered from severe economic insecurity; thus they were probably easily "converted" to working-class views on politics. In any case, although we found consistent political differences between workers of working-class origin and workers whose fathers were petite bourgeoisie or salaried employees, these differences are small. Whatever their social origins the revolution secured the support of the majority of the workers.

It received the support of the majority of the workers even in plants the Communists had never been able to organize. The prerevolutionary structure of industry, with a predominance of small shops, impeded the political and economic *organization* of the workers employed in them. But the small plant milieu tended to create a nascent radicalism—even revolutionary ideology—among its workers. Historically, these workers had formed the base of anarchosyndicalism in the working class. And this revolutionary socialist ideology may have continued to exert influence among them right up to the revolution itself. Working in small shops, and convinced that they had the requisite skills and knowledge to run them without their bosses, an ideology which called for workers' control and ownership of the factories probably had special appeal to them. The relative marginality of these small shops, their inability to expand and provide secure employment to the workers, also probably furthered the conviction that no solution for their problems would be possible in the existing system. This was a "lesson" they could learn even without the presence of a political organization to transmit it. The larger plants, on the other hand, were more easily organized by the Communists, whose influence tended to be greater there. These plants provided a milieu before the revolution in which discussion of grievances and political issues could go on almost entirely between the workers themselves. They were unlikely, within the plant, to be subject to political cross pressures, to points of view or sources of information that competed with those coming from union and/or radical sources. They strengthened each others' opinions and definitions of their situation and were much more likely to reach a consensus about their common problems and interests, and a common course of action to defend those interests. Thus the revolution could draw simultaneously on the nascent but nonpoliticized radicalism of the workers throughout the numerically predominant small factories, and the organized, politicized, socialist consciousness of the Communist workers found more frequently in the larger plants.

The direct impact of nationalization on social relations in the plants was of profound importance to many workers. The revolution gave new public esteem and respect to manual labor and abolished the private appropriation of the workers' products. In-plant relations became radically egalitarian. Nearly three quarters of the workers we interviewed who were dissatisfied with their work for one reason or another before the nationalization of industries told us their attitudes toward their work had been transformed since nationalization. Socialization of the means of production transformed their work commitment, and in turn heightened their support for the revolution. Eight out of 10 of the workers whose attitudes were changed positively by nationalization support the revolution compared to about two out of three of those whose attitudes had not changed. Moreover, the workers who thought of themselves as "estranged" from their work before the revolution, and who attribute their changed work attitudes to the abolition of their alienation from the organization and products of production, are a distinct group of revolutionary workers. Every one of the 25 in our sample support the revolution.

Not only did the revolution generate its own support in the working class, but it also had the prerevolutionary politicization of the workers to count on. When the revolutionaries came to power it was a "simple historic fact"—as Weber might have put it—that the workers had long been led by Communists and that revolutionary socialist ideology had penetrated into the very fibre of the working-class political culture. The Cuban Communists had won the support of many workers, as we have seen, who superficially had no "objective reason" (who were relatively better off materially than other workers) to support or join them.

What Guenther Roth has said of the meaning of the pre-World War II labor movement in Germany for the Social Democratic workers applies equally, I think, to the Communist workers of prerevolutionary Cuba:

> Inversely corresponding to the class cleavage in Imperial Germany and *the alienation of the Social Democratic workers from the dominant system* was the extraordinary personal impact of the labor movement for many of its members. . . . The ideological props [of Marxism] alone would not have meant much if the labor movement had not offered the concrete experience of

solidarity and of social recognition within a group of like-minded peers. Of course, Marxism provided a good rationale for the solidarity of the working class, but the collective experience was primary.[1]

Moreover, if this statement applies to the Communist workers of prerevolutionary Cuba, it is even more apt as a description of what the revolution has meant to the workers. Many of them expressed this in words like the following: "Never before has there been such fellowship between the workers and the administration and other Cubans." Thus it is understandable that the revolution is supported by all sectors of the working class. Almost regardless of what controls are made, or what combination of variables is considered, a majority of the workers in each subgroup (in most cases a majority of two-thirds or more) are revolutionaries. Whether in small plants and communities or big ones, whether the sons of urban workers or of sugar central workers, of peasants and agricultural laborers or from "middle-class" families, whether they were employed or unemployed before the revolution, are working more regularly since the revolution or not, skilled, semiskilled or unskilled, satisfied or not with their work, man or woman, black or white, and whatever their generation, the majority of the workers are with the revolution.

The Revolutionary Government has support in the working class which cuts across all the normal divisions, all the expectations derived from research on workers' political support of the Left in capitalist countries. The transformation of the old order has all but swept aside these divisions, these strata, these internal variations in the working class. The revolution has unified and solidified the workers behind the revolutionary leadership. For, aside from all the array of

[1] *The Social Democrats in Imperial Germany: A Study in Working-Class Isolation and National Integration* (Totawa, N.J.: The Bedminster Press, 1963), pp. 193-203. (My italics)

factors that distinguish workers from one another, what unifies them and defines them and makes them what they are and what they can be is the fact that they are, indeed, workers—that before the revolution, as one worker told us, "we produced riches that we could see but never touch; for we were the exploited and the trampled on. That has ended here."[2]

The revolution in Cuba has made citizens of the workers —black and white alike. For them the basic political issue of the revolution, their "incorporation into the legitimate body politic, has been settled"; with the revolution, "the workers have achieved industrial and political citizenship." The revolution has given them a sense of "basic human equality, associated with full community membership" that they never had in the prerevolutionary epoch.[3] In the past, they felt themselves to be neither human nor citizens; they were alienated from control over their lives, not fully a part of society. They rejected, and were rejected by, the ruling and dominant institutions. They were ruled, in the words of a sugar mill worker, by "individuals who, after destroying the Constitution submitted the Republic to the abyss of viciousness and corruption." Before the revolution, they expected, as another worker said, "nothing but ill treatment and theft" at the hands of government officials. Now, they

[2] In this connection, it is significant that the youngest generation of workers for whom prerevolutionary struggles, even prerevolutionary society, are mere "history," were less likely than the older workers to support the revolution. Many of them were not even workers before the revolution, and essentially were just entering the working class when the revolution occurred. Thus, they could not "understand" the revolution in the same sense as older workers, or appreciate to the same extent the changes the revolution had wrought in the workers' collective existence.

[3] Cf. Seymour Martin Lipset, *Political Man* (Garden City, N.Y.: Doubleday, 1960), pp. 92-93, 406-409, *passim*; T. H. Marshall, *Citizenship and Social Class* (London: Cambridge University Press, 1950), p. 77, *passim*, on the process of achievement of working-class citizenship in the Western capitalist democracies.

believed, this had changed. If we can justifiably infer their feelings toward the Revolutionary Government from their expectations of how they would be treated by government officials, there is little question that the workers of Cuba now thought themselves part of the "civic culture."[4] The vast majority of them now expected equality of treatment with all other Cubans—a proportion, in fact, as great as or greater than in five other nations. When workers in Cuba, the United States, England, Germany, Italy, and Mexico were asked whether they thought they would be "treated as well as anyone else" by government officials to whom they had to take a question for solution, only the workers of the advanced capitalist democracies of the United States and England came close to the proportion of Cuban workers who expected equal treatment (Table 11.1); and the Cuban workers were far more likely to expect equal treatment than were workers in Italy and Mexico, where the majority are "alienated in their expectations of treatment at the hands of governmental authority and police."[5] The workers believe the revolution has ended the old system of exploitation and social inequality, and with it the old politics of class struggle. The struggle for social justice would continue, of course, but it would now be a struggle in which their revolutionary ideology, their Red flags and May Day parades would take on a new meaning, a new significance, as symbols of what they had won, rather than of what they were yet to win. For with the triumph of the revolution in Cuba, with their achievement of citizenship, Cuba had entered, many workers believed, a new phase of its history—a "post-politics" phase. In the words of a textile worker, "We have put aside politics for

[4] See Gabriel Almond and Sidney Verba, *The Civic Culture: Political Attitudes and Democracy in Five Nations* (Princeton: Princeton University Press, 1963). Professors Almond and Verba kindly made the cards and codebook for their study available through the resources of the Inter-University Consortium for Political Research, and I gratefully acknowledge their kindness.

[5] *Ibid.*, p. 107.

administration in our interests—[administration of] a just
society where we are all equal."

The workers' sense of citizenship, moreover, was intimately linked, now as before, with their sense of their
country's sovereignty. A fundamental source of the workers'
revolutionary political attitudes, more so perhaps than all
the deprivations to which they were subject, was the quasi-
colonial status of their country and the political economy
they believed resulted from that status. United States political and economic control of their country fed and sustained
a sense of exploitation in the working class. Their sense of
exploitation was inseparable from the national colonial
status not only because they had an abstract idea that their
own exploitation and oppression was traceable to this status,
but also because the concrete class struggle inevitably took
on nationalist content. Imperialism was not an abstraction

TABLE 11.1

Workers' Expectation of Treatment by Governmental Bureau,
by Nation[a]

PERCENT WHO SAY	CUBA	U.S.	U.K.	GERMANY	ITALY	MEXICO
They expect equal treatment	89%	80%	82%	60%	48%	38%
They don't expect equal treatment	3	11	9	9	18	52
Depends	—	5	6	23	18	7
Other	—	—	—	—	4	—
Don't know	7	5	2	8	11	2
Total percent	99	101	99	100	99	99
Total (N)	(202)	(456)	(349)	(220)	(229)	(314)

[a] The question: "Suppose there were some question that you had to take
to a government office—for example, a question about a housing regulation.
Do you think you would be given equal treatment—I mean, would you be
treated as well as anyone else?"

The wording of our question is slightly different from that in the Almond-
Verba study. The middle part of theirs reads: "—for example, a tax question or housing regulation."

or an ideology that leftist leaders used to motivate them to action, nor was it a "scapegoat" on which they blamed their society's ills. For the workers' fight to win full citizenship in their society, their struggle to enlarge their social and political rights and to improve their conditions of life was in the main directed against foreign economic interests, essentially those of American corporations.

The Batista regime was interlocked with United States interests; its central responsibility was the maintenance of order and protection of the rights of private property—especially American-owned property. United States capital had a degree of political and economic security and played a strategic economic role in Cuba quite unlike any it had elsewhere in Latin America.[6] Private United States investors owned Cuba's major industries entirely, or to an extent that gave them control. In the words of a writer for the U.S. Department of Commerce:

> The only foreign investments of importance [in Cuba] are those of the United States. American participation exceeds 90 percent in the telephone and electric services, and about 50 percent in public service railways, and roughly 40 percent in raw sugar production. The Cuban branches of United States banks are entrusted with almost one-fourth of all bank deposits. . . . Cuba ranked third in Latin America in the value of United States direct investments in 1953, outranked only by Venezuela and Brazil.[7]

The sugar central workers, spread out on American-owned property throughout the country and in constant contact with

[6] Henry Christopher Wallich, *Monetary Problems of an Export Economy* (Cambridge: Harvard University Press, 1950), p. 14.

[7] U.S. Department of Commerce, *Investment in Cuba* (Washington, D.C.: U.S. Government Printing Office, 1956), p. 10. Private U.S. capital also owned the most important cattle ranches, the copper mine, the major tourist facilities and hotels, and together with British capital, almost the entire oil business.

rural labor, the miners of Matahambre, the utilities, oil, and communications workers, the nickel refinery workers, the bank employees and railroad workers, the most organized and most combative, the most politicized workers were compelled to fight American-owned companies to achieve what they believed to be their rights. "For years," as Charles A. Page has pointed out, "the Cuban workers' bloodiest strikes were against the intransigence of certain American enterprises."[8] Several of the most militant strikes that grew into demonstrations against the Batista regime in the years before the revolution were, like the major sugar workers' strike of 1955, strikes against largely foreign-owned industry.

United States government intervention, moreover, whether through direct military suppression or indirect diplomatic measures, was responsible for (or at least blamed by the Cubans for) the support of the corrupt and oppressive regimes under which they suffered; for the obstruction of attempts at social reform; and, notably, for the abortion of the profound 1933-35 revolution. This revolution, we now know, decisively affected the political consciousness of the workers of that generation and made them the major prerevolutionary generational base of the Communists. The fact that capital was foreign and had behind it the political and military power of the United States thus strengthened the link between the working class's sense of being exploited and its nationalist sentiment. "For the fifty-seven years of its independence," an outstanding American correspondent has written, "Cuba has lived more as an appendage of the United States than as a sovereign nation."[9] The former American ambassador to Cuba has stated that

[8] Charles A. Page, *The Development of Organized Labor in Cuba,* unpublished dissertation (University of California, at Berkeley, 1952), p. 167.

[9] Tad Szulc, "Profile of a Revolution," *New York Times Magazine,* April 24, 1960, p. 9.

   . . . the United States, until the advent of Castro, was so overwhelmingly influential in Cuba that . . . the American Ambassador was the second most important man in Cuba, sometimes even more important than the President [of Cuba].[10]

Ambassador Smith may have misperceived the situation or been misinformed, but even so, perhaps it is understandable how the Cuban workers might arrive at essentially the same conclusion about the relationship between their government and the government to the north.

It is understandable that their nationalist desire for sovereignty, their impoverishment and unemployment, their struggle for citizenship, the economic vulnerability of the country as a whole and its stagnation, might become linked intimately in the workers' political consciousness and provide a firm base for the earlier anarchosyndicalist and later Communist leadership of labor—as well as for the consolidation of the power of the Revolutionary Government.

The new national pride that Cuban workers now express and its relationship to their support of the revolution is reflected in what they told us they were most proud of in Cuba. We used the same question, and the same categories to classify the Cuban workers' answers to it that Almond and Verba used in their five-nation study, and found the following (Table 11.2):

Cuban workers are second only to those in the United States and England (only slightly less so than in England) in naming governmental or political institutions spontaneously as the objects of their pride in nation. (This is the major variable defined by Almond and Verba to gauge "system affect.") It is hardly surprising, of course, that the German workers, having lived through a war imposed on

10 Earl E. T. Smith, before Senate Internal Security Committee, quoted in U.S. Congress, Internal Security Subcommittee of the Committee on the Judiciary, *Hearings, Communist Threat to the United States through the Caribbean,* 86th Cong., 2nd Sess., Aug. 30, 1960, p. 700.

TABLE 11.2

Aspects of Nation in Which Workers Take Pride, by Nation

PERCENT WHO SAY THEY ARE PROUD OF	CUBA	U.S.	U.K.	GERMANY	ITALY	MEXICO
Governmental, political institutions	44%	82%	48%	7%	2%	35%
Social legislation[11]	3	10	12	7	—	3
Position in international affairs	23	8	12	3	2	3
Economic system	34	24	11	36	5	30
Characteristics of people	—	3	17	32	13	13
Spiritual virtues and religion	—	3	—	1	5	6
Contributions to the arts	—	1	4	9	10	8
Contributions to science	—	1	9	9	3	1
Physical attributes of country	7	3	9	17	25	18
Nothing or don't know	11	3	4	6	11	2
Other	11	3	11	6	25	13
Total percent of responses[a]	133	141	137	133	101	132
Total percent of respondents	100	100	100	100	100	100
Total (N)	(202)	(456)	(349)	(220)	(229)	(314)

[a] Percentages exceed 100 because of multiple responses.

[11] "Social legislation" is not really a meaningful category in the context of the revolution in Cuba, and the figure of three percent in Table 11.2 simply represents "educational accomplishments of the regime." In fact, of course, it was exceedingly difficult to categorize answers as representing pride in either the governmental and political *or* the economic institutions of the country, given their close identity at this stage of the revolution. So some degree of overlap must be taken into account in reading the table. It might be pointed out that Almond and Verba use the term "system affect" to apply only to the governmental and political institutions of a country, which may be quite valid when concentrating on the political system as such; if our interest is in attachment to the social structure of the country, including not only political but also economic institutions, social legislation, and the country's position in the world as its citizens perceive it, then the relative positions of the countries shift somewhat, with the objects of pride in nation in these four categories (the first four in Table 11.2) being mentioned more often by Cuban workers than workers in any of the other countries except the United States, which retains first place, but with a smaller margin of difference with Cuba than by comparing only mention of the political institutions as an object of pride in nation.

them by the Nazis, and knowing of the horrors perpetrated by their recent Nazi government officials, including the murder of many of their own labor leaders, are comparatively low in affection for their governmental system. Nor is the response of the Italian workers unexpected, given the fact that the Communist Party is the major party of the Italian workers. The Mexican workers, in contrast, are high in system affect. As Almond and Verba point out:

> Mexico has had a symbolic, unifying event: the Mexican Revolution. This revolution . . . is the crucial event in the development of the Mexican political culture, for it created a sense of national identity and a commitment to the political system that permeates almost all strata of the society.[12]

This statement, of course, applies with equal force to the impact of the Cuban revolutionary experience on Cuban workers. What is most important in this context, however, is that the Cuban workers were far more likely than the workers of any other country to refer to Cuba's *new position in international affairs*, its newly won sovereignty, as a major source of their pride in nation. "I feel prouder than ever of my country now," said an oil refinery worker, "because now we have our independence. Now we Cubans are masters of our own deeds and our own actions." A brewery worker said: "I am proud to be a Cuban now. Before the revolution, we were not Cubans." The words of a worker at the Enidio Díaz sugar central in Campechuela echo the nationalist combativeness heard from many Cubans: "I am proud to belong to a people that knows how to respond 'I am here!' each time that imperialism tries to break the revolution." Of course, some workers could be proud of their country's sudden capture of world attention, consider their country to be independent and sovereign since the advent of the revolution, and

[12] *Civic Culture*, p. 503.

yet be wary of the Leftward and pro-Soviet course the revolution was taking. As one worker explained his views:

> The revolution triumphed after many years of struggle against the tyranny. The revolution is the strength of the Cuban people. We fought for the liberty of Cuba, as in José Martí's doctrine. Of course, we needed social reform, but not so profound. The Cuban people knew nothing of Marx and Lenin, but only of Martí. We should be ruled in accord with his doctrine, but we now have a Marxian doctrine. We suffered many years of hardship to gain our sovereignty, and we need Martí's doctrine, not a doctrine of the Left or the Right. We need to assert our nationalism—nothing more. . . . We have to fight for us, not send our sons to work for Nikita Khrushchev. . . . The ideals of the revolution are good, but we are taking a curve in the road. . . . I am a *mestizo*. I am in between black and white, just as I am in between imperialism and communism.

For most workers, however, their radicalism and nationalism and newly won sovereignty are inseparable. The revolution has created a "commitment to the political system that permeates" all sectors of the working class, a commitment that cannot be explained more than partially by the particular personal gains or prerevolutionary situation of individual workers. "When a Cuban feels honor and pride in his heart for his nation," as a brewery worker told us, "this means more than material benefits." This new sense of nationhood and their own emancipation were spontaneously linked by worker after worker in our interviews. Though we never asked a question in which the word "imperialism," appeared, and though we had no question on Cuban independence as such, the workers themselves raised the issue in one context or another.

One of the most frequent contexts was related to our question: "What kind (*clase*) of people governed this country before the revolution?" The vast majority of responses indicated how alienated the workers were from the prerevolutionary system, but many of them went further. Their former rulers and "imperialism" were seen as connected. "This was a Yankee colony," one said, "where they did what they wanted. We were ruled by politicos, people of the most evil type, assassins, such as Fulgencio Batista, the ex-dictator of our country, who was sold to imperialist gold, who only thought of taking advantage of Cuba at the cost of the blood of its best sons and daughters." Another said: "Imperialism. Quite clearly our country was controlled by another country's government." "Those who governed this country before," another put it, "were exploiters allied with foreign monopolies that carried away the riches of the nation." Similar remarks were made in a variety of different contexts. For example, when we asked how their attitudes toward work had changed since nationalization and why, many replied in words similar to those of a sugar worker who said: "Before the benefits of the industry were carried out of the country and now they remain in the country for the construction of factories. I don't work for thieves now or an American company."

One worker explained at length why he believed there had been no strikes in the factories since they were nationalized:

Well, now there is no reason to strike. Are you going to strike against yourself? The factories and all belong to the people. Any problems are discussed in the factory. Why strike? The people have nurseries for their children. We are enthusiastic about the new system that exists here. The principal achievements for which we yearned for years are already in hand. Before the revolution, for example, we needed a merchant fleet—but we had none. We had United Fruit instead. Grau, for instance, once tried to do something about it. He got five or six boats. They are now functioning. They never functioned before.

Grau could do nothing because the American companies would have been affected. [The American Companies] agreed that if a new Cuban fleet were established, they would not trade with those who used the fleet. There is no longer such external capitalist coercion over our country.

Thus, the workers' achievement of full citizenship in their country, and their country's achievement of sovereignty, were intimately interrelated in their conception of the revolution. The revolution had abolished their alienation from the means of production, from government, and from nation. The revolution, many asserted, had abolished their alienation from themselves. As a cigar worker told us: "The principal thing that has happened since the revolution is that I am working for my nation and for the collective benefit of all. I am not exploited as I was before. The revolution is pursuing the future—a future in which the working classes, having taken control of economic and political power for themselves, will reach for the full happiness of mankind, a society in which there will be no exploitation of man by man." "Before the revolution," said another, summing up the revolution's meaning for himself and his fellow revolutionaries, "a worker was an insignificant Cuban. Now he is a human being!"

Index

administrators, plant: and Ernesto Ché Guevara, 191; origins of, 191; workers' views of, 192-94
Adorno, Theodore W., 259n
Agramonte, Ignacio, 217
agrarian reform: Bolivia, 275n; Mexico, 275n; National Institute of (INRA), 23n; and prerevolutionary economic structure, 274-75
agricultural equipment industry, unemployment in, 51; administrators of, 191
agricultural workers, 169; and anarchosyndicalism, 147; and Church, 148; and Communists, 147, 152; fathers' occupation, 11, 57, 103, 118, 194; in France, 136; politicization of, 289; radicalization of, 149. See also anarchosyndicalism
Alexander, Robert J., 161n, 275n
alienation: and politics, 283; Chap. 8 passim. See also work attitudes
Alienes y Urosa, Julián, 48n
Allende, Dr. Salvador, 121
Almeida, Juan, 232
Almond, Gabriel, 33, 232n, 253, 286n, 287n, 290, 292
Alonso, Alicia, xlv
Álvarez, León, 70
anarchosyndicalism, 8, 281; and agricultural workers, 147; appeals of, 166-68; and cigar workers, 43; and Communists, 7, 167; and guild system, 162; ideology of, 3; and labor movement, 52, 92, 93, 104, 290; and Social Democrats, 159-60; in France, Italy, Spain, 160-64
anti-Batista movement, 30, 34, 220, 238; and Communists, 8, 76, 235, 238; and Fidel, 76; leadership of, 238; and Negroes, 70; and Oriente Province, 70; and political generations, 278; and 26th of July movement, 8, 214; and workers, 12, 226ff, 278; and youth, 225; See also Fulgencio Batista
anti-imperialist movement, 3
anti-Machado struggles: and workers, 104. See also Machado regime

A/P ratio: effects of, 179-84
Argelia Libre sugar central, 193
Argentina: and communism, 160-61; working-class movement in, 161-62
Ariguanabo textile plant, 124, 165, 170; administrators of, 191
Arredondo, Alberto, 48n
Arufat, Anton, xlv
Australia: plant size and politics in, 159; and skill level, 91, 106
"autenticos," 215-16
auto workers: and alienation, 190
Aveling, Eleanor Marx, 163
Avila, Leopoldo, xlv
Aymara language, 68

Bakke, E. Wight, 47n
Baliño, Carlos, 93
bank employees, 289
Banner of the Heroes of Moncada (award), xviii, xxxi, xxxiv
Baran, Paul. xliv
Barnett, Clifford R., 71n, 93, 100n, 122, 137, 149n, 165n, 252n
Barton, Allen, 45n, 189n, 211n
Batista, Fulgencio, xi, xxxviii, 37, 38, 42, 216, 220n, 237, 294; and Communists, 234; and labor, 53n; ousting of, 235; patronage system, 72; regime of, 30, 223-25, 278; and revolution of 1930s, 70; and strikes, 289; U.S. interest in, 288; and women's vote, 121-22. See also anti-Batista movement
Bauer, Otto, 66
Bauer, Raymond, 211n
Baum, Warren C., 160n
Bauta, see Ariguanabo
Bay of Pigs invasion, ix, 13
Bednarik, Karl, 189
Behrendt, Reinhard, 212n
Belloc, Hilaire, xliv
Bendix, Reinhard, 67n, 91, 106, 108, 110-11, 118, 132n, 133, 142, 243n, 244n, 259n
Bequer, Conrado, xxvi
Berelson, Bernard, 133n, 213n
Berger, Bennet, 212, 236
Bianchi, Andres, 23n
Biblioteca Nacional de Cuba, 19
Blackburn, Robin, 53n

Blauner, Robert, 94-95, 177n, 180-81, 185n, 194n, 197n
Bohemia, 66. See also Karl Marx
Bolivia: agrarian reform, 146, 275n; and mestizos, 68; peasantry in, 145
Bottomore, T.B., 189n
Braga, Georgio, 136
Brazil, U.S. investment in, 288
Bremme, Gabriele, 120n
Brennan, Ray, 226
brewery workers, 31, 36-37, 138, 195, 206, 249, 292-93; in Havana, 35; in Manacas, xii-xiii, 34, 191, 193; and unemployment, 51; and working-class aristocracy, 115
Brodbeck, Arthur J., 134n
Brody, Richard A., 151n
Bronfenbrenner, Urie, 258n
Brown, James, 186n
Brown, Marion, 130n
Buell, Raymond Leslie, 153
Bull, Edvard, 135n, 152
Burdick, Eugene, 134n
Bureau of Commerce, U.S., 48

Camaguey: and sugar strike (1955), 154, 226
cane cutters: and unemployment, 49. See also sugar workers
Cantril, Hadley, 18, 151n, 189
capitalism: and prerevolutionary social structure, 271-74
Cárdenas paper plant, 33
Castro, Fidel, vii, ix, x, xi, xxxv, xlviii, xlix-l, li, 29, 30, 35, 36, 41, 47, 52, 53n, 213, 217-18, 220n, 223, 225, 232, 267, 268n, 269, 273n, 290; and anti-Batista movement, 76; and civil liberties, 21; denunciation by Communists, 18, 234; and generation of '53, 227; and Moncada assault, 234; and race relations, 71, 74; and sectarianism, 18; sex appeal, 125; support for, 15, 18
Castro, Raúl, 21, 220n, 232
Casuso, Teresa, 213, 220n, 225, 228
cement workers, xvii-xviii, 44, 248; and unemployment, 51
Centers, Richard, 46n, 91, 133n, 190n, 240n
Central University of Las Villas: library of, 19
centrales, 145. See also sugar workers
Chaloner, W.H., 91, 148n, 158n
Chaplin, David, 100n

chemicals plant, Santa Lucia: administrators of, 191
chemical workers, 247-48; and unemployment, 51
Chibás, Eduardo, 173-74
Chile: and communism, 160-61; and 1958 elections, 121; women's politics in, 120; working-class movement in, 160-62
China, 21, 61
chinchales, 23, 164. See also size of plant
Chinoy, Ely, 189n, 190, 190n, 204, 210
Church: base of, 122-23, 149; and counterrevolution, 272; influence of, 148; and Mexican Revolution, 148; and peasants, 272; and women, 122-23
Cienfuegos, Camilo, 34, 220n
Cienfuegos, Osmany, 220n
cigarette factory, Vedado: administrators of, 191
cigarette workers, 36, 74; and working-class aristocracy, 115-16
cigar workers, 34, 43, 248, 295; and anarchosyndicalism, 43; in Florida and New Jersey, 167; and unemployment, 51; and women, 124
"civic culture": and working-class equality, 286
civil liberties in Cuba, 16-22; Chap. 10 passim
class consciousness, 74; in Detroit workers, 82; and foreign investment, 147; and imperialism, 287-88; and marriage, 130; and nationalism, 287ff; and racial consciousness, 74, 79-88; and sugar production, 147; and unemployment, 82-88; and unionization, 82-88
class origins, see social origins
Cole, G.D.H., 160n
Coleman, James, 176n
Colombia: peasantry in, 144
Committee of Advanced Workers, xxxviii
communication, intra-class, 178-79
communications workers, 289; and working-class aristocracy, 115
Communism and the Conscience of the West (Sheen), xliv
Communists, 93, 217n, 224; and agricultural workers, 147, 152; and anarchosyndicalism, 7, 159, 167; and anti-Batista movement, 8, 76, 238; apparatus in Integrated Revolutionary Organiza-

tions (ORI), 13; appeals of, 246; in Argentina, 160-61; and Ariquanabo textile plant, 170; and Batista, 234; and Castro, 18, 31, 234; Central Committee, xli, xlviii-xlix; in Chile, 160-61; and Constitutional Convention (1940), 261; and Fascism, 245; and general strike (April 9, 1958), 235; index of attitude toward, 56; and insurrections, 153; in Italy, 292; and labor movements, xxv-xxvi, 3, 6, 11, 52, 55, 56n, 93, 104, 159, 224-26, 245, 261-62, 290; and libertarianism, 260-65; and left-wing politics, 159; and Negroes, 70; new, 13; and Nicaro nickel plant, 170; in 1948 elections, 173; old, 13, 269; sectarianism of, 18; and race relations, 72, 74; in revolution of 1930s, 224; and sugar strike (1955), 154; and sugar workers, 151, 154

community size, see size of community

compañero meaning of, xxi

Con Mi Silencio Hablo: la Historia del Cardenal Mindszenty (Shuster), xliv

conscript labor, utilization of, xxxvii

conservatism, political, 80; and peasants, 61

Constitution of 1940, 251; and Communists, 122, 261; and workers' rights, 261; and women's rights, 122

construction industry, xiii

Contradicciones del Comunismo (Nagy), xliv

copper mine: in Matahambre, 115, 144, 165; administrators of, 191

copper miners, 37, 43, 206, 248, 289; in Matahambre, xxvi, 34, 37; and unemployment, 51

Costa Rica: peasantry in, 144

counterrevolution, social bases of, 272-73

coup of March 10th, 216

Cowley, Malcolm, 211n

craft workers, see skill level

Cristo y el Comunismo (Jones), xliv

cross-pressures, political, 178

Crutchfield, Richard S., 231n

CTC, 192, 261; and Communists, 3, 225, 261; and discrimination, 72;

and Mujal, 30; purge of Communists, 223-24; and unions today, 30. See also labor movement

Cuba Socialista (journal), xli

Cuban Communism (ed. Horowitz), ix

Cuban Revolution and Latin America, The (Goldenberg), xlv

Cuban Revolutionary Party: "autentico," 215-16

Czechoslovakian workers, 66

de Man, Hendrik, 60

Democratic Party (U.S.), 62

Denmark: labor movement, 135

deprivation: and politics, 10, 58ff, 87-88, 123; sex differences in, 123; and Negroes, 107. See also income; wages; relative deprivation

Detroit: auto workers in, 190; Negro and white workers in, 82-83

Dewart, Leslie, 149n

Dicks, Henry V., 259n

Disraeli, Benjamin, 157

Djilas, M., xliv

dock workers, 63

Dogan, Mattei, 120n

Draper, Theodore, xlv, 54

DuBois, Jules, 220n, 226n

Dulles, Allen, 233

du Pont, Irénée, xx

Dutton, E.P., 162

Duverge, Maurice, 120n, 130

Echevarría, José Antonio, 233

economic structure, prerevolutionary, 48-51, 81-82, 271-75, 280

Eder, Richard, 268n

education: and libertarianism, 253-54, 265; sex differences in, 124-25; and skill level, 95-96; and social origins, 141, 143; and unemployment, 69

educational system, prerevolutionary, 252

Edwards, Hugh, 155n

egalitarianism, xvi, xx-xxi, xxxiii

Eisenberg, Philip, 46n

Eisenhower, Dwight D., 62, 233

Eisenstadt, S.N., 211n, 214

Elcelsior (publication), xliv

elections, 42; in Chile (1958), 121; in 1948, Communist strength in, 173n

electrical workers, 37-38, 75, 195,

247, 249; in Matanzas and plant administration, 193; in Santiago, 192-93; and unemployment, 51; and working-class aristocracy, 115-16

Elkins, Stanley, 71n

Engels, Friedrich, 3n, 66, 132, 157, 158n, 172, 177, 185, 187, 242, 268n; and agricultural workers, 147; and American working class, 66; and industrial revolution, 134; and "labor aristocracy," 90. *See also* Karl Marx

England: capitalist development in, 134; and skilled workers, 91, 106; voting determinants in, 133; workers' views of government officials, 286; working-class politics, 62-63

Enídio Díaz sugar central, 193, 292

Epstein, Leon, 159n

Escalante, Aníbal, xlviii-xlix

Espín, Vilma, 220n

Esso-Shell refinery in Regla, 31, 193

Estado, Servil, El (Belloc), xliv

estrangement, Chap. 8 *passim. See also* work attitudes; alienation

ethnic relations, *see* race relations

Eulau, Heinz, 62

Evan, William, 212n

Facultad Obrera-Campesina (school), xv, xlv

fascism, 245

Fagen, Richard R., 151n

family patterns: and libertarianism, 257-60, 266

farmer origins: in Germany, 136; and size of plant, 176

Farewell to Revolution (Martin), xx

food rationing, xi-xii, xvi

father's occupational status, *see* social origins

Fegiz, Luzzatto, 125n

Fernández R., Carlos, 192

Feuer, Lewis S., 3n, 5n, 66, 132n, 158n, 185n, 187n, 212n, 243

Finland, voting determinants in, 133

Florida, Cuban tobacco workers in, 167

food industry, women in, 124

Foreign Affairs (publication), x

foreign investment, 288; and class consciousness, 147; and counter-revolution, 272. *See also* imperialism

Fort Moncada, xi

Foster, Walter, xxxviii

France, 99, 102; anarchosyndicalism in, 160-64; agricultural workers in, 136; plant size and politics in, 159, 163-64; and skilled workers, 91-92; women's politics in, 120

Free, Lloyd A., 18, 151n

Frente de Acción Popular (FRAP): Chile, 121

Frente Cívico contra la Discriminación, 72

Friedmann, George, 189n, 200

Fromm, Eric, 259n

Fundamental Law (1959); and women's rights, 122

Galenson, Walter, 135, 152, 160n, 197n

Gans, Herbert, 109n

García, María, 262n

García Menócal, Mário, 37

general strike (April 1958), 70, 226-27; and Communists, 235; and Negroes, 70; of 1935, 213

generations, *see* political generations

Germany, 118; class and status in, 107, 110; labor movement in, 283-84; revolution of 1848, 66; voting determinants in, 133; workers in, 62, 66, 106, 110, 286

Gerth, Hans, 81n, 212n, 241

Glazer, Nathan, 256n

Goldenberg, Boris, xlv, 53-54

Gómez, Máximo, 233

Gompers, Samuel, 92

González Pedrero, Enrique, 216n

Goodman, Paul, 189n

Gouldner, Alvin, 256

Granma (newspaper), xli

Grau San Martín, Ramón, 215, 217n, 220, 224, 294

Grievance Commissions (*Comisiones de Reclamaciones*), xxv, 191-192

Greèn, Arnold, 259n

Greenbackers, 46n

Grievance Commissions (*Comisiones de Reclamaciones*), 191-92

Guanajay: shoemakers in, 75-76

Guatemala: and *mestizos*, 68; peasantry in, 144

guerrilla struggle, 70. *See also* anti-Batista movement

Guevara, Ernesto "Ché," 21, 28n, 30, 34, 191-92, 220n, 232, 267

Guevara, Alfredo, xlv
Guevara, Ernesto "Ché," vii, viii, ix, x, xxv, xxix, xxx, xxxii, xli, l-li, lii, liii, 21, 28n, 30, 34, 191-192, 200n, 232, 267
Guido Pérez brewery, xxxix-xl
guild system: and anarchosyndicalism, 162
Guiteras, António, 217, 233
Gusfield, Joseph R., 212n
Guttman scale, 44

hacienda system, 145; and prerevolutionary Bolivia and Mexico, 146
Haiti: and Negro immigration, 68
Hall, O. Milton, 46n
Hamilton, Richard F., 46n, 61n, 62, 91-92, 102-103, 109-10, 124, 128, 129n, 136, 159, 163, 190n, 221-22, 240n, 251
Hart, Armando, 220n
Hartley, E.L., 258n
Havana: brewery workers in, 195; and Communists, 173; Hilton Hotel, 74; restaurant workers in, 116; Riviera Hotel, 74; sugar strike in 1955, 154, 226; unemployment in, 137; University of, 19
Henderson, W.O., 91, 148n, 158n
Herberle, Rudolf, 212n, 219, 222n
Hernández, Agustín, xiii, xxviii
history: and sociology, 240; and survey research, 6
Hitler, Adolf, 255
Ho Chi Minh, 233
Hodges, Donald Clark, 189n
Holmes, John Clellan, 211n
Hoover, J. Edgar, xliv
Horton, John, 185n
Hoslett, S.S., 197n
Hoy (newspaper), xli
Huberman, Leo, 146n
Hyman, Herbert H., 212n, 236n, 239

I Chose Freedom (Kravchenko), xliv
identification cards, worker, xlii
imperialism, 288-90; and class consciousness, 287-88. *See also* foreign investment; intervention, U.S.
income: and politics, 10, 61-64, 279. *See also* wages; deprivation; relative deprivation
index of attitude: toward Communists, 56; toward revolution, 30-44; of political radicalism, 7
Indians: in Oriente Province, 68
"In Difficult Times" (Padilla), xlv
industry, small-scale, 23. *See also* *chinchales*; size of plant
Inkeles, Alex, 211n
INRA (National Institute of Agrarian Reform), 23n
Institute for International Social Research, 18
Integrated Revolutionary Organizations (ORI): Communist apparatus in, 13
International Bank for Reconstruction and Development, 47, 52, 56n, 86n, 145n
intervention, U.S., 228, 289
interview methods, 26-30; and internal situation in Cuba, 16-22. *See also* survey research
*intra*class social differentiation: effects of, 8-9
Italy: anarchosyndicalism in, 160-64; plant size and politics in, 159; and skilled workers, 91; and women's politics, 120; Communists in, 292; workers' views of government officials, 286

Jahoda, Marie, 270n
Jamaica and Negro immigration, 68
"Jim Crow" laws: in Cuba and U.S., 71
Jiménez, António Nuñez, 68n
Jolly, Richard, 23n
Jones, Eli Stanley, xliv

Kautsky, Karl, 45, 158, 242n, 243
Kecksckemeti, Paul, 212n
Kennedy, John F., 233
Kerr, Clark, 159n
Key, V. O., 159n
Khrushchev, Nikita, 233, 293
Knowles, Ruth, 15
Kolko, Gabriel, 61n
Kornhauser, Arthur, 159n, 197n
Kravchenko, Victor, xliv
Krech, David, 231

labor aristocracy, 89-90, Chap. 4 *passim*
labor brigades, xxxvii
labor force: women in, 123-24
labor movement, 135; and anarchosyndicalists, 52, 92, 104, 290; and Batista, 53n; and Commu-

nists, 11, 52, 55, 56n, 104, 224-26, 261-62, 290; in Germany, 283-84; and Negroes, 70; and political generations, 12, 104-106
landowners: and traditionalism, 60-61
Las Villas, Central University of, see Central University of Las Villas
Law No. 270, xxxiv, xxxv
Law No. 1225, xlii-xliii
Lazarsfeld, Paul, 45n, 46n, 47, 133n, 189n, 211n, 213n
leather factory at Managua: administrators of, 191
leather workers: and unemployment, 51. See also shoemakers
Left voting, 45. See also political radicalism; voting determinants
Leggett, John C., 46n, 47n, 82-83
Lenin, Nikolai, viii, xxix, 233, 268n, 293; and labor aristocracy, 89-90
libertarianism, Chap. 10 passim. See also civil liberties
libraries, xliv
"life chances": by race, 69; sex differences in, 124-25; and skill level, 95; and social origins, 140, 143
Lindzey, Gardner, 46n, 189n, 211n
Linz, Juan, 45n, 47n, 61n, 120, 136, 159, 176, 189n, 190, 211n
Lipset, Seymour Martin, 45n, 46n, 67n, 80, 91, 106-108, 110-12, 118, 128n, 130n, 132n, 133, 142, 154n, 159n, 176n, 177-78, 189n, 197n, 211n, 240n, 243n, 244-45, 250, 255n, 258n, 259n, 260, 262-64, 266, 270n, 285n
Lipsitz, Lewis, 251, 259
Lockwood, David, 109n
Lorwin, Val R., 160n
Los Angeles Times (newspaper), xliv
Low, J.O., 61n
Luxemburg, Rosa, li

Maccoby, E.E., 258n
Maceo, Antonio, 217, 233
MacGaffey, Wyatt, 71n, 93, 100n, 122n, 137, 149n, 165n, 252n
Machado regime, 166, 215, 217n, 222, 224, 226, 228, 237, 278. See also anti-Machado struggles
McEwan, Arthur, xl
McPhee, William, 133n, 213n
Magoon, Charles, 48

Manácas: brewery workers in, 31, 34, 191, 193
Managua: leather factory in, 191
Mannheim, Karl, 187n, 212
Mao Tse Tung, 233
Mariel: Portland Cement plant, 34
Marquand, H.A., 160n
marriage, class barriers to, 110; and politics, 126-30
Marshall, T.H., 285n
Martí, José, xliv, 115, 217, 233, 293
Martin, Everett Dean, xx
Martínez Sánchez, Augusto, 220n
Marxism-Leninism, xlv
Marx, Karl, 3n, 11, 45, 132, 157, 158n, 162, 172, 177, 185-90, 203-204, 242n, 268n, 293; and German labor movement, 283-84; and German revolution, 66; theory of alienation, 202ff. See also Friedrich Engels
Masó, Calixto, 262n
mass culture, 243
mass media: Cuban, 21
Masters of Deceit (Hoover), xliv
Matahambre copper mine, 26, 34, 37, 115, 144, 165; administrators of, 191. See also copper miners
Matanzas: electrical plant in, 193; Province, 174n
Mella, Julio António, 217
Mendoza, Miguel, xiv
Menéndez, Jesús, 70
Merton, Robert K., 230n, 231n, 270n
mestizos: in Bolivia, 68; in Cuba, 70n; in Guatemala and Mexico, 68
Mexico: and agrarian reform, 275n; and haciendas, 68; and mestizos, 68; peasantry in, 144-45; workers' views of government officials, 286; revolution and Church in, 148; revolution and "system affect," 292
Miami: Cuban refugees in, 76
Michels, Roberto, 9, 90, 138, 158
militia, 13, 39n, 40, 270; influence on government, 22; and women's rights, 126
Mill, John Stuart, 157, 185-87
Miller, S. Michael, 109n, 259n
Milligan, Martin, 186n
Mills, C. Wright, 81n, 189, 241
miners, see copper miners; Matahambre copper mine
Ministry of Industries: aid this

study, 23, 27, 28n, 29n. *See also* Ernesto Guevara
Mintz, Sydney, 146
Miró Cardona, José, 233
missile crisis, ix, x, 13, 17
Moa Bay mine, 165
Moncada Fortress, 52, 76, 234
Moravia, 66
Morgenthau, Hans, x
Mujal, Eusébio, 30, 70, 225
Myrdal, Gunnar, 66

Nagy, Imre, xliv
Nation (magazine), xliv
The Nation, 27
National library in Havana, xliv
National Plan, xxxii, xl
National Workers' Confederation, 166
nationalism, 13-14, 147, 252, 290, 293; and class consciousness, 287ff. *See also* imperialism
nationalization, 282; and work attitudes, 190ff, 294
Nazis, 255, 292
Negroes, Chap. 3 *passim*; American southern, 61; and anti-Batista movement, 70; and Communists, 70, 98; and relative deprivation, 107; and skill level, 98; and unemployment, 11. *See also* race relations
Nelson, Lowry, 69, 108, 145n
Neumann, Erich, 125n
Neumann, Sigmund, 67, 212n
Newcomb, T.M., 258n
New Jersey: Cuban tobacco workers in, 167
New Politics (magazine), xliv
New Republic (magazine), xliv
New Statesman (publication), x, xliv
"New Unionism," 90
New York Times, The, xiii-xiv, xliv
Nicaro nickel plant, 30, 35, 37, 85, 144, 165, 193, 206, 248, 289; and Communists, 170; and strike (Aug. 1, 1957), 226; and unemployment in, 51; working-class aristocracy, 115
Nicholas, Herbert G., 46n
Nisbet, Robert, 185
Noelle, Elizabeth, 125n
Nolff, Max, 23n
Non-Partisans, 46n
Norway: labor movement, 135; voting determinants in, 133; women's politics in, 120

Nuestra Industria (journal), x, xli
Nueva Clase, La: Análisis del Régimen Comunista (Djilas), xliv
Nuñez Jiménez, Antonio, 68n

occupational community: and sugar workers, 101; and voting, 154
O'Connor, James, 272n
oil refinery: Esso-Shell, Regla, 31, 193; Texaco, Santiago, 36; unemployment in, 51; workers in, 31, 38, 43, 76, 195-96, 289, 292; and working-class aristocracy, 115-16
Oltuski, Enrique, 220n
ORI (Integrated Revolutionary Organizations): Communist apparatus in, 13
Oriente Province: Indians in, 68; *mestizos* in, 70n; Negroes in, 70; and strike (Aug. 1, 1957), 226
origins, *see* social origins
"Out of the Game" (Padilla), xlv

Padilla, Heberto, xlv
Page, Charles A., 87n, 154n, 262n, 289
País, Frank, 226, 233
paper mill: at Cardenas, xxi, 33, 249; unemployment in, 51
Paris Commune, 242
Parra, Jesús, xxxiv, xxxv, xxxvi
Parsons, Talcott, 134
Pázos, Felipe, 53n, 274n
Pázos, Javier, 53n
Pear, T.H., 259n
peasants, 146, 169; in Bolivia, 145; and Church, 148, 272; in Colombia, 144; in Costa Rica, 144; and counterrevolution, 272; in Cuba, 144; fathers' occupations, 11, 57, 103, 118; in Guatemala, 144; and market economy, 145; in Mexico, 144-45; in Peru, 144; and political conservatism, 61; radicalization of, 149; and skill level, 103; and sugar workers, 145; and traditionalism, 60-61, 144
Peña, Lazaro, 76
Pérez, Faustino, 220n
Pérez la Rosa, Miguel, xxxviii
Petersen, Julius, 211n
petite bourgeoisie, 151, 169; and size of plant, 176; and skill level, 109; origins in, 11, 57, 103, 150, 176
Peyre, Henri, 211n

Philip, Andre, 160n
Pinar del Rio, 26, 174n
plant administration: workers' views of, 192-94
plantación system, 145. *See also hacienda* system
plant size, *see* size of plant
Poland, 66
political crimes, vlvii-xlviii
political culture: and working class, 6, 133
political generations, Chap. 9 *passim*, 58n, 128, 219, 278; and labor movement, 104-106, 120; and skill level, 104-106
political interest, 246, 255-57; and libertarianism, 265, 269
political radicalism, index of, 7; deprivation vs. structure as determinant, 58ff; theory of, 7. *See also* anarchosyndicalists; Communists; labor movement; Left voting
Populists, 46n
Portland Cement: Mariel plant, 34
Prío Socarrás, Carlos, 215, 233
production process: workers' role in, 10. *See also* alienation; A/P ratio; size of plant; skill level
promotion opportunities: workers' views of, 194-96
propaganda, Cuban, 21
prostitution: in prerevolutionary Cuba, 125
Puerto Rico: and "rural proletarian community," 146
Pujol, Raúl, 226

Quechua language, 68

race relations, Chap. 3 *passim*; and politics, 280. *See also* Negroes
radicalism, *see* political radicalism
railroad workers, 289
Realengo 18: workers' "Soviet," 70
Rebel Army: and plant administrators, 191
recruitment, *see* social origins
reference individuals, 233
Reflections on the Cuban Revolution (Baran), xliv
refugees: in Miami, 76
Regla, Esso-Shell refinery in, 31, 193
Reissman, Frank, 109n, 259n
relative deprivation, 106ff. *See also* deprivation; income; wages

religion, xlv
Renourard, Yves, 211n
restaurants, xix
restaurant workers, 116
Reston, James, xiii-xiv
Revolución (newspaper), xli
revolution of 1933-35, 3, 12, 118, 213, 217n, 222-24, 289; and Batista, 70; and Communists, 224; intervention in, 228; and Negro leadership, 70; and workers, 104-105. *See also* political generations
Revolutionary Government: accomplishments of, 14; consolidation of, 15; economic difficulties of, 14; and "family life," 125; and individual liberties, 271-74; and race relations, 73-75, 77; and women's rights, 126
revolutionary process: and individual liberties, 267-76
Riesman, David, 256n
Riera, René, xxxviii
Rintala, Marvin, 212n
Risquet, Jorge, xxxi, xxxii, xxxiii
Roa, Raúl, 20, 220
Roca, Blas, 20
Rodríguez, Carlos Rafael, xi, xxix
Rodríguez Morejón, Gerardo, 220n
Rosenberg, Bernard, 244n
Roth, Guenther, 283
Rubel, Maximilen, 189n
rum workers, Bacardí, 115
"rural proletarian community," 146
Russia: uneven development of, 135
Ryder, Norman B., 219n, 231n

salaried employees, 151, 169; father's occupation, 57, 104; wage scales, xix
sampling method, 23-26
Sánchez, Emilio, 93
Sanial, Lucien, 161
Santa Clara, 1955 sugar strike in, 154, 226
Santa Lucía chemicals plant: administrators of, 191
Santamaría, Haydeé, 220n
Santiago: electrical workers in, 192-93, 195; and general strikes, 70, 226-27; oil workers in, 195-96; strikes in, 278; Texaco oil refinery in, 36; and unemployment, 137
Schattschneider, E. E., 67n

Scheer, Robert, 268n
Schlesinger, Arthur M., Jr., xliv, 39n
secret police, vlvii
Seeman, Melvin, 185n
Seers, Dudley, 22-23
sex and politics, Chap. 5 *passim*
Sheen, Fulton, xliv
Shell-Esso refinery, *see* Esso-Shell refinery
shoemakers, 34-35, 247; in Guanajay, 38, 75-76
Shuster, G. N., xliv
Siegel, Abraham, 159n
size of community, 12, 98-99, 172-73; and skill level, 100, 118
size of plant, 12, 98-99, 164, Chap. 7 *passim*, 281-82; and social origins, 176; and traditionalism, 177; and unemployment, 58n
skill level, 11, 70, Chap. 4 *passim*, 65, 89-91, 175, 279; in France, 99; and race, 70, 86n; sex differences and, 124-25; and social origins, 143; and unionization, 11, 87-88n; and unemployment, 69, 175; and wages, 93
slavery, 67-68, 70-71
Slavonic populations, 66
slums, elimination of, xiv
Smith, Robert F., 228
Smith, Earl E. T. (U.S. ambassador), 290
Social Democracy, 136, 159; and anarchosyndicalism, 160; appeals of, 161; and German labor movement, 283
social deprivation, *see* deprivation
social differentiation: *intra*class, 8-9
socialism, 46n; in Castro's speeches, 270; ideology of, 4; and labor movement leaders, 6; and race relations, 74. *See also* anarchosyndicalism; communism; nationalization; political radicalism; Social Democracy
socialist morality, concept of, xxxiii-xxxiv
social mobility, *see* social origins
social origins, 11, 57, 99-104, 118, Chap. 6 *passim*, 176, 281; of plant administrators, 191. *See also* agricultural workers; farmers; peasants; petite bourgeoisie; salaried employees; sugar workers
sociology: and history, 240
solares (urban slums), 69
Sombart, Werner, 161-62

Sorge, Friedrich A., 66
Soto, Jesús, xxvi, 170, 192
Soviet Union, 273n; in Cuban mass media, 21; and nuclear testing, 21. *See also* Russia
Spain, anarchosyndicalism in, 160-64
Spargo, John, 161-62
Stein, Maurice, 185n
Stokes, William, 174n
Stouffer, Samuel, 44, 244
Strauss, Anselm, 241
Street, David S., 47n
strikes: and Batista regime, 226-27; and ethnic relations, 66; and sugar workers in 1955, 153; in U.S.-owned industry, 289. *See also* general strikes; labor movement; unions
sugar *centrales*, 165; administrators of, 191
sugar workers, 37-38, 43, 63, 75, 117, 145, 153-54, 193, 206-207, 248-49, 277, 285, 292; and class consciousness, 147; and Communists, 55, 151, 154, 225; conscript labor, xxxvii; and fathers' occupations, 101-102; and industrial unionism, 93; and Jesús Menéndez, 70; and labor movement, 86n, 87n; and nationalism, 147; and occupational communities, 101; and peasants, 145; and political education, 101, 118; as radical social base, 146; and skill level, 100; and slavery, 68; strike (1955), 153-54, 226, 289; and unemployment, 49-51
Sugar Workers Union, xxvi
survey research: and history, 6; and internal situation in Cuba, 16-22
Sweden, 118; labor movement in, 62, 106, 135; skilled workers in, 91; status differences in, 107; voting determinants in, 133
Sweezy, Paul M., 146n
syndicalism, *see* anarchosyndicalism
"system affect," 290-92
Szulc, Tad, 289n

Taber, Robert, 220n
Tannenbaum, Frank, 71n
Technical Advisers Councils (*Consejos Técnicos Asesores*), 53, 191
Tejera, Vicente, 93
television, xliv
Ten Years' War against Spain, 217n

Texaco oil refinery at Santiago, 36, 76, 115, 195-96
textile plant in Ariguanabo, xii, xix, xxvii; administrators of, 191
textile workers, 124, 165, 170; and Communists, 170; and women, 124; and unemployment, 51
Thompson, Charles A., 228
Time (magazine), xliv
Tingsten, Herbert, 120n, 128n
tobacco workers, *see* cigar workers
Tocqueville, Alexis de, 157, 185, 187
tourism and working-class aristocracy, 115
trade unions, *see* unions
traditionalism, 146; and capitalism, 271-73; and landowners, 60-61; and peasants, 60-61, 144; and size of plant, 157-58, 177. *See also hacienda* system
Trimestre (journal), xli
Trotsky, Leon, xxix, 135
Trow, Martin, 46n, 176n, 259n
Truslow Mission, *see* International Bank for Reconstruction and Development
26th of July movement, xxxviii, 8, 214, 216-17, 225-26, 238; denunciation by Communists, 234; manifesto of, 214-19; and Oriente Province, 226

Ulam, Adam B., 5, 135, 152, 158
unemployment, 10-11, Chap. 2 *passim*, 138, 144, 174; and class consciousness, 82-88; and education, 69; in Havana, 137; and political generations, 236-39; and politics, 79-88, 279-80; and race, 11, 69, 78; in Santiago, 137; sex differences in, 124-25; and skill level, 69, 95-96, 175; and social origins, 141, 143; and wage level, 69; and work attitudes, 203
Union of Cuban Writers, xlv
Union of Writers and Artists, xlv
unions, xxv-xxviii, 30, 93, 116; and class consciousness, 82-88; and Communists, 159; and skill level, 87n-88n; and Social Democrats, 159; in United States, 89. *See also* labor movement; names of unions; strikes
United Fruit Company, 294
United States, 275n; class differences, 110; in Cuban mass media, 21; intervention in Cuba, 228,

288-90; investment in Cuba, 288; plant size and politics in, 159; and race relations, 71-72; and skill level, 91, 106; slavery in, 70-71; and Socialist Party, 46n; strikes in, 289; sugar production in Cuba, 147; unions in, 89; urbanization in, 165; voting determinants in, 133; workers in, 62, 66, 290; workers' views of government officials, 286
University of Havana: autonomy gained, 222; library of, 19; reorganized curriculum, 21
urban slums (*solares*), 69
urbanization, 165
Urrutia, Manuel, 233
Uruguay sugar central, 31, 75, 191, 193, 248
utility workers, 289

Van Aartsen, J.P., 160
Varadero beach, 74
Vedado, cigarette factory in, 191
Vélez, Brunilda, 120n
Venezuela, U.S. investment in, 288
Venezuela sugar central, xxii-xxiii, xxviii, 43, 193
Verba, Sidney, 33, 232n, 253, 286n, 287n, 290, 292
Verde Olivo (journal), xli, xlv
Víbora, agricultural equipment plant in, 191, 194
Vidich, Arthur, 185n
Viet Nam, x, 61
Voice of America, xliv
voting determinants, 133. *See also* Left voting; political radicalism

wages, xvi-xix, 63; freeze of, 191; and politics, 61-64; sex differences in, 124-25; and skill level, 93, 95-96, 112-13; and social origins, 143; and unemployment, 69. *See also* deprivation; income; relative deprivation
Wagner, Helmut R., 212n
Walker, Barbara Ann, 261n
Wallich, Henry Christopher, 288n
War against Spain (1898), 35, 217n
Warner, Lloyd, 61n
Weber, Max, xxi, 81
West Germany: farmer origins, 136; size of plant, 159; and skilled workers, 91; women's politics in, 120
West, Patricia S., 270n

WGBS (radio station), xliv
white collar workers, *see* salaried employees
White, David M., 244n
Whyte, William Foote, 61n
Wilensky, Harold, 155n
Wolf, Eric R., 144
work attitudes, 96, 190ff. *See also* alienation
Workers Council, xxi, xxviii, xliii
working-class aristocracy, *see* labor aristocracy

Wythe, George, 161n

"youth ideology," 214

Yugoslavia, 21

zafra, 49-50; in 1962, 14; and unemployment, 54
Zawadski, Bohan, 47n
Zetterberg, Hans, 25n
Zweig, Ferdinand, 109n

70 71 72 73   12 11 10 9 8 7 6 5 4 3 2 1

Revised January, 1970

hARPER ✦ TORChBOOKS

American Studies: General

HENRY STEELE COMMAGER, Ed.: The Struggle for Racial Equality TB/1300
CARL N. DEGLER: Out of Our Past: *The Forces that Shaped Modern America* CN/2
CARL N. DEGLER, Ed.: Pivotal Interpretations of American History
Vol. I TB/1240; Vol. II TB/1241
A. S. EISENSTADT, Ed.: The Craft of American History: *Selected Essays*
Vol. I TB/1255; Vol. II TB/1256
ROBERT L. HEILBRONER: The Limits of American Capitalism TB/1305
JOHN HIGHAM, Ed.: The Reconstruction of American History TB/1068
ROBERT H. JACKSON: The Supreme Court in the American System of Government TB/1106
JOHN F. KENNEDY: A Nation of Immigrants. *Illus. Revised and Enlarged. Introduction by Robert F. Kennedy* TB/1118
RICHARD B. MORRIS: Fair Trial: *Fourteen Who Stood Accused, from Anne Hutchinson to Alger Hiss* TB/1335
GUNNAR MYRDAL: An American Dilemma: *The Negro Problem and Modern Democracy. Introduction by the Author.*
Vol. I TB/1443; Vol. II TB/1444
GILBERT OSOFSKY, Ed.: The Burden of Race: *A Documentary History of Negro-White Relations in America* TB/1405
ARNOLD ROSE: The Negro in America: *The Condensed Version of Gunnar Myrdal's* An American Dilemma. *Second Edition* TB/3048
JOHN E. SMITH: Themes in American Philosophy: *Purpose, Experience and Community* TB/1466
WILLIAM R. TAYLOR: Cavalier and Yankee: *The Old South and American National Character* TB/1474

American Studies: Colonial

BERNARD BAILYN: The New England Merchants in the Seventeenth Century TB/1149
ROBERT E. BROWN: Middle-Class Democracy and Revolution in Massachusetts, 1691–1780. *New Introduction by Author* TB/1413
JOSEPH CHARLES: The Origins of the American Party System TB/1049
WESLEY FRANK CRAVEN: The Colonies in Transition: 1660–1712† TB/3084

CHARLES GIBSON: Spain in America † TB/3077
CHARLES GIBSON, Ed.: The Spanish Tradition in America + HR/1351
LAWRENCE HENRY GIPSON: The Coming of the Revolution: 1763-1775. † *Illus.* TB/3007
PERRY MILLER: Errand Into the Wilderness TB/1139
PERRY MILLER & T. H. JOHNSON, Eds.: The Puritans: *A Sourcebook of Their Writings*
Vol. I TB/1093; Vol. II TB/1094
EDMUND S. MORGAN: The Puritan Family: *Religion and Domestic Relations in Seventeenth Century New England* TB/1227
WALLACE NOTESTEIN: The English People on the Eve of Colonization: 1603-1630. † *Illus.* TB/3006
LOUIS B. WRIGHT: The Cultural Life of the American Colonies: 1607-1763. † *Illus.* TB/3005

American Studies: The Revolution to 1860

JOHN R. ALDEN: The American Revolution: 1775-1783. † *Illus.* TB/3011
RAY A. BILLINGTON: The Far Western Frontier: 1830-1860. † *Illus.* TB/3012
GEORGE DANGERFIELD: The Awakening of American Nationalism, 1815-1828. † *Illus.* TB/3061
CLEMENT EATON: The Growth of Southern Civilization, 1790-1860. † *Illus.* TB/3040
LOUIS FILLER: The Crusade against Slavery: 1830-1860. † *Illus.* TB/3029
WILLIM W. FREEHLING: Prelude to Civil War: *The Nullification Controversy in South Carolina, 1816-1836* TB/1359
THOMAS JEFFERSON: Notes on the State of Virginia. ‡ *Edited by Thomas P. Abernethy* TB/3052
JOHN C. MILLER: The Federalist Era: 1789-1801. † *Illus.* TB/3027
RICHARD B. MORRIS: The American Revolution Reconsidered TB/1363
GILBERT OSOFSKY, Ed.: Puttin' On Ole Massa: *The Slave Narratives of Henry Bibb, William Wells Brown, and Solomon Northup* ‡ TB/1432
FRANCIS S. PHILBRICK: The Rise of the West, 1754-1830. † *Illus.* TB/3067
MARSHALL SMELSER: The Democratic Republic, 1801-1815 † TB/1406

† The New American Nation Series, edited by Henry Steele Commager and Richard B.]
‡ American Perspectives series, edited by Bernard Wishy and William E. Leuchtenburg.
a History of Europe series, edited by J. H. Plumb.
§ The Library of Religion and Culture, edited by Benjamin Nelson.
‖ Researches in the Social, Cultural, and Behavioral Sciences, edited by Benjamin Nelson.
Ϟ Harper Modern Science Series, edited by James A. Newman.
° Not for sale in Canada.
+ Documentary History of the United States series, edited by Richard B. Morris.
# Documentary History of Western Civilization series, edited by Eugene C. Black and Leonard W. Levy.
ʌ The Economic History of the United States series, edited by Henry David et al.
¶ European Perspectives series, edited by Eugene C. Black.
** Contemporary Essays series, edited by Leonard W. Levy.
* The Stratum Series, edited by John Hale.

LOUIS B. WRIGHT: Culture on the Moving Frontier TB/1053

American Studies: The Civil War to 1900

T. C. COCHRAN & WILLIAM MILLER: The Age of Enterprise: *A Social History of Industrial America* TB/1054
W. A. DUNNING: Reconstruction, Political and Economic: 1865-1877 TB/1073
HAROLD U. FAULKNER: Politics, Reform and Expansion: 1890-1900. † *Illus.* TB/3020
GEORGE M. FREDRICKSON: The Inner Civil War: *Northern Intellectuals and the Crisis of the Union* TB/1358
JOHN A. GARRATY: The New Commonwealth, 1877-1890 † TB/1410
HELEN HUNT JACKSON: A Century of Dishonor: *The Early Crusade for Indian Reform.* † *Edited by Andrew F. Rolle* TB/3063
WILLIAM G. MCLOUGHLIN, Ed.: The American Evangelicals, 1800-1900: An Anthology ‡ TB/1382
JAMES S. PIKE: The Prostrate State: *South Carolina under Negro Government.* ‡ *Intro. by Robert F. Durden* TB/3085
VERNON LANE WHARTON: The Negro in Mississippi, 1865-1890 TB/1178

American Studies: The Twentieth Century

RAY STANNARD BAKER: Following the Color Line: *American Negro Citizenship in Progressive Era.* ‡ *Edited by Dewey W. Grantham, Jr. Illus.* TB/3053
RANDOLPH S. BOURNE: War and the Intellectuals: *Collected Essays, 1915-1919.* ‡ *Edited by Carl Resek* TB/3043
A. RUSSELL BUCHANAN: The United States and World War II. † *Illus.*
Vol. I TB/3044; Vol. II TB/3045
THOMAS C. COCHRAN: The American Business System: *A Historical Perspective, 1900-1955* TB/1080
FOSTER RHEA DULLES: America's Rise to World Power: 1898-1954. † *Illus.* TB/3021
HAROLD U. FAULKNER: The Decline of Laissez Faire, 1897-1917 TB/1397
JOHN D. HICKS: Republican Ascendancy: 1921-1933. † *Illus.* TB/3041
WILLIAM E. LEUCHTENBURG: Franklin D. Roosevelt and the New Deal: 1932-1940. † *Illus.* TB/3025
WILLIAM E. LEUCHTENBURG, Ed.: The New Deal: *A Documentary History* + HR/1354
ARTHUR S. LINK: Woodrow Wilson and the Progressive Era: 1910-1917. † *Illus.* TB/3023
BROADUS MITCHELL: Depression Decade: *From New Era through New Deal, 1929-1941* ∆ TB/1439
GEORGE E. MOWRY: The Era of Theodore Roosevelt and the Birth of Modern America: 1900-1912. † *Illus.* TB/3022
WILLIAM PRESTON, JR.: Aliens and Dissenters: TWELVE SOUTHERNERS: I'll Take My Stand: *The South and the Agrarian Tradition. Intro. by Louis D. Rubin, Jr.; Biographical Essays by Virginia Rock* TB/1072

Art, Art History, Aesthetics

ERWIN PANOFSKY: Renaissance and Renascences in Western Art. *Illus.* TB/1447
ERWIN PANOFSKY: Studies in Iconology: *Humanistic Themes in the Art of the Renaissance. 180 illus.* TB/1077
HEINRICH ZIMMER: Myths and Symbols in Indian Art and Civilization. *70 illus.* TB/2005

Asian Studies

WOLFGANG FRANKE: China and the West: *The Cultural Encounter, 13th to 20th Centuries. Trans. by R. A. Wilson* TB/1326
L. CARRINGTON GOODRICH: A Short History of the Chinese People. *Illus.* TB/3015

Economics & Economic History

C. E. BLACK: The Dynamics of Modernization: *A Study in Comparative History* TB/1321
GILBERT BURCK & EDITORS OF *Fortune*: The Computer Age: *And its Potential for Management* TB/1179
ROBERT L. HEILBRONER: The Future as History: *The Historic Currents of Our Time and the Direction in Which They Are Taking America* TB/1386
ROBERT L. HEILBRONER: The Great Ascent: *The Struggle for Economic Development in Our Time* TB/3030
FRANK H. KNIGHT: The Economic Organization TB/1214
DAVID S. LANDES: Bankers and Pashas: *International Finance and Economic Imperialism in Egypt. New Preface by the Author* TB/1412
ROBERT LATOUCHE: The Birth of Western Economy: *Economic Aspects of the Dark Ages* TB/1290
W. ARTHUR LEWIS: The Principles of Economic Planning. *New Introduction by the Author*° TB/1436
WILLIAM MILLER, Ed.: Men in Business: *Essays on the Historical Role of the Entrepreneur* TB/1081
HERBERT A. SIMON: The Shape of Automation: *For Men and Management* TB/1245

Historiography and History of Ideas

J. BRONOWSKI & BRUCE MAZLISH: The Western Intellectual Tradition: *From Leonardo to Hegel* TB/3001
WILHELM DILTHEY: Pattern and Meaning in History: *Thoughts on History and Society.*° *Edited with an Intro. by H. P. Rickman* TB/1075
J. H. HEXTER: More's Utopia: *The Biography of an Idea. Epilogue by the Author* TB/1195
H. STUART HUGHES: History as Art and as Science: *Twin Vistas on the Past* TB/1207
ARTHUR O. LOVEJOY: The Great Chain of Being: *A Study of the History of an Idea* TB/1009
RICHARD H. POPKIN: The History of Scepticism from Erasmus to Descartes. *Revised Edition* TB/1391
BRUNO SNELL: The Discovery of the Mind: *The Greek Origins of European Thought* TB/1018

History: General

HANS KOHN: The Age of Nationalism: *The First Era of Global History* TB/1380
BERNARD LEWIS: The Arabs in History TB/1029
BERNARD LEWIS: The Middle East and the West ° TB/1274

History: Ancient

A. ANDREWS: The Greek Tyrants TB/1103
THEODOR H. GASTER: Thespis: *Ritual Myth and Drama in the Ancient Near East* TB/1281

2

A. H. M. JONES, Ed.: A History of Rome through the Fifth Century # *Vol. I: The Republic*　　　　HR/1364
Vol. II The Empire:　　　　HR/1460
SAMUEL NOAH KRAMER: Sumerian Mythology　　　　TB/1055
NAPHTALI LEWIS & MEYER REINHOLD, Eds.: Roman Civilization *Vol. I: The Republic*　　　　TB/1231
Vol. II: The Empire　　　　TB/1232

History: Medieval

NORMAN COHN: The Pursuit of the Millennium: *Revolutionary Messianism in Medieval and Reformation Europe*　　　　TB/1037
F. L. GANSHOF: Feudalism　　　　TB/1058
F. L. GANSHOF: The Middle Ages: *A History of International Relations. Translated by Rêmy Hall*　　　　TB/1411
HENRY CHARLES LEA: The Inquisition of the Middle Ages. || *Introduction by Walter Ullmann*　　　　TB/1456

History: Renaissance & Reformation

JACOB BURCKHARDT: The Civilization of the Renaissance in Italy. *Introduction by Benjamin Nelson and Charles Trinkaus. Illus.* Vol. I TB/40; Vol. II TB/41
JOHN CALVIN & JACOPO SADOLETO: A Reformation Debate. *Edited by John C. Olin*　TB/1239
J. H. ELLIOTT: Europe Divided, 1559-1598 *a* °　　　　TB/1414
G. R. ELTON: Reformation Europe, 1517-1559 ° *a*　　　　TB/1270
HANS J. HILLERBRAND, Ed., The Protestant Reformation #　　　　HR/1342
JOHAN HUIZINGA: Erasmus and the Age of Reformation. *Illus.*　　　　TB/19
JOEL HURSTFIELD: The Elizabethan Nation　　　　TB/1312
JOEL HURSTFIELD, Ed.: The Reformation Crisis　　　　TB/1267
PAUL OSKAR KRISTELLER: Renaissance Thought: *The Classic, Scholastic, and Humanist Strains*　　　　TB/1048
DAVID LITTLE: Religion, Order and Law: *A Study in Pre-Revolutionary England. § Preface by R. Bellah*　　　　TB/1418
PAOLO ROSSI: Philosophy, Technology, and the Arts, in the Early Modern Era 1400-1700. || *Edited by Benjamin Nelson. Translated by Salvator Attanasio*　　　　TB/1458
H. R. TREVOR-ROPER: The European Witch-craze of the Sixteenth and Seventeenth Centuries and Other Essays °　　　　TB/1416

History: Modern European

ALAN BULLOCK: Hitler, A Study in Tyranny. ° *Revised Edition. Illus.*　　　　TB/1123
JOHANN GOTTLIEB FICHTE: Addresses to the German Nation. *Ed. with Intro. by George A. Kelly* ¶　　　　TB/1366
ALBERT GOODWIN: The French Revolution　　　　TB/1064
STANLEY HOFFMANN et al.: In Search of France: *The Economy, Society and Political System In the Twentieth Century*　　　　TB/1219
H. STUART HUGHES: The Obstructed Path: *French Social Thought in the Years of Desperation*　　　　TB/1451
JOHAN HUIZINGA: Dutch Civilisation in the 17th Century and Other Essays　　　　TB/1453

JOHN MCMANNERS: European History, 1789-1914: *Men, Machines and Freedom*　TB/1419
HUGH SETON-WATSON: Eastern Europe Between the Wars, 1918-1941　　　　TB/1330
ALBERT SOREL: Europe Under the Old Regime. *Translated by Francis H. Herrick*　TB/1121
A. J. P. TAYLOR: From Napoleon to Lenin: *Historical Essays* °　　　　TB/1268
A. J. P. TAYLOR: The Habsburg Monarchy, 1809-1918: *A History of the Austrian Empire and Austria-Hungary* °　　　　TB/1187
J. M. THOMPSON: European History, 1494-1789　　　　TB/1431
H. R. TREVOR-ROPER: Historical Essays TB/1269

Literature & Literary Criticism

W. J. BATE: From Classic to Romantic: *Premises of Taste in Eighteenth Century England*　　　　TB/1036
VAN WYCK BROOKS: Van Wyck Brooks: The Early Years: *A Selection from his Works, 1908-1921 Ed. with Intro. by Claire Sprague*　　　　TB/3082
RICHMOND LATTIMORE, Translator: The Odyssey of Homer　　　　TB/1389
ROBERT PREYER, Ed.: Victorian Literature **　　　　TB/1302

Philosophy

HENRI BERGSON: Time and Free Will: *An Essay on the Immediate Data of Consciousness* °　　　　TB/1021
H. J. BLACKHAM: Six Existentialist Thinkers: *Kierkegaard, Nietzsche, Jaspers, Marcel, Heidegger, Sartre* °　　　　TB/1002
J. M. BOCHENSKI: The Methods of Contemporary Thought. *Trans. by Peter Caws* TB/1377
ERNST CASSIRER: Rousseau, Kant and Goethe. *Intro. by Peter Gay*　　　　TB/1092
MICHAEL GELVEN: A Commentary on Heidegger's "Being and Time"　　　　TB/1464
J. GLENN GRAY: Hegel and Greek Thought　　　　TB/1409
W. K. C. GUTHRIE: The Greek Philosophers: *From Thales to Aristotle* °　　　TB/1008
G. W. F. HEGEL: Phenomenology of Mind. ° || *Introduction by George Lichtheim* TB/1303
MARTIN HEIDEGGER: Discourse on Thinking. *Translated with a Preface by John M. Anderson and E. Hans Freund. Introduction by John M. Anderson*　　　　TB/1459
F. H. HEINEMANN: Existentialism and the Modern Predicament　　　　TB/28
WERER HEISENBERG: Physics and Philosophy: *The Revolution in Modern Science. Intro. by F. S. C. Northrop*　　　　TB/549
EDMUND HUSSERL: Phenomenology and the Crisis of Philosophy. § *Translated with an Introduction by Quentin Lauer*　　TB/1170
IMMANUEL KANT: Groundwork of the Metaphysic of Morals. *Translated and Analyzed by H. J. Paton*　　　　TB/1159
WALTER KAUFMANN, Ed.: Religion From Tolstoy to Camus: *Basic Writings on Religious Truth and Morals*　　　　TB/123
QUENTIN LAUER: Phenomenology: *Its Genesis and Prospect. Preface by Aron Gurwitsch*　　　　TB/1169
MICHAEL POLANYI: Personal Knowledge: *Towards a Post-Critical Philosophy*　TB/1158
WILLARD VAN ORMAN QUINE: Elementary Logic *Revised Edition*　　　　TB/577
WILHELM WINDELBAND: A History of Philosophy *Vol. I: Greek, Roman, Medieval*　TB/38

3

Vol. II: Renaissance, Enlightenment, Modern
TB/39
LUDWIG WITTGENSTEIN: The Blue and Brown Books ° TB/1211
LUDWIG WITTGENSTEIN: Notebooks, 1914-1916
TB/1441

Political Science & Government

C. E. BLACK: The Dynamics of Modernization: A Study in Comparative History TB/1321
DENIS W. BROGAN: Politics in America. *New Introduction by the Author* TB/1469
ROBERT CONQUEST: Power and Policy in the USSR: *The Study of Soviet Dynastics* ° TB/1307
JOHN B. MORRALL: Political Thought in Medieval Times TB/1076
KARL R. POPPER: The Open Society and Its Enemies *Vol. I: The Spell of Plato* TB/1101 *Vol. II: The High Tide of Prophecy: Hegel, Marx, and the Aftermath* TB/1102
HENRI DE SAINT-SIMON: Social Organization, The Science of Man, and Other Writings. || *Edited and Translated with an Introduction by Felix Markham* TB/1152
CHARLES SCHOTTLAND, Ed.: The Welfare State ** TB/1323
JOSEPH A. SCHUMPETER: Capitalism, Socialism and Democracy TB/3008

Psychology

LUDWIG BINSWANGER: Being-in-the-World: *Selected Papers.* || *Trans. with Intro. by Jacob Needleman* TB/1365
MIRCEA ELIADE: Cosmos and History: *The Myth of the Eternal Return* § TB/2050
MIRCEA ELIADE: Myth and Reality TB/1369
SIGMUND FREUD: On Creativity and the Unconscious: *Papers on the Psychology of Art, Literature, Love, Religion.* § *Intro. by Benjamin Nelson* TB/45
J. GLENN GRAY: The Warriors: *Reflections on Men in Battle. Introduction by Hannah Arendt* TB/1294
WILLIAM JAMES: Psychology: *The Briefer Course. Edited with an Intro. by Gordon Allport* TB/1034

Religion: Ancient and Classical, Biblical and Judaic Traditions

MARTIN BUBER: Eclipse of God: *Studies in the Relation Between Religion and Philosophy* TB/12
MARTIN BUBER: Hasidism and Modern Man. *Edited and Translated by Maurice Friedman* TB/839
MARTIN BUBER: The Knowledge of Man. *Edited with an Introduction by Maurice Friedman. Translated by Maurice Friedman and Ronald Gregor Smith* TB/135
MARTIN BUBER: Moses. *The Revelation and the Covenant* TB/837
MARTIN BUBER: The Origin and Meaning of Hasidism. *Edited and Translated by Maurice Friedman* TB/835
MARTIN BUBER: The Prophetic Faith TB/73
MARTIN BUBER: Two Types of Faith: *Interpenetration of Judaism and Christianity* ° TB/75
M. S. ENSLIN: Christian Beginnings TB/5
M. S. ENSLIN: The Literature of the Christian Movement TB/6
HENRI FRANKFORT: Ancient Egyptian Religion: *An Interpretation* TB/77

Religion: Early Christianity Through Reformation

ANSELM OF CANTERBURY: Truth, Freedom, and Evil: *Three Philosophical Dialogues. Edited and Translated by Jasper Hopkins and Herbert Richardson* TB/317
EDGAR J. GOODSPEED: A Life of Jesus TB/1
ROBERT M. GRANT: Gnosticism and Early Christianity TB/136

Religion: Oriental Religions

TOR ANDRAE: Mohammed: *The Man and His Faith* § TB/62
EDWARD CONZE: Buddhism: *Its Essence and Development.* ° *Foreword by Arthur Waley* TB/58
H. G. CREEL: Confucius and the Chinese Way TB/63
FRANKLIN EDGERTON, Trans. & Ed.: The Bhagavad Gita TB/115
SWAMI NIKHILANANDA, Trans. & Ed.: The Upanishads TB/114
D. T. SUZUKI: On Indian Mahayana Buddhism. ° *Ed. with Intro. by Edward Conze.* TB/1403

Science and Mathematics

W. E. LE GROS CLARK: The Antecedents of Man: *An Introduction to the Evolution of the Primates.* ° *Illus.* TB/559
ROBERT E. COKER: Streams, Lakes, Ponds. *Illus.* TB/586
ROBERT E. COKER: This Great and Wide Sea: *An Introduction to Oceanography and Marine Biology. Illus.* TB/551
WILLARD VAN ORMAN QUINE: Mathematical Logic TB/558

Sociology and Anthropology

REINHARD BENDIX: Work and Authority in Industry: *Ideologies of Management in the Course of Industrialization* TB/3035
KENNETH B. CLARK: Dark Ghetto: *Dilemmas of Social Power. Foreword by Gunnar Myrdal* TB/1317
KENNETH CLARK & JEANNETTE HOPKINS: A Relevant War Against Poverty: *A Study of Community Action Programs and Observable Social Change* TB/1480
LEWIS COSER, Ed.: Political Sociology TB/1293
GARY T. MARX: Protest and Prejudice: *A Study of Belief in the Black Community* TB/1435
ROBERT K. MERTON, LEONARD BROOM, LEONARD S. COTTRELL, JR., Editors: Sociology Today: *Problems and Prospects* || Vol. I TB/1173; Vol. II TB/1174
GILBERT OSOFSKY, Ed.: The Burden of Race: *A Documentary History of Negro-White Relations in America* TB/1405
GILBERT OSOFSKY: Harlem: The Making of a Ghetto: *Negro New York 1890-1930* TB/1381
PHILIP RIEFF: The Triumph of the Therapeutic: *Uses of Faith After Freud* TB/1360
ARNOLD ROSE: The Negro in America: *The Condensed Version of Gunnar Myrdal's An American Dilemma. Second Edition* TB/3048
GEORGE ROSEN: Madness in Society: *Chapters in the Historical Sociology of Mental Illness.* || *Preface by Benjamin Nelson* TB/1337
PITIRIM A. SOROKIN: Contemporary Sociological Theories: *Through the First Quarter of the Twentieth Century* TB/3046
FLORIAN ZNANIECKI: The Social Role of the Man of Knowledge. *Introduction by Lewis A. Coser* TB/1372